"You can see absolutely no one in the audience. It is alienatingly black. Then you realize it is all up to you. You are a performer. The long years were worth it. The miraculous magic of expression overrides everything. Once again you realize you are everything you are aware of. You are part of the audience. They are part of you. You and they are one expressing talent. The talent of giving and receiving, of resonating to a greater spirit by means of the body; the talent of souls appreciating one another creating life on a larger scale. The talent of understanding the shadow awareness that makes us all one, part of a divine perfection which is the essence of sharing. You are dancing with God. You are dancing with yourself. You are dancing in the light."

—Shirley MacLaine

Dancing in the Light

Shirley MacLaine

BANTAM BOOKS

TORONTO · NEW YORK · LONDON · SYDNEY · AUCKLAND

DANCING IN THE LIGHT
A Bantam Book / October 1985

Bantam hardcover edition / October 1985

A selection of the Literary Guild and
Doubleday Book Club.
An excerpt of this book appeared in Cosmopolitan magazine,
January 1986.
11 printings thru December 1985

Bantam paperback edition / November 1986

Library of Congress Cataloging-in-Publication Data

MacLaine, Shirley, 1934–
    Dancing in the light.

    1. MacLaine, Shirley, 1934–   .   2. Entertainers—
United States—Biography.   3. Spiritualists—United
States—Biography.   I. Title.
PN2287.M18A32   1985   791.43'028'0924   [B]85-47621
                  ISBN 0-553-25697-1

Published simultaneously in the United States and Canada

PRINTED IN THE UNITED STATES OF AMERICA

KR   0   9   8   7

Dear Reader,

From the time I was very small, I remember having the impulse to "express" myself. At the age of three I attended dance classes because I wanted to express myself physically. As a teenager, I went from dancing to singing, which seemed a natural and logical extension of that self-expression. Later, as an adult, I carried that impulse for expression even further, into acting, and experienced a greater form of expression. I loved the intricate mystery of being another character, sorting out background and motivation and meaning, exploring my own feelings and thoughts in relation to another person.

Then I found writing—an outlet that enabled me to express more intricately and specifically my experiences. I wrote to know what I was thinking. I wrote to understand my profession, my travels, my relationships, and, in fact, my life. Writing helped to whet an already insatiable appetite to understand the *why* and *how* of everything.

I like to think of each of my books as a kind of map depicting where I've been and where I'm going. *Don't Fall off the Mountain* described how I learned to spread my wings as a young artist and began to take charge of my personal destiny. In a series of expeditions to Africa, India, the Himalayan Kingdom of Bhutan, and to the land of my daughter Sachi's namesake, Japan, I first reached out to touch the unknown—and was changed by it. The personal period profiled in *You Can Get There From Here* was one of great internal, intellectual, and political growth for me. The star system had come to an end in Hollywood, so I ventured into the quicksands of television. The result was disastrous and the impact on me profound. It drove me to test myself in the political arena during the presidential election of 1972, when I campaigned for George McGovern against Richard Nixon. That experience motivated me to pursue a desire few Westerners had been allowed to fulfill in the early 1970s. I led the first women's delegation to China to study the remarkable evolution of a brand-new culture from the ashes of an ancient and little-known land. The experience of adjusting to an alien culture brought us smack-up against ourselves. We learned about our own evolution as well, and even more about what the human will, properly directed, can accomplish even against great odds. All of this prepared me to return to my performing career with a greater enthusiasm and appreciation for the craft by which I earned my living, and to explore what new levels of creativity I could bring to it. I believe this experience also helped to drive home another lesson: Anything is possible if you believe you deserve it.

I thought for a long time before I published *Out on a Limb* because it is the written expression of a spiritual odyssey that took me further than I ever expected to go, into an astonishing and moving world of psychic phenomena where past lives, the existence of spirit guides, and the genuine immortality of the soul became more than concepts to me—they became real, true parts of my life. I think of this book as my spiritual diary opened to the eyes of those who also seek an inner understanding, and as my statement to those who taught me and opened my eyes that I accept their gifts with gratitude and humility.

I like to think of *Dancing in the Light* as a celebration of all my "selves." It was a fulfilling and satisfying exploration of the promises I made to myself in *Out on a Limb*. In it I look with pleasure, humor, and some contentment upon my experiences as a daughter, a mother, a lover, a friend, a seeker of spiritual destiny, and a voice calling for peace in the world. I think it expresses my great personal joy at reaching this important point in my life, as well as the strengthening of my sense of purpose. But the story is not yet finished, for I am still a woman in search of myself, the lives I might have lived and the inner heart of my being.

If my search for inner truth helps give you, the reader, the gift of insight, then I am rewarded. But my first reward has been the journey through myself, the only journey worth taking. Through it all I have learned one deep and meaningful lesson: LIFE, LIVES, and REALITY are only what we each *perceive* them to be. Life doesn't happen to us. We make it happen. Reality isn't separate from us. We are creating our reality every moment of the day. For me that truth is the ultimate freedom and the ultimate responsiblity.

Love and Light,

Shirley MacLaine

Wu Li = Patterns of organic energy
Wu Li = My way
Wu Li = Non-sense
Wu Li = I clutch my ideas
Wu Li = Enlightenment

Master = One who begins at the center, not the fringe

To dance with God, the creator of all things, is to dance with oneself.

The Dancing Wu Li Masters
Gary Zukav

Part One

The Dance Without

Chapter 1

On the morning of April 24, 1984, I woke up in my New York apartment to realize I was going to be fifty years old at 3:57 that afternoon. I felt there was some kind of dramatic flair to reaching the midcentury mark in 1984 and of course I couldn't, anymore, accept the synchronicity of my personal event as merely accidental. As I had told everybody I knew, I no longer believed there was any such thing as accident. Everything that happened was a result of some form of cause and effect and therefore had an underlying reason.

For example, the slight headache I now had. I knew it was from the prebirthday bash the night before.

My friend, the lyricist Christopher Adler, had thrown a party for a few thousand of my closest friends. Since I had to work the night of the twenty-fourth, we pretended my birthday was the twenty-third. Chris had decorated the Limelight with white and crystal. The invitations required white dress, and a few people came in jogging togs and sheets because white was not part of their city wardrobe.

The Limelight was an old church done over into a hot, Fellini-like disco. After the church owners had moved out, it had become a drug rehabilitation center for a while, and it was the Limelight people who prevented the building from being torn down. Due to my spiritual proclivities, I thought it very fitting that my birthday party was being thrown in a rescued church. Perhaps we could help add a new dimension to its original purpose. To dance in a church seemed to be as good an idea as praying. In fact, they were the same thing to me. As I remembered, it seemed to me no dancing was allowed in the basement of the Baptist church in Virginia where I grew up. My Catholic friends, on the other hand, could dance and even drink beer in their church basements. It was a sort of double standard both ways. The Baptist church was informal upstairs, and formal downstairs. The Catholic church was the other way around. But my so-called Baptist background (which was actually negligible) never really influenced me. After my first church picnic, I opted for necking on hayrides instead. So my religious propensities were determined more by my libido than my higher self. But then everything depends on how you look at it.

However, my disco prebirthday party was an event, religious or otherwise, in anybody's language. Each guest was met at the door by a white-clad escort (some decorated with sequins or crystals) who then ushered us through the passageways from rectory to library to meeting rooms all bowered in white flowers. There was laughter, warmth and joy ringing through the rooms where crystals hung from eight-foot floral arrangements of white lilies, white roses and white freesias, while clouds of white balloons drifted about the ceiling, rippling in the air currents. The walls were draped with crystal studded white silk. Eighteenth-century chamber music reverently accompanied us into the cocktail reception room. I privately wondered how long it would take before the night cut loose into what, I was sure, would be a full-blown exercise in la dolce vita.

I turned over in bed, stretched my legs, massaged the place on my right foot where some overly religious photographer had dropped his camera. I thought of Elizabeth Taylor's description of her experience at Mike Todd's funeral. She told me there had been people eating their lunch off the gray slabs of tombstones while waiting to get pictures of the grieving widow. There had been a hot, ghoulish feeling of excitement—the same kind of excitement that is generated by bad accidents. Accidents? Was Mike's death in a plane crash an accident? Oh dear, tell the one who's left alive it isn't. What possible good could death play? I wished I had known then what I knew now. Perhaps I could have been more help to Elizabeth.

I gazed out my bedroom window across the East River. Images of the night before still skipped in my mind . . . the friends who had come in from various parts of the world to help me celebrate being half a century old, the toasts of endearment they had offered me as, shyly, they stood to declare what they thought of me. It was one of those nights when you are faced with whether or not you have the grace to accept compliments without self-judgment, without false deprecation, and without embarrassment. But my daughter Sachi really did it to me. As only children, who basically speak from feelings and not from intellect, always can, she brought the tears fully spilling from my eyes when she stood up and said, all in a breath, "Happy birthday to my mother whom I love more than I can say and she is also my role model."

Mercifully, Christopher wheeled in the birthday cake (I had asked for carrot—my favorite), and as I blew out the candles I found myself struggling with how to thank everyone. I stared down at the cake for some time. The room was silent. I was deeply touched by the tributes of these, my dearest friends and colleagues, and was having trouble clearing my throat. Also I wanted very much to say something meaningful, for this was indeed a special occasion, a special time for me, a special outpouring of love.

Then I got a picture in my mind and spoke it out loud—after I blew my nose. "Friendship is like a ship on the horizon," I said. "You see it etched against the sky, and then as it moves on, the ship dips out of your vision, but that doesn't mean it's not there. Friendship is not linear. It moves in all directions, teaching us about ourselves and each other.

"That's why, over the period of long friendships, as with most of the people in this room, we are there for each other, even if we are not always seen." I wanted to say more, but choked up and so came to a stop. And discovered I was very hungry as we all plowed into white asparagus in pastry shells, roast veal, green vegetables I had never heard of, morel mushrooms, and mixed salad with herbs only a health food store would recognize, all topped off with that divine carrot cake.

Dinner over, we repaired to the public rooms to join a cast of apparently thousands thronging the nave of the ex-church. From a floodlit balcony overlooking the milling, shouting, cheering, singing audience we watched delightedly as a roster of extraordinary entertainers joyfully tore the night apart.

I definitely was treated to a coruscating birthday in a Love and Light temple out of one of my old Atlantean lifetimes!

I gazed out at Welfare Island as I thought about the night before, wondering what other people's perceptions of the party had been. I always loved to speculate on whether others were seeing through their eyes what I was seeing through mine. Truth and reality were so relative, I mused, residing only in the mind's eye. I wondered how others felt about being fifty. Did they look back and inward as much as I, wondering how life to that point had happened? Did others also speculate on lives they might have led before which brought them to the life they were leading now?

I rolled over and lifted my legs out of bed—my

dancer's legs—my two-shows-a-day-on-the-weekend legs—my twenty-five-years-apiece legs. I knew the reality of these legs in this life, this morning, all right. They were killing me. They needed a hot shower to make a transition into a less painful reality.

Jesus, I thought as I shuffled like a fifty-year-old toward the bathroom, was pain real or something I just figured I should have because I was working hard and was half a hundred years old?

I looked full-face into the mirror. Pretty good, I thought. Clear, translucent-pink skin ever since my last hicky disintegrated just before my daughter, Sachi, was born, and hardly any wrinkles, except the laugh lines sprinkled around the eyes which I considered my badges of positive thinking. I tilted my head downward slightly so I could observe the part in my hairline. Did I need a touch-up; how visible was my own streaked red hair from Clairol's version? It was fine. I had another week or two. My mind flashed to the pared-down basics I enjoyed when traveling, out of touch with the technology of twentieth-century beauty aids, and challenged to rely on my own resources. The experience of living in huts in the Himalayas, or the Andes of Peru, or in tents on the plains of Africa, or in shacks in the backwoods of the American South, was etched in my memory—a sharp contrast to the life I was leading now in New York as a musical-comedy performer in my own show at the Gershwin Theater.

I flipped the shower curtain closed and turned on the hot water. Hot water is a dancer's trump card. I hadn't learned how important it was to me until the last ten years. It worked liquid miracles on the body. And fast too. I didn't have to contend with the scheduling of the eucalyptus steam room in a health club. I had an immediate hot, wet therapy in my own bathroom as long as I knew how to use it.

I checked the positions of my four quartz crystals sitting on each corner of the tub. I had been

learning to work with the power of crystals and that
discipline had become part of my daily life. I stepped
into the tub and let the steaming water run over my
face, hair, and body. I could feel the sleep conges-
tion in my chest loosen up and the muscles along
my spinal column become more pliable. I did a quick
chiropractic back adjustment, feeling the vertebrae
slip into place, and breathed deeply, inhaling and
exhaling the steam about ten times. I leaned over
and poured some sea salt into a warm glass of shower
water and began another disciplined ritual which I
did every day. I put my nose to the edge of the glass
and sniffed in the salt water. My grandmother, and
several other people's grandmothers, had used this
method to purify the nasal, throat, and sinus tracts.
It worked, too, as far as I was concerned. Whenever
I did happen to catch a rare cold, sniffing the salt
water usually nipped the cold in the bud the first
day. Natural, holistic approaches worked better for
me than medicines or drugs. In fact, I no longer had
a family doctor. Experience had taught me that orthodox Western medicine relied far too heavily on
drugs.

   I touched my thumbs and forefingers together
and prepared to do my chanting mantras. By closing
the thumb and forefinger together, the energy circulated through my body in a cycle, nourishing each
cell as the frequency of the sound waves of my
chanting increased. I loved the feeling of sound waves
coursing through my body. I had first understood
the power of the frequency of sound when I began
singing lessons years ago. The vocalizing during
warm-ups actually made my body feel more aligned
than before. Physical therapists had used diathermy
(circulated sound waves) on any injury I had in-
curred as a dancer. It was quite effective. So it made
sense to me that one could use sound therapy on
oneself without a machine by simply chanting as the
Hindus have done in their temples for centuries, or,
for that matter, as thousands of people have done,

joyously caroling in bathtub and shower for generations, ever since plumbing was adopted by the West. And no doubt the Romans did it too.

As I chanted my Hindu mantras I visualized white light flowing through my bloodstream. It made me feel centered and balanced. I had learned to draw in white light that I visualized coming from some source above me, and with the sound vibrating through my body, the light traveled through me causing a sensation of calm alignment. I had no doubts about what the AMA would think of my morning discipline as a contribution to maintaining health, but some members of even that august body were using visualization techniques with their terminally ill patients—when there was nothing to lose.

I rubbed some salt on my throat and down the front of my chest. Salt is a basic purifier. Nature knows what it is doing. Any negative energy I was carrying from the tumult of the night before I would purify while chanting with the salt. Again, it might have seemed "new age" faddistic, but it worked for me.

I chanted and visualized the white light for about five minutes. That's all it took. Five minutes out of my morning life every day. I don't think I would have continued with these techniques if I hadn't gotten practical, functional, concrete, solid results from them. I have always been a pragmatic person. When you're trained as a dancer, you have to be.

Your orientation is earthbound because pain is a reality you live with. Dancing, using the body in creative ways, is one of the oldest arts known to man. But sophisticated forms force and strain the body, challenging its apparent limitations to become unlimited. A good dancer always knows that challenge to the capability of the body involves far more than an orientation to the physical. A superb athlete always understands that there is a dimension of mind and spirit necessary to realize the full potential of the body. So, *esoteric*, *holistic*, *mysticism*, might be words that sound unpragmatic, but when translated into physical terms, the practitioner understands that he or she is simply learning how to use invisible energies to their best advantage.

I stepped out of the shower. The phone rang. People seemed to know when I was up. I let it ring until the service picked it up. I had learned how a simple phone call could interrupt the alignment of energies for the rest of the day. If I waited until I finished, all news was good news.

I put on my yoga tape and began my twenty-five postures, feeling the pliability from the hot shower elongate my muscles. The yoga took about fifty minutes, or seven more phone calls, to complete. I felt energized and proud of myself that I had not been seduced by contact from the outside world.

Now I was ready. I called my service and picked up many messages; among them, that my publisher (Bantam) was expecting to give me a birthday present. They hoped that afternoon would be suitable.

I dressed and went downstairs to the living room. Sachi and my friends Sandy and Dennis Kucinich were out.

I felt neglected because no one was there to wish me a real happy birthday. Spoiled rotten, I thought to myself, after the lavishing of affection the night before.

Simo walked into the living room from the kitchen with a dish of his homemade apple compote and a cup of decaf coffee. Simo worked for me. He did everything. He was my friend, runner of the household, and companion in spiritual quest. We had met through the metaphysical community in Manhattan, and the spiritual path he was treading had reoriented his life as much as it had mine. He just laughed wisely when I introduced him as my wife, because before he came to work for me, I had said, "Look, what I need is a wife in every respect but the bedroom." He had said, "I'm your man. I've always wanted to take care of someone." So that's the way it was with us.

"So, did you sleep after all that last night?" he asked.

"Yeah," I answered. "Have you ever seen anything like it?"

He shook his head, and his tummy jiggled up and down as he laughed and joked about what had happened.

"You know," he said, slowly rocking on his heels, looking up at the ceiling as though he could snare some elusive thought up there. "You know," he murmured again, "they just wanted to touch you to remind themselves that somebody like you is real, didn't they?"

"What do you mean?" I asked.

"Well," said Simo, "Christopher said the same thing. After everything that has happened to you over the past year, people wanted to see for themselves that you were not an illusion, not a myth. That you had a wart or two and still, as they say, put on your pants one leg at a time."

"Yeah, maybe," I said. "I guess that's why celebrities are hot items. We're some kind of symbol that anything is possible—good or bad."

"It's everything," said Simo. "Your Oscar, the success of all that stuff you're talking about in *Out on a Limb*. How it's so obviously working for you on the stage with this hit show. They feel you have an answer they would like to be a part of. And the people that said you didn't have all your paddles in the water a year ago are beginning to wonder what they might have missed."

I smiled to myself. Gloating was not one of my things. In fact, I despised it. I could never stand people who said, "I told you so," to me, so I wasn't about to do it to anyone else. I didn't even like I-told-you-so's when they agreed with me. It is so prejudicial and self-serving and ultimately arrogant.

Simo picked up some dirty napkins from the

coffee table and put one hand on his hip. "Well," he said, "I don't know. My former friends who thought I was weird because I understood it are really hard for me to communicate with now. We don't have anything to say to each other." He hesitated a moment. "But then," he went on, "there are others who are beginning to see what I was talking about, and I find it easier to be with them." He walked into the kitchen.

I looked out the window down First Avenue. It seemed so simple to me, as it did to Simo or to any of us who were pursuing our self-search from a karmic point of view. *The concrete difference between the karmic spiritual perspective and the earth plane, "prove it," materialistic perspective was self-responsibility.* When we realized *we* were responsible for everything that happened to us, we could get on with living in a positive and contributive way. And that went for everything, whether it was a love affair, a death, a lost job, or a disease. *We* choose to have these experiences in order to learn from them—and to me, that is what life is about: learning. Learning and enjoying the knowledge that life is all about lessons.

I remembered how I had felt just prior to the publication of *Out on a Limb.* A few of my friends had said it would be a "career buster." Was it really necessary to be so public about my beliefs? Couldn't I have them in private just as well?

I'd thought a lot about that. Of course I could have safely kept my thoughts and feelings to myself. But my life had been about expression. From the time I was three years old, I was attending dancing classes because I loved to express myself physically. And when, as a teenager, I went from dancing to singing and musical comedy, that expanded experience was a natural and logical extension of self-expression.

When I carried expression even further, into acting, I felt a different kind of joy, the delight of becoming more specific through the use of words and language, which painted a more detailed portrait than song and dance could accomplish. I loved the intricate mystery of being another character, sorting out background and motivation and meaning, exploring my own feelings and thoughts in relation to this new person.

Writing became, yet again, another logical and natural extension of understanding and explaining my thoughts and feelings, of trying to understand the thoughts and feelings of others.

When my internal explorations began to take a metaphysical and spiritual turn, I felt, at first, that this was a purely private matter, a curiosity, something which I would write about only for myself. But then the discoveries I was making began to take on significance and importance not only for me, personally, but as a philosophy with a power of its own. To sit on my fresh awareness would have meant curbing the expression of a whole set of concepts new and vital in my experience. For me, such repression would be tantamount to paralysis. I could not have lived with myself if I had failed to write, or had calculated my writing according to what the market would bear. I would then have been living my life to the dictates of some amorphous public "image." And *that* was not in my lexicon of behavior.

I may have been raised in a middle-class, WASP, "don't-rock-the-boat" environment as far as behavior was concerned, but the free exploration of thinking was another matter altogether. Both my mother and father encouraged the expansion of curiosity in human thought, mine and everyone else's. They may have had their concerns about appearances, but never once did they curtail what I might want to *think*. They were the single most encouraging factor in my development as a free, uninhibited thinker. Nothing was preposterous to them when it came to the natural, spongelike seeking of a young mind, all questions were not only permitted but welcomed and explored, and no restrictions were imposed just as long as I was polite and made a fairly "good impression" as a person. Their open-mindedness in regard to philosophic and spiritual exploration was free-flowing, unthreatened, and unthreatening. As they often said, "If you keep your feet on the ground and your head in the stars, you will be fine." Their reality was up to them, as mine would be up to me. And mine was out in the open.

So, as I began my book tour to publicize *Out on a Limb,* I knew I would be discussing reincarnation, spiritual guides, the possibility of the existence of extraterrestrials, and the "reality" of other dimensions in public, and, happily, I found that the open-mindedness of my parents wasn't all that unusual.

For me, that was a new kind of liberating miracle, and one that I think could have happened only in America. I was enthralled by how genuinely curious and open-minded Americans really were. I encountered an ingratiating friendliness on the part of talk-show hosts, audience participants, feminists, journalists, students, even doctors and psychiatrists who questioned my point of view without rancor or judgment. The doctors and psychiatrists often said, yes, they sensed there was another dimension to deal with when they treated their patients, but as empirical practitioners of science they had to rely on what they had learned. But I loved the genuine human curiosity that most people displayed. And the humor! So much of it made me laugh. And as soon as it was clear that my own sense of humor had not deserted me while floating down the spiritual path, people relaxed and had fun.

The male journalists usually questioned me about "proof." How do you know you have a soul? How do you measure this God-force? How do you know you've lived before? Don't you feel you're fantasizing these things because civilization has reached the point of collapse and this just makes you feel better? The men were less *self*-involved. They externalized their reactions, not allowing a personal evaluation to come forth regardless of what it might be. It was an object lesson in left-brain (yang) orientation. They weren't comfortable exploring their right-brain (yin) intuitive intelligence. They were shy about their "feelings" and didn't consider them credible. Intuition and feelings were the domain of the female.

I had known many of the journalists personally throughout the years. They were familiar with my feminism, political activism, antiwar position, antinuclear stance, and my attitudes toward personal and sexual freedom. They knew how opposed I was to drugs and that I couldn't even swing smoking a joint. I was "down to earth" and forthright.

So when I explained spiritual search as a natural extension of personal and intuitive curiosity, they put it down to *my* reality, *my* perspective, and *my* need to look for more in life than meets the eye.

The women were another story. Most of them seemed hungry for validation of feelings they had wondered about, been exploring, or possibly even expressing, but were embarrassed to expose. Quietly, in small personal ways, they were on their own search. In private they were comfortable engaging in discussions and consciousness-raising sessions relating to their spiritual lives. Chakkra energy, holistic healing, meditation, and karmic truth were subjects that commanded their attention more and more.

Exploration might have begun as a search for identity, but it had rapidly evolved into identity assertion. For generations, as women, they had been in pursuit of intuitive understanding, a fundamentally female (right-brain) path to recognizing that truth may exist on an *unseen* as well as a seen level. Women had been surviving within the male power structure for eons on that basis. Their yin strength was now becoming more developed, more visible, and was steadily accelerating.

So the female journalists related to their questions with the heart. The men with the mind. Both were a lesson for me. Both were necessary. The men motivated me to become more articulate, which isn't easy when describing matters of the soul. The women motivated me to just be myself, which, alas, isn't easy when your task is to find out what self is.

The letters had poured in. I read many but I knew from the beginning that I shouldn't and couldn't offer any explanations. It was each individual's responsibility to look into his or her own soul and find the answer. Meditate, I suggested. Allocate time every day to "knowing" yourself better. If someone was interested in spiritual channeling, I told them to read books by Edgar Cayce, or Jane Roberts, or Ruth Montgomery. If they were interested in having a more positively functioning body, I suggested they read books on holistic medicine, or food combining, or yoga exercise. If they were interested in opening up the seven chakkra energy centers down the spine, I recommended they go to metaphysical bookstores in their community and ask for advice from the owner. I had found that one book usually leads to another anyway, just as one shared conversation leads to many more.

I was reluctant to recommend spiritual guides and teachers or trance medium channels because I felt that most people should be guided to their own source of learning. When the student is ready, the teacher appears.

I cherish the response, but have since come to realize that, for the letter writers, the act of having expressed themselves and shared their feelings was what was important to them.

I didn't want to become anybody's guru, nor did I want to lead or form a spiritual movement. Spiritual self-searching was something a person did on their own, in their own way, at their own pace. Each individual reacts and responds differently to these personal truths. Each person is their own universe of understanding and it doesn't work in terms of comparative progress. One person might *seem* more advanced than another, but who could ever really know? Knowledge of self is a lifetime job, and not just this lifetime either. So there is no way to assess progress in a linear fashion. There isn't a comparative pecking order. A spiritually evolved person in a former lifetime could choose to have the experience of spiritual blindness in this lifetime, just to act as a catalyst for someone like me who needed to be more articulate about what I had come to realize.

And here I was at fifty, still questioning, still curious, hopefully still evolving, and certainly still doing it all out in the open. What made me the way I was? I no longer questioned whether I had lived before or whether I would live again. I was now questioning how and why.

Relationships were the heart and core of everything we were. So did we *choose* to have relationships with people in order to learn? Did we make these choices before we were born? Indeed, did we choose the very parents we wanted to belong to?

When I went over my life from that point of view, the relationships I had with my mother and father and daughter and friends took on another dimension—a dimension that would help me see them and myself in another light. Yes, life was a dance which was just beginning to come into the light for me.

I heard voices in the front hall. Sachi and Dennis and Sandy were home.

"Happy birthday," they caroled as they came into the room and kissed me.

"Thank God the stores were open," said Dennis. "We were so caught up in the celebration yesterday, we didn't have time to get you a present."

"You are the present," I said, looking at one of the most daring and unorthodox politicians in big-city politics—housed in the body of a twelve-year-old kewpie doll. His eyes were round brown saucers, his hair teenage thick, and his way of walking that of a prancing track star certain that he would win every race possible because he knew he was borne by the winds of his own destiny.

Dennis Kucinich and his blond wife, Sandy, had a young two-year-old named Jackie to whom I was the godmother. Dennis was positive I had known Jackie in another life and was possibly the only one, later on, who would be able to handle her in this one.

Behind Dennis and Sandy came came Sachi.

"Hi, Mom," she said, lighting up the room as she did every time she walked into one. She leaned over and hugged me and kissed me on my cheek. "Happy birthday," she said. She handed me two gift-wrapped boxes. "This says it better than I can," she said.

I opened the boxes. One was my favorite perfume (and hers too) and the other was a morning coffee mug which said: I LOVE YOU, Mom, every morning.

I poured what was left of my decaf into her mug and sat back and looked at her.

She bubbled on about the crowded balcony the night before and Christopher popping out of a plaster-of-paris cake in the middle of the show they put on. She laughed at the spectacle of Liberace wearing a cloak that a royal queen would have killed for, and the sweet humor of Marvin Hamlisch as he dedicated the heretofore unheard overture to *Chorus Line* to me.

As she recalled the theatrical excitement of the celebration I watched her in delight and reveled in the truth that this pure, lighthearted flower child was really my daughter.

Sachi had had an international education, having grown up with me in America until she was nearly six, with her father in Japan until she was twelve, and at her request, in boarding schools in England and Switzerland until she graduated. We had spent three months every summer together as well as six weeks during the Christmas and Easter holidays. As she put it once, "It's the quality of the time you spend with someone. Not the quantity."

I was so proud as I watched her. She had a pristine innocence about her. When she was happy in her soul, there was no one I had ever met who brought me more joy. She was nearly twenty-eight years old, but gave the impression of being barely out of her teens. Yet she was shrewd and canny when she knew what she wanted. Long, free-flowing corn-silk hair hung around her freckled, button-nosed face, and when she blinked her porcelain-blue eyes, a minihurricane was stirred up by her very long, thick, absolutely ridiculous eyelashes. Her naïveté had a quality of joyous wisdom. She continually marveled at the wonder of the world around her, and the lives of people who came in contact with her were caught up by her infectious gaiety.

But Sachi had a depth of understanding which was sometimes stupefying. She empathized with others on levels that made me continually question where her talent for sensitivity came from. I guess parents are always the last to comprehend their children's discriminating maturity and I was no different. Sachi also had a clear understanding of what she wanted to convey and I had often been on the receiving end of her convictions. In other words, as guileless as she seemed, I knew in my heart that most of the time she knew exactly what she was doing. In fact, that was probably what I, and many others, found so attractive in her. She knew she was a creature of light and she wanted to stay that way. . . . A complicated process, since the world around her was becoming more and more disheartened.

Sachi was also working with spiritual and metaphysical principles. Most of her friends were too. They meditated, practiced their yoga, and visualized light techniques for healing. They were careful about junk food, and prowled the health food stores looking for food from natural sources, experimenting with no salt, sugar-free brownies, and bee pollen and wheat grass for even more energy.

I always knew when Sachi had been shopping. The refrigerator was stacked with carrot juice and organic fruits and vegetables. To her, a good dinner was a load of raw vegetables surrounding a dish of lemon and mustard dressing, all nestled on a large wooden plate.

She was also, however, a gourmet cook. She had studied *haute cuisine* in Paris and in Tokyo and could whip up a masterpiece for the palate out of leftovers. The night she sautéed thinly sliced chicken in a wild-mushroom and butter-wine-shallot sauce, I was mystified. I thought she had discovered some new kind of veallike meat, but it was a thawed-out frozen chicken breast. She never liked having me in the kitchen when she was cooking because that was her perfectionist domain. And she sipped dry vermouth on the rocks while she cooked, just as I had heard the chefs of Europe do. I think she doesn't like me in the kitchen because she doesn't want anyone to know how many weight-gaining ingredients she uses to achieve the effect that is so delectable.

For a while, my diet called for a lot of baked apples. Whenever *I* made baked apples, I used brown-sugar substitute and nothing else. They were fair. When Sachi made baked apples, they had been prepared with melted butter, cinnamon, nutmeg, and real sugar. There was no comparison. She loved watching me enjoy the baked apples, but was most upset when I walked in and realized how she did it!

Because of her international education, Sachi had thought of becoming a translator at the United Nations. She spoke and read and wrote fluent Japanese and French plus some Cantonese Chinese. She could read many Oriental newspapers but Japanese was the language she translated the alphabet into. She was socially sensitive in both Eastern and Western cultures and was sometimes confused by the reality that East and West did have a complicated time making the twain meet.

Soon after she completed her French studies in Paris, she came to Malibu to live. One night we were discussing what she might want to do with her life. I remember she was cutting a piece of fruitcake. She was in a wistful mood that night, and as she gently pushed the knife into the cake, she sighed and said, "Oh, Mom, life is so mysterious, isn't it?"

I couldn't help it. She was so adorable, I laughed out loud. She looked up at me, startled, and said, "What?"

I said, "Excuse me, sweetheart. Yes, life is certainly mysterious, but could you cut into that fruitcake again, and deliver that line the same way once more?"

"Deliver the line?" she asked, mystified.

"Yes, I mean, just do what you did again, saying what you said exactly the same way. Do you remember how you did it?"

"Yes," she said. "I always remember how I do something."

Oh my, I thought. This could be revealing.

So, once again, with no preparation, she repeated the "scene."

It was uncannily identical.

She looked up at me. I blinked. I sensed this was an important moment. So did she.

"I see," said I.

I hesitated. Should I pursue this or not? I went on.

"Okay, now," I said. "Let's have some fun. Do the same thing with the fruitcake and deliver the same 'life can be mysterious' line, but make me feel sad as though your heart is breaking."

"Sure," she said without even thinking. Again, with no preparation or emotional adjustment, she cut a little more hesitantly into the cake and seemed to be choking back tears as she said, "Oh, Mom, life can be so mysterious," as though she had been sentenced to die at dawn. She really moved me. As a professional, I thought, oh dear, should I really tell her how talented she is? Her kind of expressive capacity was instantaneously evident. I felt almost guided to go on.

"Okay," I said, "let's do something else."

"Sure," she answered, knowing that not only was this fun, but she might be on to something.

"Let's do an improvisation," I suggested.

"What's that?"

"Well, here's the outline. You go outside. Knock on the door. I'll answer it, and your task is to tell me that you have found someone out on the street who has been injured somehow and desperately plead for me to help them. And make me believe it."

"Oh," she said, her face lighting up. "Just knock on the door and then launch into all that?"

"Yep."

"Okay."

She walked outside and closed the door. I heard her descend the stairs that led to the beach below. About one minute elapsed before she ran up the steps and pounded on the door. As soon as I heard the intensity of the pounding, I knew how it was going to develop.

"Mom, Mom," she screamed. "Open up! Open up!"

I opened up.

"There's a man, a really sweet man, outside on Malibu Road. He's been hit by a car and he needs help. He's bleeding, Mom. He's losing so much blood, we need to call the paramedics before it's too late." Her eyes filled with desperate tears as she pulled on my arm to come and look. "Please, Mom, come and look for yourself if you don't believe me. Come, really. This isn't acting. He's really there. Maybe you should look at him before you call the doctors so you can tell them what to bring. But hurry, he's really in pain. I'm not acting now. Come on. Don't just stand there."

It was all I could do *not* to bolt down the stairs and beeline it for the street. I stood astonished in the doorway.

Sachi stared at me.

"What are you doing, Mom?"

"I'm wondering if there really is a man on the street."

"No, Mom," she laughed, the tears gone now. "You said make you believe it. I did, didn't I?"

"Yes, darling," I said. "You certainly did, especially when you said, 'This isn't acting.' You're shrewd too."

"Is this acting?" she said.

I put my arm around her and closed the door. "This is more than acting," I said. "This is believability."

She skipped back to the fruitcake. "Then is acting making someone believe what you say, whether it's true or not?"

"Yes," I sighed, thinking of Ronald Reagan.

"Well," she said, "maybe I should go into that. I've been doing this sort of thing all my life!"

In five short minutes, the course of her life had been changed and we both knew it. With stunning alacrity, she understood that she had stumbled across a form of expression that was natural for her. The question was, would she have the discipline to realize that acting took more than talent?

Within two weeks, Sachi had enrolled herself in one of the finest acting schools in Hollywood and found herself working beside already established actors and actresses who had returned to class to brush up on their honesty. She had no problem being known as my daughter, although she never mentioned it unless someone else did. And before I knew it, she was rehearsing, memorizing lines, wading through my closet for costumes and props, and carrying on long detailed conversations with her scene partners about what was expected of them the next day.

Word began to filter back to me about her talent. But more than that, people loved having her as friend. Of course, most of the new friends she made were struggling, using ingenious methods to make ends meet, and learning to adjust to the emotional cruelty of the oppressive competition of show business. It made no difference to Sachi. She *knew* she was in the right business and she would make it one day.

There was also a profound aspect of therapy in relation to what Sachi derived from acting. During all her years in Japan and England, she had suffered from the cultural requirement to repress her feelings. She was an American, not a Japanese or an English person. The double standard had begun to weigh heavily on her heart. She *needed* to express her feelings, her latent fears, angers, and confusions. She needed to mirror herself somehow, pulling out her emotions so she could confront them. She found acting to be a perfect forum, and because she was once removed from feeling "real," she allowed herself free rein in searching out who she was.

She soon became a participant in the positive aspects of California culture. She went for long walks in the Calabasas mountains, waded in the ocean, learned all the backstreet shortcuts in the Valley, Beverly Hills, and Santa Monica areas, and haunted the health food stores.

She was repulsed (thank goodness) by the cocaine toots and never drank more than a Kir (white wine and cassis) before dinner or her vermouth when she cooked. She met a young man who was also a fellow actor, whose family lived in Santa Barbara, so she treated herself to time away from her classes for walks along the trails and mountains, and she camped out under the stars with him.

At first I was concerned about the drug scene I knew she was bound to encounter in Hollywood. Sending her to school in Japan in the first place had been one way of avoiding that problem, particularly when I was on location most of the time anyway. Her father and I had discussed that early on. As soon as she was of school age, we had agreed that being educated away from Hollywood would afford her the opportunity to have a multicultural support system, avoiding what could potentially have been a tragedy for the child of a movie star. Who knows whether we made the right decision. I'm sure there were other confusions that plagued her as a result of being separated from me so much as a child, and I knew she had been through lonely hours as she searched for herself. But we often talked about that search being one you had to make on your own, and as I gazed at her in front of me now, bubbling with wondrous fun, I was comfortable in the certainty that she was a happy person, full of optimism, and that our relationship had survived the confused stickiness that plagued so many mothers and daughters.

Sachi and Dennis and Sandy and I celebrated for an hour. We talked of how important it was to celebrate oneself. We talked of how we could each make whatever we desired happen in our lives if we believed it enough. If we couldn't celebrate ourselves, how could we celebrate someone else? If we didn't love ourselves, how could we really love anyone else? If we felt good about ourselves, we'd feel good about others. It had taken me fifty years to reach that state of mind, and I wasn't about to change it even if such an attitude seemed self-aggrandizing. It was real to me. It was working for me. I also felt, and still do, that as long as I keep a positive attitude, it's only the unlimited beginning.

Chapter 2

I dressed in a warm knit suit, said good-bye to Sachi and Dennis and Sandy for a few hours, and went over to Bantam.

The first person I saw as I walked into the offices was Betty Ballantine, my editor on *Limb*. I call her G.A. because she was my guardian angel as she shepherded me through weeks of the nine hundred-odd pages that were ultimately cut down to 372! Betty and her husband, Ian Ballantine (the grand old man of publishing), took me under their wings and encouraged me to have heart when I feared that the New York intellectuals would ridicule me. "Just write your personal experience," they would say. Or, "It's *your* reality. Be honest about your own experience and let it grow out of that. We want to read how it happened to *you*." So I did. I began to call Ian the Gremlin because he could invisibly maneuver any situation into a positive reality.

"Well, there you are," said Betty, walking toward me with her arms outstretched and her snow-white curls winding around her heart-shaped face. "Many happy returns, dear heart," she said, beaming as though she had said something particularly significant.

"Thanks, G.A.," I said. "Why do you look as though you've just eaten a canary?"

"Oh," she laughed, "I've been thinking and

thinking what to wish you on your birthday and it suddenly struck me." She looked at me intently.

"Many happy returns," she said again, with emphasis. "It's an old saying. What do you think it means?"

Many happy returns, I said to myself and then the penny dropped.

"Do you mean that it could relate to each incarnation we choose to return to earth with?"

"Could be," she said. "Anyway, I thought it a particularly appropriate wish for you."

I thought again. "I don't know. Couldn't it mean that you hope someone is happy every time their birthday returns?"

"Well," she countered, "maybe, but we're already here, so what does the return part mean?"

I stood stock-still in the hallway. "Well," I said, "you've just given me the title of the next book I want to write and I think I'll begin it on this birthday."

"Good," said the Gremlin, who had invisibly appeared behind me. "When can we have it?"

"As soon as I close my show I'll begin. I'm supposed to do a picture, but I think I'll postpone it. I've been waking myself up at night with ideas. I just didn't know how to structure them. I think I know how now."

The Gremlin beamed and rattled the change in his pockets.

"You two are once again responsible for making my agent a very unhappy man!" I chided. "He thought he had finally gotten me back into show business and then you pop up again."

We put our arms around each other and I knew that it would be another year before I went in front of a camera again. When I saw something clearly that felt right for me, it didn't take me long to make up my mind.

Jack Romanos, publisher at Bantam, and Stuart Applebaum, chief of publicity, who had accompanied me on my book tour the summer before, walked toward us. "Everyone is ready," said Jack. "Let's go on in for your birthday presentation."

I walked into the main conference room, where several dozen intelligent, literary-type people stood with champagne glasses in hand waiting to see what I was like.

Jack stood on a chair and talked about how apprehensive some people at Bantam had been before *Limb* came out, then said that if the response was any indication of what people wanted to read these days, it was a case of how the public was ahead of the publisher. Lou Wolfe, Bantam's President, then presented me with a dozen roses and two beautifully leather-bound books, one of the hardback and the other of the paperback edition of my book, housed in a magnificent keepsake box. The crowd from Bantam applauded, then asked to hear from me. I looked at my watch. It was 3:55 P.M. In two minutes it would be my birth time. A spiritual guide had told me that the energy one inherits on one's birthday is very powerful, because the sun and its complementary planets are emitting the same aligned energy that they did the moment you were born. You "own" that energy. It is yours to use in projecting whatever you want of it for the following years. In 1983 I had gone to a mountaintop in Colorado and "projected" positively what I wanted; the success of *Terms of Endearment*, the Oscar, *Out on a Limb*, and my Broadway show. I had tried not to allow any doubt or fear to enter my mind. I needed to "know" that what I had projected would come to pass. Everything that I had projected happened. Now, as I stood before the Bantam crowd, I remembered my projections the year before. There was no mountain this time and I couldn't be alone, so I stood on the chair and thanked everyone. I explained what I had done on my birthday the year before at exactly 3:57, and I asked everyone if they would please take one minute and, in a collective mood, send me some positive thoughts about the book I was going to begin writing as soon as I left the building. No one bowed their heads, but nearly everyone closed their eyes. Some probably thought I was a lunatic, but they indulged me anyway, and I have had enough to do with audiences to know that this one genuinely wished me well.

I sopped up the positive goodwill I could feel in the room and for one minute we were silent with each other. It was a kind of collective projection.

When the minute was over and I was officially one year older, I applauded them for going along with me, thanked them, and went out to get some looseleaf notebooks and new smooth ball-point pens.

Betty and Ian knew they wouldn't have to nudge me and I was satisfied that I knew what I'd be doing for the next year.

As soon as I got back to my apartment, I called Mort, told him what I was thinking, and he hung up the phone.

"I'm very busy," he said. "I'm writing my memoirs. I don't have time to talk to you."

Betty and Ian Ballantine had been pressing me to write more about the relationship I had had with my mother and father. They said they were anxious to know how my childhood had contributed to my life, and what had been the interplay among us. I resisted because I didn't want to invade the privacy of my brother, Warren. My parents never minded when I wrote about our life together; as a matter of fact, they seemed to revel in hearing how important they had been to me.

I understood what Ian and Betty wanted, and had been exploring that approach. One's fiftieth birthday is for sure a time for assessment. However, my thinking had gone along slightly different lines. I wasn't interested simply in searching out more of my childhood, I was interested in discovering what my parents and I might have meant to each other long before I was born. *That* was why Betty's title had appealed to me so much.

Mom and Dad and I had talked about that too— believe it or not. It all started when I took them the manuscript of *Out on a Limb*. Mother had just gone through a cataract operation on her eyes and couldn't read. I wanted them to hear simultaneously what I had written. So I sat them down for three days and read it to them myself. They promised they would keep their hearing aids turned up to maximum and that they wouldn't argue, either with themselves or with me, until I was finished. I explained that I was going to dedicate the book to them so I wanted them to be the first people to know what I had written.

"We are the first to know?" asked my mother. It was, as I had surmised, important to her.

"Yeah, you sure are," I answered, wondering whether they would be shocked to realize what their daughter was into now.

"Gosh, Shirl," said Mom, "this is wonderful. Your daddy and I will really concentrate because we know how hard this will be on your voice."

"Okay, Monkey," said Daddy. "Do your stuff. What new things will you say about us this time?"

He was smiling in such a good-humored way, as though he adored being a leading character in all of my books. He cherished the influence he knew he had been on me, and to have me state it publicly seemed to mitigate the disappointment he felt in the unfulfilled potentials of his own life. There were many adventures he had longed to pursue, but he had curtailed his own driving passions ("which might have led to nothing") in order to be a good provider, a husband, and a father to Warren and me. Yet, when he was a young violinist, long before he married Mother, a famous teacher had plucked him out of an amateur symphony orchestra in Front Royal, Virginia, and offered to take him to Europe to teach him and start him on a career as a soloist. But Dad had decided against it, fearing that after long years of musical training, he might just possibly end up playing in the pit of some Broadway show.

"The competition was too rough, Monkey," he had explained to me. "And that would have been no way to make a living. It wouldn't have been dependable. Sure, I would have seen Europe, maybe been wined and dined by royalty, but if I had done it, I probably wouldn't have met and married your mother and we wouldn't have had you and Warren. So I think I did the right thing."

Somewhere underneath that story I had always sensed a deeper reason, something much stronger than his fear of competition, but I couldn't put my finger on it. Obviously, I had had nothing to do with his career decision. Yet I had felt a sense of inevitability when he first told me the story as a teenager. Indeed, there had been an inevitability to everything he had done with his life, and in that I was certainly a participant. Whenever I looked at Dad, I felt that our relationship had been almost preordained.

Mother gave me the same feeling too. It was as though she had *chosen* to meet Dad and marry him. There was a quality of intense predetermination about the way they related to each other. Or so it always seemed to me.

Many times Mother had described to me the moment when she said good-bye to her mother in Canada. Her father had died when she was a teenager. She had adored him and had done all she could to help her mother with the raising of the rest of the children (two girls and one boy). Mother was the responsible one. But she had met a professor of psychology and education at Maryland College where she had come to teach dramatics. His name was Ira Owens Beaty. He was intelligent, witty, had a good set of values, and a warm sense of humor, and she had fallen in love with him. And felt compelled to marry him.

She had brought her new love to Canada to meet her family. His mother came with them, and as

Mother was saying good-bye to her mother, setting off on a new life in America, she was horrified at the raucous argument Ira and his tyrannical mother were having while packing up the car. Mother told me that for the first time she felt a flicker of fear. She knew Dad had had an "unhappy" childhood and she was now a chilled witness to some of the drama he had grown up with.

"Am I making a mistake?" she remembered asking herself. "There's no telling what kind of damage that woman has visited upon her son—and I will very likely inherit it." She wondered if she should make a life with someone who had a mother like that.

But she said she couldn't help herself. It was something she *had* to do, not only because she loved him and it had already gone too far, but because she also felt Dad needed her. Over the course of her life Mother was always willing to sacrifice herself when she felt she was needed by others.

So, she stuffed herself in the car with the new family she was marrying into and had a torturously confusing trip back to Virginia.

She felt compelled to endure each mile of that journey. The dynamics set in motion by meeting Dad were somehow beyond her control. She just *knew* what she was doing was right, even though so much of it seemed questionable. Again she said she felt "this compulsion" to go through with it. She couldn't let anybody down. And then when Warren and I came along, she understood why.

I have always been interested in what caused the "compulsion." Of course there are all the psychological explanations: the need to sacrifice herself, attraction to chaos, attraction to another family which was volatile and sometimes violently explosive. I remember watching Dad's mother, armed with a huge metal skillet, chase his father around their Front Royal house with every intention of hitting him over the head; whereas Mother's Canadian upbringing had been controlled, placid, and preeminently polite. There were many complicated reasons for Mom and Dad deciding to make a life together, not the least of which was their love for one another. But I always sensed there was some other subtlety to their relationship. Let me just say for the moment that from the time I was very small, I wondered whether I had in fact been adopted. There was an element beyond being a daughter that I was picking up. It is one of my enduring childhood memories. There seemed no reason for me to have what psychologists would call "an orphan psychology." But I would often sit and gaze at them and wonder who they *really* were. I didn't know what I meant by that then. I do, however, think I know now.

So I sat down in the sun room of our Arlington, Virginia, home, with the creaking of the wicker chairs interfering with their hearing aids, and began to read them the manuscript of *Out on a Limb*. Dad gave me his rocking chair next to the pipe rack and Mother brought me some tea with lemon in one of her china cups. They leaned forward with bright, inquiring eyes and smiles on their lips. We had agreed that I would read aloud slowly until I was tired. It took about five hours a day for three days. They sat openmouthed as I described my affair with a married English M.P. and my useless battering at his rigidly closed mind, the search for enlightenment through spiritual questing, my curiosity about reincarnation and trance medium channeling sessions where I spoke to entities on the other side, Peter Sellers's description of his own death and his attraction to the loving glow of the white light, my trip to the Andes where I talked with someone who said he had met an extraterrestrial being from the Pleiades, my growing conviction that all of us had lived before and would live again, and my own out-of-body experience which served to validate the answers to many questions—the surest knowledge being derived from experience.

At the end of the third day, I read the last page and put the manuscript down. I looked up at Mom and Dad. They were both crying. I wondered if they were humiliated.

"Well, Monkey," said Dad, "I certainly am proud to know you." He choked back more tears and tried to go on. "You could get a Ph.D. with that manuscript," he said. Then he couldn't talk anymore.

I turned to Mother. "Oh, Shirl," she said, "what courage that took to write. There is a lot of it I don't understand, but let me tell you something." She brushed away her tears with her long fingers and straightened up in her chair, fingering the frilly blouse around her neck. "You know," she began, "this is the first time that I've understood the expression on my father's face when he died. Did I ever tell you about it?" she asked.

"Not really," I answered. "Not in detail."

"Well," she began, "I had been out playing tennis with my friends. I knew my father was sick but I wasn't prepared for what happened. He sent for me. Why me, and not the others, I don't know. But I went to him. I remember being concerned that I was keeping the tennis game waiting. Daddy was lying in bed. He looked over at me when I walked in and beckoned for me to sit beside him. I did. He took my hand, and then, as though he had only been waiting for me, he squeezed my hand and looked up into my face. Something was happening to him that I didn't understand. I remember I was nervous and I giggled. I would have much preferred to have been playing tennis. I've been guilty about that feeling ever since. His eyes took on the most beatific glow. I have never seen anything like that since. Then, with his eyes still open, he became almost transfigured— with an expression of such beauty it took my breath away. And he said, 'Oh, darling, it is so beautiful, it is so, so beautiful.' Then he closed his eyes and died."

Mother had a faraway expression on her face as

she remembered, lost in vividly recalling the emotions of a major event in her life. Then she came back to the present and looked slightly confused for a moment. "Do you suppose," she asked, "that I was watching my father's soul leave his body and what he described as 'so beautiful' was the same thing that Peter Sellers and those other people in your book also describe? Was he seeing that white light that the others said they saw? Why else would he say it was so beautiful? Does that mean death is nothing to be afraid of and old people like your daddy and me should not be so anxious about dying?"

My breath caught in my throat. What on earth do you say to the woman who gave you life, when her honesty about death is so blazingly open-minded? Here was my darling, self-sacrificing touchstone, a frail eighty years old, breaking a bone every month or so, knowing that her days were numbered, facing sleep every night wondering if she would wake up in the morning, questioning *me* about what to expect and realizing, and acknowledging, that I had touched on another dimensional reality which might possibly mean there would be no such thing as her death. I had not anticipated such wondrously unlimited courage. I couldn't speak.

Daddy came to my rescue, realizing what he was doing.

"Okay, Monkey," he said strongly, "now I'm going to tell you something *I've* never told anyone, not even your mother."

I sat back in my chair. Both of my parents unceasingly surprised me.

"Remember," he began, "when I had my car accident about twelve, fifteen years ago?"

"Yes," I answered.

"Well," he continued, "I died that night. I literally died. I was dead to the doctors in the ambulance that came. I saw the police say another drunk driver had bitten the dust. But I didn't see them from inside my body. I was outside of my body. I was above my body watching the whole scene. I saw them all scrambling and milling around, but I knew I was not dead. I felt myself rise out of my body and begin to soar. I saw my body below me. I remember the conversations I heard. Then I saw the most beautiful white light above me. I can't describe how that light felt. It was warm and loving and *real*. It was real and it was God or something. I wanted to go to that light more than anything I've ever wanted. I was prepared to continue toward the light—and then I thought about your mother and I thought about Warren. I knew they needed me. I knew I couldn't leave. I knew I had to come back into my body. I didn't think about you, Monkey, because I knew you didn't need me. But they did. And as soon as I felt any doubt about leaving, I felt myself come back into my body. Suddenly my body felt heavy and broken and painful. I don't know how long I was gone, but when I opened my eyes, all the folks around me were surprised. So when you tell me about out-of-body experiences and Peter Sellers and the soul being separate from the body, I know just what you're talking about because it happened to me."

When he finished, Mother was looking at him as though she had just met him for the first time and understood everything he was saying.

"Yes," she said, "I can understand what you're saying. Why didn't you tell me before?"

"Because," said Daddy as he filled up his pipe, "I didn't want you or anyone else to think I was crazy. If Shirley hadn't written this, I would still have it locked inside of me. And something else, Scotch [his nickname for Mother was related, I think, more to her heritage than her attitude toward his booze habits], whenever you people get upset with me because I'm sleeping so much, what I'm really doing is a little bit of what happened to me back then."

This was a truly amazing statement. Mother's

mouth dropped open, but whether or not she realized my father was saying he *deliberately* spiritual-
traveled, I don't know. What she said was, "Well, I
still think you should get up earlier so I can clean
your room. It's a mess and the dust from it flies all
over the house."

"Now, Monkey," said Daddy, "I want to tell
you something else. You know how long I studied
philosophy at Johns Hopkins University?"

"Yep."

"Well, every Sunday morning after we had finished a week of what they said we should learn, we
would all sit around and discuss the things you're
talking about. Why, I remember everybody having a
story or two about believing or experiencing these
other dimensions. Why, only a fool would categori-
cally claim they don't exist. I remember the custo-
dian of our dormitory telling us about the vision he
had had of the death of his son. He was a nice
lookin' boy who served in World War II, and one
night his father had a vision that his son appeared at
the foot of his bed. Scared the bejesus out of him
because the son was real. And he knew the son was
in Europe. But the son said, no, he was here saying
good-bye to his father because he had just died. The
old man jumped up and came to me in the middle of
the night to tell me about it. I suspected what had
happened, but I couldn't be sure. A week later the
old man got the telegram saying that his son had
died at precisely the same time that he had appeared
at the foot of the bed."

"So what do you think of all this, Daddy?" I
asked, never having anticipated that my *parents* would
be people I could talk to about this stuff.

"Well," he said, loving the introduction of meta-
physics into our relationship, "I think we should
stay open-minded about everything there is to learn.
You may be blazing a trail here, to make it more
acceptable to discuss. I mean, read your Plato, or
Socrates, or your Freud and Jung for that matter.

How do we know unless we explore? Of course, we can't explain it in presently acceptable terms, but who knows how those terms will change? Nobody believed there were microbes crawling around on the skin until someone came up with the microscope. We are each our own microscope."

I got up and stretched and went to look out the familiar sun-room window. Had I sensed this capacity for metaphysical truth in both my parents while growing up? Were they the reason I now found such speculations easy and thrilling to comprehend? Had Ira and Kathlyn Beaty been silently instrumental in the forming of this bent of mind I now had? I knew I had responded more to their feelings than to their words during the years we had lived together— emotional truth being more vivid and influential to me than intellectual truth. But never, not once, had I consciously speculated that they might be thinking about the same possibilities I was. I thought *I* was the only one.

Mother watched me at the window.

"You know, Shirl, remember your old Bible?"

"Yes," I said. "Why?"

"Well," she answered, "you were always reading it and underlining your favorite verses. I have it here, if you want to see it. You have been interested in this spiritual side of life since you were a little girl."

"Really?" I asked, not remembering.

"Yes, you were never much on religion or church or any of that stuff. You wanted to know what was underneath what they were teaching. You really liked reading about Christ. I remember you used to call him a spiritual revolutionary."

"I did?" I asked.

"Sure," she answered proudly. "Your friends were going to church and you were reading books about religion. You know, both you and Warren could read before you ever went to school. Your daddy and I read to you every night until you began to be able to do it yourselves. You were insatiably curious. Your minds were always clicking over."

Yes, I remembered the books, and the discussions that Mom and Dad shared with us.

Mother always encouraged self-reflection and reverence for nature. I remembered the many times she would suggest a long walk by the stream near our house so that I could commune with myself in the company of the birds and trees and rushing water. During an unhappy interlude in a young teenage love affair, she would say, "Shirl, stop worrying about your boyfriend and what he's doing. You should be out in the wind and the rain. Go stand under a tree and then wonder and think about yourself. You're too young to be so intensely involved with 'going steady.' There's a magical world of nature out there that you're missing. You'll know more about yourself if you allow nature to be your teacher."

And Dad, as a teacher himself, regarded education as a dedication. He believed knowledge was power. Knowledge was freedom. To help inspire a young mind to search for truth had been the cornerstone of his life. He not only lived up to that dedication in his chosen profession as a teacher and principal and superintendent of schools in Virginia, but he brought that dedication into the home. There was no question I could ask that he would casually brush away.

Daddy lit his pipe and crossed one leg over the other as though he were about to launch into a lecture.

"Monkey," he said, "do you know the definition of the words 'education' or 'educate'?"

"No," I said, "I've never thought about it."

"Well, they come from the Latin words *ed*, out of, and *ducar*, to lead. *Educar*, to lead out of, or to bring out that which is within. What does that mean to you?"

"I don't know. Maybe it means to lead out of yourself the knowledge you already know."

He smiled gently. "Yes, it could. But what do you mean?"

"Well, if we really never die, if we just leave the body like you did, and then if we do continually come back or reincarnate into new bodies, then we must have done that many times. If we have done that many times, then we each must have tremendous knowledge and experience from lives we've led before. So maybe the ancients realized that education was just helping people get in touch with what they already knew. And maybe our higher selves already know everything. Isn't that what Plato and Socrates believed?"

Daddy thought a moment. "Yes," he said, "I think you could put it that way. Plato professed to know that other civilizations such as Atlantis existed. Maybe he was having an imaginary vision or maybe he was speaking from former knowledge of those times. I'm not sure what the difference is. Possibly imagination is simply a form of memory. Most of our great thinkers have professed to have had an intuition or guidance that they couldn't describe, something they ultimately called a force or God or a higher recognition of truth that required a quantum leap of inspired faith. As Carlyle put it, 'The unfathomable SOMEWHAT which is not WE.' Or as Matthew Arnold said, the 'not ourselves' which is in us and all around us."

I had never heard my father talk like this. Was this the man whom I had mentally dubbed a prejudiced bigot when he, perversely, insisted on calling black people "niggers"? Was this the man I believed had rotted his brains with booze so much that he reduced me to tears?

"Art is the same thing," said Mother. "Who knows where great art comes from? Who knows what inspiration and talent are?"

"What do you think they are, Mother?" I asked.

"I think," she answered, "that everything comes from God."

"And what is God, then?" I asked.

"I don't know," she answered. "But I know it's there."

Daddy cleared his throat with a commanding *hurrumphhh*. He always did that when he was vitally interested in something.

"What are you getting at, Monkey?" he asked with genuine curiosity on his face.

I chose my words carefully. I wanted to convey what I was thinking as succinctly as possible even though I realized there were not many words that could define what I felt.

"Well," I began, "since so many new ideas are surfacing these days, I'm wondering whether they are, in fact, *new*, or instead are really rather ancient. I'm wondering if all the old masters weren't actually more in touch with the 'real' spiritualization of mankind, meaning that they understood that the soul energy of man is eternal and infinite. That they *knew* that the soul goes on and on. That it never dies and in fact cyclically reembodies itself in order to learn and grow while alive in the body on the earth plane."

"You're talking about reincarnation, then," said Dad.

"Yes, and if the soul is the repositor of all its accumulated knowledge and experience, then education is only the process of drawing out what it already knows."

Dad flicked some lint from his shoulder, a ploy to give himself time to consider a point.

"Well," he said, "I understand that nothing ever dies. High school chemistry proves that. Matter only changes form. So I could even go along with your belief that the body becomes the eternal soul after death, but I don't know if I can go along with reincarnation."

"But Dad," I said, feeling my voice rise as it had whenever, as a child, I wanted to get a point across to him, "you actually had the experience that your soul was *separate* from your body. How can you say the body *becomes* the soul?"

"What do you mean?"

"Well, if you have already experienced death, then you know that death is only the experience of the soul leaving the body, right?"

"Right."

"Then if the soul is separate from the body, why not stretch a little bit further and contemplate what the soul does after it's been out of the body for a while. Or if there's no old body to go back to."

"Well, Monkey, the way I felt about that white light that I saw, I'm not sure I'd ever want to leave it to come back again."

"Oh," I said, understanding that his version of the white light was so glorious, there would be no future necessary after that.

"So, you'd just hang around up there basking in the glow forever?"

"I think so, yes." He laughed. "I certainly wouldn't have to worry about the dust in my room, would I?"

"Oh, Ira, be serious now," Mother chimed in. "Shirl," she said, "if you believe that we have all lived before, then you and your father and I have lived before too?"

"Yes," I answered, "that's what I believe. And I think that our family, and every family for that matter, is a group of souls very closely connected because we have been through many incarnations together. I think we *choose* to be together, to work out our drama. We choose our parents, and I think the parents choose the children they want to have before they ever come into an incarnation."

"You do?" said Mother, astonished at the thought and realizing, at the same time, the implications of what I'd said. "You mean you believe you chose to have your father and me as your parents?"

"Yes," I answered, "and I believe that we all agreed to be a part of this family unit before any of us were born. That's why I feel your marrying Daddy seemed inevitable to you. Your higher self knew as soon as you met him that you had already agreed to have Warren and me for children with him."

"Oh, my goodness," exclaimed Mother. "You believe all of this was preordained?"

"Yes, and not by God, but by each of us."

"Oh my. I have to fix myself a drink," said Mother. "Ira, do you want a glass of milk?"

"Look at that," said Daddy. "The boss won't even let me share in a drink with her after we planned our lives together from the spiritual plane."

I laughed and thought of all the incarnations they must have had together. If there were ever two people who were joined at the hip, acting as catalysts for one another's learning process, it was my mother and father. They had a kind of George and Martha *Who's Afraid of Virginia Woolf* relationship. They couldn't live happily with each other, and they couldn't live happily without each other. From my very first memories, I felt there was a profound experiential drama going on between the two of them. They could push each other's buttons more effectively than anyone I had ever witnessed. But then they were my mother and father. So of course I would be affected as intensely as all children are by their parents. Surely the human drama with our parents (or the reverse, a total lack of it) is the most influential element in our lives? The drama within the family unit had to be the underpinning for the way we regarded life in the world from then on.

Yet, if the purpose of life was to experience, the better to appreciate the growth and understanding of the soul, then everyone we met, to a greater or lesser extent, was a means to that end. To realize oneself fully meant the necessity of experiencing all the possibilities available to the human condition.

The lessons in living which triggered our most profound reactions dealt with our feelings toward authority, helplessness, loss of control, material com-tort, survival, manipulation of fear, restriction of freedom, attitudes toward possessions, attraction to the opposite sex, attraction to the same sex, closeness of living, passion, violence, and love.

What better place to learn those lessons than within the family unit? The family constellation was a microcosm of the overall human family. Work out the problems within the family and you might very well have the capability, training, conditioning, and tolerance to work out problems on a global level.

Families are all about karma.

Therefore, one's karmic requirements began at birth within the association of parents and siblings. Within the family environment was every human conflict that could ultimately lead to a willingness, or a nonwillingness, to wage war. Most attitudes of, and toward, violence and hostility are spawned in the family. Just as attitudes of love and compassion are. No one knows better than parents and children how to set off the trigger points in each other. Feelings of suspicion, fear, and doubt are a direct result of family attitudes. Those who "brought us up" to know ourselves chose to help us with life's lessons. Nowhere could a teacher be more effective than in the body of a parent. If the parent and the child chose to make it so.

The reverse was true also. Don't we learn as much from our children as we ask them to learn from us?

Ideally, parents and children could help each other with their self-realization. What we would do then, out in the world, would be an extension of that realization. In actuality, too often the pattern gets skewed or dulled, so that growth and the ability to cope with one's self and the world don't develop.

Mother brought two wet martinis and a glass of milk from the kitchen.

"I know he'll go sneak some Scotch anyway." She shrugged. "So he can put it in the milk."

I took a sip of the martini and watched my mom and dad as I would a good situation comedy. More and more I saw them from the karmic perspective, but when I was growing up, the intense emotional environment in the home had had several effects on me.

First, I was the amused, sometimes astonished and confused, child witness to their dramatic and theatrical human interplay. Often I didn't understand the intricacies of their scenes, or the meaning of the outcome, but I learned on a subtle level to read their emotional tones and their detailed shifts in mood and expression.

Unconsciously, I was receiving an exquisite education in the nuances of manipulation.

Therefore I believe it was inevitable that I would, later on in life, put this understanding and knowledge to work in an art called performing.

Second, the spectrum of expression that I saw exhibited at home, both positive and negative, inspired me to want to express myself. My parents were locked in their own battles of interplay so intensely that Warren and I needed to seek out our own turf for expression. Mine, at a very early age, was dancing class but escalated later into the expression of acting and writing.

So the development of my discipline in early life was in direct ratio to the emotional need I felt to express myself. My "discipline" was not difficult for me. On the contrary, it was my support system for being heard: because my parents were clearly the stars of our household, co-starring with each other, Warren and I were the supporting players constantly working for a chance to star ourselves. Considering the refined, high-level art of manipulation exhibited by my parents with one another, it was inevitable that Warren and I would go into a business where we could confidently apply what we had learned. Show business was a profession made to order for us. And self-expression became as necessary as air.

It wasn't that they didn't allow us to express ourselves in the home. Not at all. It was more that the level of their expression overpowered our capacity as children to express ourselves. They were our teachers by example and inspired us by triggering our sense of survival. We were forced to step into the spotlight just to assure ourselves that we were real. And our desires to be recognized were lovingly acknowledged and supported—that is, whenever Mom and Dad took a little time off from their own starring drama.

As I said before, I believe now that all of it was karmically preordained by the four players involved. And *that* interested me more than anything I had explored in a long time.

"Well, I really like your book, Monkey," said Dad. "I don't think the metaphysical stuff will be any problem. But I do see another problem."

"Oh?" I asked. "What is it?"

"The love affair with that British politician. He's still married, isn't he?"

"Yes, but he's had several other affairs since me."

"Well, I think the people are going to want to know about that, because after all, his wife is still around."

"You really think that will cause an uproar?" I asked.

"Well, it's something to think about. By the way, who is Gerry?" Daddy asked with a mischievous gleam in his eye.

"Margaret Thatcher."

Daddy's stomach undulated as he laughed.

We talked long into the evening about how and why I had written the book. Karmic overload came around midnight. We all went to bed. As I was falling asleep, I heard Mother say to Dad, "Ira, I wish you had heard what Shirley was talking about." Daddy seemed astonished.

"What are you talking about, Scotch? It's you I can't hear because you don't want me to."

Leaving them to their own karma, I fell asleep,

wondering if Dad had been right about the "Gerry" relationship.

The week the book was published in America, Margaret Thatcher called an election in Britain. An enterprising English journalist based in New York City read it, saw an opportunity to have some fun, and spiced up an otherwise dull election by sending his editors in London the juiciest chapters relating to the love affair I had had with a Socialist M.P. who wore a newsprint-stained trench coat and socks with holes in the heels, and had lost the tip of one finger. The story hit the front pages of every newspaper in London and the campaigning English politicians were called upon to hold up their five fingers and remove their shoes, the implication being that if they did qualify as my British lover, they'd get votes, not lose them.

Gallant M.P.'s claimed sadly they didn't qualify, but wished they had. One said he'd chop off a finger if it would help. Another said he was happy it was only the finger missing. Another said it must have been a Tory, not a Socialist, and his name was Marble because that was clearly what he was missing.

When members of the London press tracked me down in Dallas, I countered by regretting that Fleet Street cared more about my "in-body" experience than my "out-of-body" experiences, but that they could rest assured the gentleman's real identity would go with me to the grave—unless I decided to incarnate very soon again to help elevate a future British election.

Dad, in his old-fashioned country-boy wisdom, had hit the nail on the head more accurately than he realized.

Chapter 3

Sachi and Dennis and Sandy were busy dressing for my show when I got back from Bantam. As I walked into the living room, Simo stopped me.

"Your mom called," he said. "I think there might be a problem. She didn't want me to say anything to spoil your birthday, but I think you should know."

"What kind of problem?" I asked with a twinge of fear. "What happened?"

"I don't know. She just came from the doctor," he answered haltingly.

I tried to stay calm. It was one of those moments you have thought about, and expect, but are never ready for.

I reached for the phone and dialed. Mother answered. "Mother?" I could hear myself pleading for good news. "What's going on? How are you?"

"Happy birthday, darling," she said. "Are you having a nice day? You know I sent your present to Malibu."

"Yes, Mom. I know," I said. "Thank you. I loved the lavender color, and the fabric of the sweater is really soft."

I waited.

"Well, listen, darling," she began. "I don't want to upset you with all you have on your mind, but I just got home from the doctor's office. He did an

EKG on me. I thought it would be routine, but in the middle of the EKG my heart started to go. They did an X ray and found a clot on my lung moving toward the heart. So the doctor is putting me into the hospital to try to dissolve the clot. I don't want to mince my words, but it's serious."

Actually she had never made a drama over her health and aches and pains, even while steadily, in old age, pursuing a course of broken bones. I could feel the honest concern in her voice; she wanted to prepare me for the worst.

I didn't know what to say.

"Well, what does the doctor think?" I asked lamely.

"He just says I have to go to the hospital immediately. So I'm leaving in five minutes. I'm glad you called back before I left, so I could tell you myself what it's all about."

"What time did the heart trouble happen?" I asked, not really knowing why. "I mean, when did the machine register the problem?"

"Oh"—she thought a moment—"I remember I looked at my watch. It was a few minutes before four, about one and a half hours ago. Why?"

Then I realized why I had asked.

"Because, Mom, that happened at exactly the moment I was born fifty years ago," I said.

She thought a moment. "Oh, I'm not surprised," she said casually. "I've always known I've lived my life through you. You've done what I always wanted to do, so that makes sense to me."

I felt myself gasp slightly over the implications of what she said. I didn't want to ask if she was feeling it was, therefore, time to die, but I could sense she was considering it.

"Now listen, darling," she said rather commandingly, "whatever will be, will be. I've led a wonderful life and if it's time, it's time. I want you to know how much I love you, and do real well tonight on the stage. You just remember I've been working hard on my broken shoulder so that I can come up to New York and see you before you close. And I mean to do that. So don't you worry."

My throat ached so painfully that I couldn't breathe.

"Oh, my goodness," I finally said. "Is Daddy taking you to the hospital?"

"Yes. Your daddy is going to take me."

She gave me the hospital name, telephone number, room number, et cetera. Then she said, "Darling, don't let this interfere with your work. If I'm supposed to go, that's just what'll happen. And that'll be because it's supposed to."

I could apply my karmic understandings with no trouble at all in the abstract, but now I was getting the test of my beliefs personally. The impending death of the mother you love couldn't be more specific.

Again, I found it hard to reassure her because of my own pain. I couldn't find any appropriate words. I didn't want to say, "Oh, it'll be all right," because she was beyond that kind of social inanity.

"I love you, darling," she said, "more than I can say. And I always have. So say a little prayer for me."

"I love you, Mother. I love you so much," I said, my voice breaking to a hoarse squeak as I held back the tears and wished I had said I loved her so many more times than I had.

"So do a good show tonight and we'll talk tomorrow, okay?"

"Okay," I said.

She gently hung up and I collapsed in the chair with the receiver resting on my lap. I wasn't even aware I hadn't hung up.

I felt Sachi walk into the room behind me.

"Mom?" she asked. "What's wrong?"

I began to sob.

"Grandmother had a kind of heart attack or something," I said, crying. "I mean, there is a blood

clot on her lung, really close to her heart. She's
going into the hospital."

Sachi's face crumbled. She had not spent much
time with her grandparents, and had been feeling
lately that she wanted to make up for lost time
before they got too old.

She put her arms around me and felt me fall
apart. I could feel her identify with the situation,
wondering what she would do if she had gotten the
same news about me.

"What do you think, Mom?" she asked. "What
do you sense?"

I blew my nose and thought about it. "It might
be time for her to go now. There was something
about how she said 'whatever will be, will be.' She's
never talked that way before."

I got up and paced the floor. I tried to approach
what was happening with objectivity. My mom had
lived for over eighty years. The last five had not
been easy. She had had an operation for an aneurysm, a broken pelvis, two cataract operations, a hip
transplant, a broken arm, and she was diabetic. We
had all openly commented that Mother appeared to
be doing herself in. Either that or she was testing
herself for a hundred-year run. This was only the
latest crisis in her struggle to overcome.

I calmed down and breathed deeply.

"You know, it's funny, Sach," I said. "She's
been through so much with her health for the last
three or five years that it became almost abstract to
me. She never complains, yet she keeps doing these
things to herself. I'm beginning to feel the impact of
what she's trying to tell us very strongly now."

"You mean, you think she's saying she wants to
go?"

"Yes, but I think she's conflicted about it, she's
worried about leaving my dad behind. She always
says she hopes he goes first because he'd never be
able to get along without her."

Sachi blinked quickly.

"But wouldn't Granddaddy go right away?" she asked.

"Sure, I think so. And I don't feel he's afraid of that. As a matter of fact, I get the feeling he's just waiting for her to go, so he can go back to the white light with a clear conscience!"

Sachi laughed. I had told her about Dad's out-of-body experience and she understood.

I blew my nose again.

"Mom, you'd better get dressed or you'll be late," she said. "Will you be able to work tonight?"

Sachi possessed a combination of sensitivity and practicality at moments of crisis. I remembered how she had passed her stewardess examination for Qantas Airways with a top score. What put her over the top were her reactions to the simulated crash-landing test. She had been the only one who stayed calm and collected. She was showing me a bit of that now.

I did a deep knee bend to see how my body felt.

"Sure, I can work," I said, knowing that nothing would keep me from doing a show when the audience expected me to be there. A kind of inbred professional ethic always prevented me from canceling a show. It was literally impossible for me to indulge myself that way. I remembered the night I had done two shows in Vienna, when I was on tour in Europe, with a 106-degree fever. By the end of the second show, my temperature was normal. I had sprained my ankle on New Year's Eve in Vegas. The doctor told me I shouldn't even walk on it for three weeks, nor dance on it for two months. It was purple-black. But I went on anyway—and never missed a show for the rest of the engagement. When I was sixteen years old, I had *broken* the same ankle and danced a complete ballet on point rather than miss a show. I think I wouldn't be able to live with myself if I couldn't live up to my professional obligations. It was my gypsy-dancing training, I guess. But really, I think it was more that I didn't want to displease anyone. I was my mother's daughter, all right. So I really understood her sincerity in not wanting to upset me. I had come to understand that conducting myself according to what others might think was not a trait to be admired, but when it came to an audience waiting with the expectation of seeing me, some kind of workhorse professionalism took over. *I would be there.*

"Mom," said Sachi, "don't you think you'd be more comfortable wearing slacks tonight?"

I wondered what she meant. "No," I said, "I don't feel like changing. I'll just keep on this knit suit. It's okay. Besides, why should I wear slacks to our dinner afterward?"

"Oh, I don't know," she said vaguely.

I didn't know what that was all about.

Simo came in tapping his watch.

"Why don't you put on some slacks so we can get going?" he said casually.

"Why does everybody want me to wear slacks?" I said.

"No reason," he said. "Just thought with all that's going on, you'd be more comfortable."

I brushed it all aside, picked up my pocketbook, yelled for Sandy and Dennis, and we all piled into the limo to go to the theater.

The crosstown traffic was congested. With each red light and delay, thoughts of my mother crowded my mind. Sad childhood memories. How I would feel when I could never touch her again. What it would be like walking into the house without seeing her rush toward me, her long arms outstretched. I pushed the thoughts away. I had a show to do. But as we pulled up to the stage door, I realized I was quietly crying.

Crowds of people milled around the stage-door entrance. Many more than usual.

' What's going on?" I asked.

"Well, it's your birthday," said Simo.

"Yeah, but why all this?" I asked.

I looked into the crowd more carefully. I saw three television camera crews.

"I don't understand," I said. "I'm not Queen Elizabeth."

"Well, I hope not," said Simo. "She wouldn't know what to do with this."

"With what?" I asked, really becoming curious now.

My company manager, Michael Flowers, flanked by two policemen, guided me over to the huge stage-door elevator that was used for loading equipment into the theater.

"Why are you taking me this way?" I asked.

And with that, the elevator door opened. The crowd began to applaud. I turned to them. I didn't know why they were applauding. Someone pointed behind me. I turned around.

Towering over me was a huge Indian elephant with her trainer from Ringling Brothers Circus beside her.

Lee Guber, the promoter for my show at the Gershwin, said, "You said the one thing you had never done was ride an elephant. Well, happy birthday! Here's your chance."

I quickly wiped my eyes, took a deep breath, entered the scene, and we were "on." Lee was right. The night I had won the Academy Award, I was interviewed by Joel Siegel. He had concluded that I had done just about everything there was to do in my life and he wondered if there was anything I hadn't done that he didn't know about. It didn't take me long. "Oh," I said, "I've never ridden an elephant."

So, here she was, along with several hundred people who were now going to watch me do it.

"What's her name?" I asked the trainer.

"Tananya," he said tenderly, as though she were his lumbering daughter.

I looked up into the huge pachyderm's eyes. She blinked like the shutter of a low-speed camera. I liked her immediately. She seemed kind. I had always loved elephants. I had elephant knickknacks, brought back from India, all over my apartment.

Tananya nuzzled me with her trunk and moved me into position. She clearly had the idea she was going to pick me up. The crowd roared. Then, before I realized what was happening, she scooped me up in her powerful trunk and held me aloft for all of Fifty-first Street to see. The people applauded. Tananya had a new performing partner. She gently returned me to earth and knelt down.

On my toes I reached for the flap of her ear and lifted it. "I think I have met you before," I said into her ear. "But I can't isolate which lifetime it was. It was either you or your great-great-grandmother. And if you guys have the memories everybody says you do, maybe you can remember when it was."

She nuzzled me again with her trunk. The television cameras ground away.

"Well," said the trainer. "How about a ride? That's what we're here for."

With that, Tananya knelt lower and I realized why Sachi and Simo had wanted me to wear slacks.

Well, I picked up my knit skirt, grateful that I was wearing thick black panty hose, grabbed one of her ears gently, stepped as lightly as possible on the crook in her bent knee, and whipped my right leg over her massive head. I scrambled the rest of me to the top just as Tananya lurched to her feet. The crowd adored it and all I could think of was the Carmen Miranda shot that the TV cameras must have gotten. (There was a famous shot taken during the Second World War of Carmen Miranda out dancing one evening. She had evidently forgotten her underwear and the camera proved it. There were legions of soldiers who claimed that that shot, posted on their lockers, was what brought them back alive.)

Tananya proceeded to break into a fast, head-bobbing shuffle—the same rapid movement they use on stage; she knew damn well what this was all about—and headed down Fifty-first Street with me hanging on to my birthday life for all I was worth. Several Russian cab drivers couldn't believe what they were seeing. If for no other reason, it had been a good move for them to renounce the oppression of communism and try the bizarre expression of New York City.

Tananya and I were a hit. We could have taken our act on the road. I definitely understood why her other mistresses wore leotards, especially leotards which were beaded in the crotch.

We made several rounds of Fifty-first Street. I had a flash that Mother would be watching this on *Entertainment Tonight* from her hospital bed, and if anything would convince her that she had lived to see it all, it would be this.

Tananya finally came to a triumphant halt. She knelt down again, and then I saw the reason why . . . a huge chocolate birthday cake waited for me with candles lit and the crowd singing. I jumped from her back and blew out the candles, making a wish for Mother's recovery as fast as I could. It wasn't fast enough. Tananya nuzzled me out of the way, neatly scooped up half the birthday cake in her trunk, and did away with it in one fell swoop. I doubled over laughing.

Someone handed me a knife. I trimmed away the unevenness of her trunk-scoop and passed out the rest of the cake to the crowd.

Sachi was hugging herself with glee as we disappeared into the stage door.

There was only half an hour left for me to make up and warm up. But I had long since learned that having fun was more important than being prepared. It had been a painful lesson to learn, but I was much happier with the knowledge that living in the moment was everything.

When I walked out onto the stage, the audience yelled "Happy birthday," and when the ovation stopped, I told them what had happened with the elephant. Some of them had been on the street and were still eating the cake. Others, who never hung out around stage doors, realized what they had missed. One man yelled from the audience wondering why we hadn't brought the elephant on stage. I said if he could have seen what happened in the freight elevator, he would realize that I wouldn't have been able to dance on the stage for a week.

I did the show and had the time of my life. When it was over, I sat happily exhausted in my dressing room and called Dad.

"Hi, Monkey," he said. "We saw you on television. You had yourself a big time, didn't you?" He was laughing and spirited.

"How's Mom, Daddy?" I asked.

He hesitated a moment. "I don't know. We'll see. I think she's all right tonight. She's asleep now."

"Did she see me on the elephant?"

"Oh, yes. She had a big time watching you too."

"What do you think, Daddy?"

"Well, Monkey, you know how I feel about this. I'm prepared for whatever happens. If she goes, I won't be far behind."

The celebration joy receded. It was such a contrast in two realities. He was really talking about the Big Moment.

"I think maybe your mother is not as prepared for the hereafter as I am. But since my experience I told you about, it's fine with me. I'm just waiting for her."

"Would it be okay with you if she died?" I asked, hardly believing that such a question had come out of me.

"Oh, sure," he said. "We all have to go and it's certainly getting to be that time for both of us. I'm not afraid for her. She's worried about me, but she shouldn't be. I'd be free to go, too, if she'd just go ahead and do it."

I began to tell him something I had wanted to say for a long time.

"You know, Daddy, that when you both go we'll be able to spend much more time together than we do now."

"Oh, yes, Monkey. I know that."

His agreement surprised me.

"I mean," I went on, "that when you leave the body and become just a soul again, I will always know you're there."

"Yes, I know."

"I mean, there won't be this separation of cities and countries like there is now. When you're on the other side and out of your body, you can talk to me all the time and I'll hear it, because I really understand how that stuff works now."

"Oh, yes," he said, "I know. And I won't have to wear these damn fool contraptions in my ears to hear you either. I know what you're talking about. That's why I'm not afraid." Oh God, I wondered, did other fathers and daughters talk like this when death was near?

"Bodies are difficult to live in, right?" I asked.

"Very difficult," he answered. "Especially when you know how it is to be out of one."

"So, if she goes, don't think you have to hang on to staying alive just for Warren and me."

I heard him breathe an audible sigh of relief. "Monkey?" he asked, "if I could only believe that your brother feels this way, too, it sure would be easier on your mother and me."

"Well," I said, barely able to talk, "he's a big boy too. You don't have to worry. If you want to go—go ahead. Then you can help both of us from the other side. Maybe you'll be one of those spiritual guides I talk to. You always did know more than you let on, you know. Why should it stop now?"

"That's right," he answered, needing to say nothing more.

"Right."

"And you and Warren can save a lot of money on plane tickets. All you'll have to do is close your eyes and we'll be there. You can do your work anywhere in the world and we'll be able to talk to you and see how you're doing. It would be much better than this because we don't see enough of you now."

I couldn't stand it anymore.

"Okay, Daddy," I said, feeling my voice pinch into that raspy squeak. "I think I'd better go now. I'll call you when I wake up."

"Okay, Monkey," he said. "Thank you. Tell me, did that pachyderm take a dump on the street or in that elevator?"

"In the elevator," I answered. "She was trained to be polite in public, just like me."

"Yes," he said, "you always were right much of a lady. Were you glad you wore those black stockings?" He laughed that maddeningly teasing laugh of his, the laugh that also drove Mother crazy.

"Yes, I was glad," I said to him, "but when you're on top of the world like that, it really doesn't matter what you have on."

"Yeah, I reckon you were always a child of nature, weren't you?"

"Bye, Daddy. I love you."

"I love you too, Monkey. Happy birthday."

We hung up. I dressed for a birthday dinner, but all the restaurants were closed. A group of us ended up bringing home delicatessen food, which Sachi arranged deliciously, but I was so done in by the implications of the day's events that I eased upstairs and went to bed. It was all very well to be metaphysical in the abstract, but the personalization of the earth-plane reality when it came to my mom and dad got me right where I lived. I was exhausted and, above all things, I needed sleep. Before I shuttered down, I had time to be grateful for my fiftieth birthday and glad it wouldn't happen again. This time.

Chapter 4

Two days after Mother went into the hospital, I took the Eastern shuttle and went to Virginia to visit her. Sachi had gone the day before on her way back to California. Neither Mom nor Dad wanted me to do anything that would jeopardize my time or health. "Wait until your day off," Dad had said. But that was a week away. I felt I couldn't.

As I walked into Mother's hospital room, I found her in remarkably high spirits. Seeing her lying helplessly in bed had become a familiar sight to me over the last few years. I couldn't help feeling that she was desperately trying to convey that life had become too trying for her. Yet she was always a favorite of the doctors and nurses and seemed to flourish and bloom with their attention. She cared much more about the well-being of the hard-working hospital attendants than she did about herself. "You go on now," she said to a young blond nurse who had a husband waiting at home, "I'll be fine. I can take care of things while you're gone." The nurse evidenced confusion because she knew her hours required her to stay anyway. Mother wanted the nurse to know that she shouldn't spend any extra energy on her, though.

"These nurses are my real friends," said Mother,

glowing from their attention as I walked into her room and leaned over to kiss her.

"Yeah, I'll bet you have more friends in hospitals than anywhere else by now, don't you?" I asked.

"Oh, no," she answered. "I have friends everywhere."

I sat down and took off the jacket of the raw-silk slack suit I was wearing.

"My goodness," said Mother, "that's a nice outfit. Where did you get that, Hong Kong?"

I explained it was from Canada and she said she loved to see me done up in clothes from around the world.

"You know, Shirl," she said, "the trips you've given us are our most cherished memories. You said they would change our lives, and they certainly did. We sit together and go over them night after night, and when we read a book about one of the places we've been, or watch a TV program and recognize the scenery, it's so much fun to know we've been there."

I sat down beside her bed and prepared for an afternoon of happy reminiscing about her travels. But I did have a particular curiosity to explore her feelings about her trips.

"Mom," I asked, "were you ever anywhere that you felt you had been before?"

"Oh, yes," she said, "I've thought about that a lot. I think it was in the hills somewhere in Scotland. I knew the look of that place so well. I couldn't understand it. I thought I had been there with your daddy. But he didn't feel it was familiar at all. So I don't know why, but I *knew* I had been there. It was the smell and the feel of the place. And when I was there, I was happy, very happy, but I can't figure out *when*."

A nurse came in to check Mother's heart monitor. She looked over at me casually and said, "Good morning," and then said, "Oh, my God. I didn't realize *you* were here."

I laughed.

"Yes, this is my daughter, Shirley," said Mother.

"Oh, my God," said the nurse, "I'm a nervous wreck. . . . Well, we really love your mother. She takes as much care of us as we do of her."

"Yes," I said, "I can imagine."

Mother looked up at her.

"Is my clot dissolving?" she asked with an almost girlish smile.

"It's not one clot, Mrs. Beaty. It's several clots and, yes, they are dissolving."

"Can you see them dissolving?"

"Well, we take the CAT scans and that's how we tell."

"See?" said Mother. "The doctors don't tell you anything."

"Oh," said the nurse, "the doctors will tell you everything if you ask."

"Isn't that nice," said Mother. "You see, that's why I love doctors."

"Well," said the nurse, feeling that she should leave, "I'll let you two visit."

She left, and Mother asked if I could get her and Dad tickets to my show when they came to New York. I laughed and said sure, wondering what else I could do or say to get these two to relax and enjoy one another more.

We sat and smiled at each other.

"You know, Mother," I began, "so many people are going through intense problems right now. Haven't you noticed it?"

Mother sat up in bed. "Yes, Shirl," she said, "that's true, isn't it? Everyone I know seems to be going through difficulties."

"Well," I went on, "we all draw to us what we need to experience, in order to grow, however that might be. So whatever we're going through is a learning process."

"That's right," said Mother. "Same as your father. He knows that whenever he takes a drink, he has to be responsible for it."

I thought about how to continue the point I was attempting to make.

"So," I continued, "whenever someone chooses to do whatever they're doing, there's really nothing much anyone else can do but allow them with love and understanding to do it."

"Yes," said Mother, "the only way to really help someone else is to be with them every minute of the day. Like your father with his drinking, I know where he is every minute. Sometimes he gets mad at me and I lose my temper, but that's the only way I can help him."

"Well, Mother, maybe his drinking really isn't that bad. I mean, he doesn't exactly get drunk. It's more that *you* think he shouldn't drink at all because of what *you* feel it does to him."

"But it does, Shirl. He's not happy when he drinks."

"But he says he is. And at this age, why not let him do it? It can't be too terrible for him."

She shook her head stubbornly.

"Nope," she said, "it's not good for him. Why, I find bottles all over the house—under the bed, in the closets."

"Well, no wonder, Mother. You won't let him drink out in the open."

"Nope."

"Okay." I let the matter rest for the time being. It was so amusingly clear to me that the issue wasn't so much about my dad's drinking as it was about control and interaction. If Dad didn't drink, I wondered what there would be for them to talk about.

"Are you eating all right, Mother?" I asked.

"Oh," she said, "I'm on a very strict diet. No sugar, no sodium. No salt, you know. Oh, yes, I have to be careful. Lunch will come in a while, then you will see."

"So," I said, "did you have a nice visit with Sachi?"

"Oh, Shirl, she is really something. She told me all about her acting and her scene partner. Did she tell you about the scene partner she had during the love scenes who stuck his tongue in her mouth?"

Both my properly raised mother and my liberally raised Sachi had an uncanny gift for stating the blunt truth without censorship.

"Oh, yes," said Mother, "the boy wouldn't leave her alone. He followed her everywhere and tried to make dates with her, but she didn't want to have anything to do with him. She's such a darling."

I laughed, wondering if not having anything to do with such a demonstrative boy was what made her darling.

As she talked, Mother seemed unaware of her fragile bones, her dry mouth, her shattered shoulder, the monitor on her heart. She was aware only of what she was talking about. I admired her focus, her concentration, her obliviousness to pain.

"Shirl?" she asked, changing the subject in that free-associative way that old people have of doing. "Do you really believe that we have all lived before?"

"Yes, Mother. I do. That's what I've been writing about."

"I know," she said. "But I wasn't sure you really thought it."

"Well, I do. I thought about it and questioned it and read everything I could get my hands on about it and, yes, I have come to the conclusion that it must be true."

"So you think we have known each other before?"

"Oh, yes."

"So, if I knew you before, then I would have known Sachi before too?"

"I think so, yes. But I can't say about anyone else. I can only speak for what I believe about me."

"Well," she went on, "I feel very close to Sachi.

Very familiar. I don't know what other mothers feel about their grandchildren. I've never discussed it with them. But I feel I have known Sachi for eons. Especially when she touches my hand. I don't know what it's all about. It's beyond me. And at a certain point, I just give up thinking about it. But I know that whenever she touches my hand, it reminds me."

I gazed at the faraway look in her eyes. She wanted to say more.

"I think," she went on, "that Warren had something like that with my mother. I remember he used to get all dressed up to come to the dinner table because he knew Mother would be dressed. She never came to the table without having dressed, with a new hairstyle and perfume. And she wouldn't use a paper napkin. She insisted on a real linen napkin. Anyway, as soon as Warren and Mother sat down, Warren would snuggle up to her and say, 'Oh, Grandmother, you smell so good.' He never left her side. There was something very profound between the two of them."

I listened, remembering the trips we had taken to Canada to see her mother. The wind-blown clam hunts along the Nova Scotia shore were my favorite times. We dug the clams and steamed them over tin pots in the cool evening sand and told stories as we dipped them in dripping hot butter and slurped happily into the night.

"You, on the other hand," Mother went on, "you would come rushing in from dancing somewhere, all tumbled and disheveled. You'd eat partly standing up as though you couldn't stop moving. Then you'd look over at Mother and say, 'Hello, Grandmother. You're looking beautiful.' And Mother would say, 'She's such a little lady.' "

I thought of Grandmother MacLean's powder-white hair, like strands of fine ivory-colored silk. She had the bearing of a dean of women (which is what she was at Acadia University, in Wolfille, Nova Scotia) and she seemed aware of every move she made and the effect it would create. She flowed when she walked, as though she had an invisible pot on her head.

"Well, what did we talk about at dinner when we were little?" I asked Mother.

"Oh, dinnertime was the time for discourse," she answered. "It was when your father flourished. You know how he loves to talk. He'd pick out a subject and then draw you and Warren out. Sometimes it went on for hours. Your father had plenty of time for it, but I was too busy."

"What do you mean, busy? Were you cooking?"

"Oh, I don't know. It seemed as though I was always busy. You know, your father never changed a didi [diaper]. It made him sick. And if either one of you upchucked, I'd have to clean it up. So I was always busy."

"We must have upchucked a lot," I said.

Mother went on. "Your father is like that now. If I'm sick now, he falls apart. So I have to do everything myself. I'm always so busy."

"Well, so what did we talk about?" I asked.

"Oh, the opera. Mother loved opera. But I hated it. She couldn't get me to go with her. But religion was something we talked a lot about. You were attracted to the Episcopalians and your Daddy and I felt you should stay within the Baptist ranks, which was stupid because people should be able to choose. But frankly, you didn't really think much of any of them. You didn't like getting dressed up to go to church. You never thought *that* should have anything to do with God. That's why you didn't go much. You thought people should be comfortable when they worshiped. But really, you didn't have much time anyway. You were always either at dancing class or rehearsing."

Mother sat up in the bed, her hands cupping her ears. "I have to have my ears repierced," she said, looking ahead to the future. "I've been sick for so long, I let them go. And I want to wear those beautiful diamond studs you gave me years ago."

There was a flurry at the door. People were greeting someone outside. Ira O. Beaty made his entrance. He sported a cane in one hand and a bunch of flowers and a brown paper bag in the other.

"Well, there himself is," I said, chuckling at how commanding he was, even using his early eighties shuffle to the utmost effect.

"Hi, Monkey," said Daddy as he walked over to Mother, leaned down, and offered his cheek to her.

"You brought me flowers, Ira?" Mother exclaimed with incredulity.

"Yes, Scotch," he answered. "Flowers from your own garden."

"Oh, Ira, did you pick them yourself?"

"I picked them with my own lily-white hands." He snuck the brown paper bag under her sheet. She noticed and stealthily looked up at him with grateful, bright eyes.

As though I hadn't observed the interchange, Dad began to make a fuss with the chair he would sit in. I said, "No, take my chair. It's much more comfortable." He said, "No, it's too much trouble." And before I realized what was happening, I, while maneuvering my chair over to him, looked up and saw Mother poke into the brown paper bag under her sheet, unwrap noisy tinfoil, and push a clump of moist chocolate cake into her mouth. Daddy continued with the diversionary tactic of the chair-moving exercise as Mother chewed voluptuously. She made no real attempt to hide what she was doing, apparently knowing that she would continue eating the obviously delicious forbidden food regardless of sugar shock.

"Daddy," I said, mockingly reproachful, "you snuck chocolate cake in here?"

"Yes, Monkey," he said guilelessly. "It's real good cake."

"There's not much sodium in this," said Mother stoutly. Why, whenever I make tollhouse cookies, I always have to add a teaspoon of salt." She seemed to feel this was an explanation.

"Real good," said Daddy. "Sachi had two pieces and Bird Brain ate the rest."

"Who's Bird Brain?" I asked, realizing that now he was using a verbal diversionary tactic in lieu of chair moving.

"The new woman who takes care of us. Mrs. Randolf."

"Why d'you call her Bird Brain?"

"Well," said Mother in between chews, "she can't keep her mind on anything."

" 'Ah forgot,' she says," said Daddy.

Mother laughed with Daddy as she fingered a piece of cake to the front of her mouth before the nurse came back. "She forgets the flour out of the gravy," she said, swallowing a tiny choke as she laughed. "But she's really a darling. Bird Brain is an affectionate name."

"Oh," said Daddy, "she's better than the TV. She'll come around the corner of the kitchen cabinet with a knife. Then she'll remember she forgot the fork and go back to the drawer and get it. Then she'll remember she needs two sets, but she only comes back with one. She walks several miles a day in that kitchen. So I guess it's good exercise for her."

Mother opened the drawer next to her bed. "They'll never notice if I put the rest of the cake here, will they?"

I couldn't resist and said no, helping her stuff it into the back of the drawer.

"Cake won't kill me," she stated positively. "And I'm not ready to die."

Daddy retrieved a piece of paper from his coat jacket. "Now *this* Bird Brain remembered," he said.

It was Mother's exercises for her previously broken shoulder. "Bless Bird Brain's heart," said Mother.

"I'm forever losing this paper, and she's forever knowing where it is."

"We'll get some different exercises when you decide what you're going to break next."

"You may think that's funny, Ira, but I don't."

"You mean falling off the piss pot is not funny?" asked Daddy with his special brand of malicious glee.

"Now, Ira," chided Mother, "I like to tell my own stories."

All my life I had been privy to the tragicomic details of my parents' life together. Bird Brain was a new chapter. I was very curious.

"Tell me," I said, "where does Bird Brain sleep?"

"In your mother's room," answered Daddy. "She sleeps in the other twin bed so she can hear it every time your mother falls out."

"Now, Ira," said Mother repetitiously. "I don't like Bird Brain sleeping in the room with me much, but she's nice and clean and was obviously brought up nicely [Bird Brain, I later discovered, was seventy-seven]. But when she takes her bath, she makes such a racket."

"What do you mean?" I asked, trying to picture Bird Brain, whom I had never met, having a raucous time in the pretty pink-tiled bathroom Mother had decorated.

"Well, for instance, the other night I was in bed about to fall asleep and Bird Brain decided she wanted to have a glass of milk. I got up and walked to the kitchen and found her in there in the dark gobbling up ice cream and cake with chocolate syrup poured all over it."

"Bird Brain puts butter and sugar on everything," said Daddy. "Even sausage."

My stomach turned over.

"Well, I left her alone and went back to bed and she still didn't come to bed herself. So I got up again and went to look for her. I noticed the door to the guest room was closed. I opened it and there was

Bird Brain asleep on *your* bed with a book over her face. I screamed at her, 'What are you doing sleeping on top of that spread? Don't you know if you sleep on that twenty-five times, I have to wash it?' Well, Bird Brain was so startled she lurched out of bed, and I said, 'This room is for my children whenever they decide to come home. *No one* sleeps in this room or on that spread.' Well, poor Bird Brain. I terrified her. So then she went in the bathroom and made a terrible racket when she was taking her bath."

It occurred to me as I listened that what she was describing would make a good senior-citizens TV show. It was, however, interrupted by the arrival of a nurse. Mother eyed her table drawer slyly. Daddy gestured it was okay.

The nurse pulled Mother gently to a sitting position and explained the exercises she was about to put her through.

"You know," said Mother to the nurse, "if I hadn't fallen and broken my hip, I would have died of my aneurysm."

The nurse lifted her arm and said sweetly, "Really?"

"Oh, yes," Mother went on, "because when they X-rayed my hip, they found the aneurysm there. So, you see, it all happened for the best. The good Lord said she's not supposed to die yet."

"What about your wrist, Scotch?" asked Daddy, deciding to tease her in front of her nurse.

"Well, I haven't figured that out yet. It was an accident. And the pelvic break came because we were in a hurry. You should never get out of a car at Christmastime in a hurry unless you know you've gotten everything out of the car with you. I was just plain stupid to get my coat caught in the car door. So I learned my lesson. I'll never do that again."

Daddy laughed. "You say you're finished breaking your bones?"

"You're darned right I am," said Mother defiantly. "I don't want to have to keep going to restaurants where they serve you that soppy food. I want to entertain in my own home. I'm going to live to be ninety. I want my friends to be able to come and see me. I don't want to retire to my bed and say I'm done."

"When did this ninety thing come up?" said Daddy, almost as though he wasn't sure he would stick around for the event.

"Well, I've been thinking about it since I came in here," said Mother.

"Why ninety?" I asked.

"Well, it seems like a ripe old age. I don't want to live to be a hundred. I might change my mind, but I doubt it. At ninety people will give you their arm and help you to a chair, but more than that would just make people exasperated. I think my legs will give out first. I'm so long-legged, you know."

I turned to Daddy, wondering how he felt about living ten more years. "What do you think about ninety as a good, ripe figure?" I asked.

Daddy ruminated. "I like that saying from Omar Khayyám. You know, the one about a jug of wine, a loaf of bread, and thou. These days the only thing I give a damn about is a loaf of bread." He eyed Mother. "But I never dispute the boss," he added.

"He'll be lying in the bed," said Mother, "waiting for me to go. Then he'll come right after me. There's no way to get away from him."

Daddy lit another cigarette. "Well, Monkey," he said, "where do you keep your Oscar?" The talk of death didn't faze him in the least.

"My Oscar?" I asked. "Well, I have it in New York on the stage with me now. I have it on the piano, covered with a black cloth. And sometimes I tell the audience that I want them to meet a person who has come into my life who is very special to me. I say he represents many qualities to me: integrity, hard work, experience, longevity, quality, and love. And besides that, I'm sleeping with him. They gasp and look around, wondering who is there. Then I take the cloth off and it's Oscar."

"Right cute," said Daddy.

"I've only done that a few times. Some people think it's too self-congratulatory though. So I'll probably stop. Some people have a problem when you celebrate yourself. They think it's tricky and smacks of flaunting your success. What do you think?"

He chuckled. "Well, it's a lot safer to sleep with Oscar than it is for some of your other people I've been reading about."

I chucked Daddy on the arm playfully.

"Warren says we should both bring our Oscars home to you so you can enjoy them. He says he keeps his in a drawer." (Warren won his Oscar for best director for *Reds*.)

"Well," said Daddy, "we certainly do have a lot of stuff in our house. Why not the Oscars?"

"No, Ira," said Mother flatly. "As it is, most of our things Warren and Shirley ought to have."

"I agree with you," Daddy said, "but since they don't have those things, because they are still in our house, then we might just as well have their Oscars too."

Dad and Mom were like a pair of vaudevillians, each endeavoring to top the other for attention and focus. Each was secure in the role they were playing and neither would call it quits and say the show was over. Their twists of mind, their upstaging tactics were more intricate than the finest melodrama the stage could produce. Mother played the tyranny of the fragile and Daddy the insecurity of the tyrant. Their games with each other left outsiders batting their heads against each other. And as I have said, Warren and I had been, in effect, outsiders. Bit players to the two stars.

They possessed an astonishing repertoire, which bewildered our impressionable minds at the same time that it entranced us. Again, it was inevitable that we would go into show business. First to elicit attention and second to attempt to dissect complicated characters, which we would play in a theatrical effort to work through, and hence comprehend, what had indeed gone on in our own home. Mother's and Dad's chickens had come home to roost.

Daddy looked at his watch. I had been there for six hours. We had had lunch (no salt, no sugar) and many interludes with charmed nurses.

"Do you want me to take you to the plane station, Monkey?"

I adored the way he mixed up words. "No thanks, Daddy," I said. "I think I'll just get a cab."

"Well, you should leave fairly soon because the shuttle will be jammed and you don't want to miss your show tonight. There's nothing worse than a dark theater when you've just begun your run."

I knew how much he had wanted to be up there during his life as a teacher and later as a well-providing real estate salesman.

"Let me go call a cab at the front desk," he said.

He left Mother and me alone together.

She looked at me longingly. "I'm going to be fine," she said. "I'm not ready to die yet. I was worried before, but I'm not now. They make this anticoagulant out of snake venom. And snake venom will dissolve these clots."

She sounded so involuntarily jarring, so piercingly discordant. Then she turned on an emotional dime and said, "Shirl, I want you to tell me something."

"Yes, Mom. What?" I asked.

"Sometimes, just before I fall asleep at night, I hear some people talking to me in my head. I know I'm not dreaming. I know a dream when I have one. This is something else."

"Oh, tell me about it."

"Well, we have real good conversations. They make me laugh. They're real funny."

"What do you talk about?"

"Oh, everything. They are such good friends. I've never told anyone else about them. Sometimes they tickle me so much that I sit up in bed. But there's no one in the room. I know I'm not crazy yet. I know they are real. Do you think they are my spiritual guides who are helping me to know what is on the other side?"

Her eyes were boundlessly deep, with a longing desperation. "And do you think they are preparing me to die?"

I didn't know what to say, yet I felt that what she was saying was true.

"Well, Mom, you know that you'll never die, even when you go. If you feel they are real, then they're real. I would say, yes, they are your friends and you are accepting them because you know you will meet them when you cross over."

"They're real sweet and they love me so much."

"Well then, why don't you relax and enjoy them until you can meet them in the flesh, so to speak."

"Oh, good," she said, "I'm so glad you understand. I love to go to bed because I know we'll have some fun. Don't tell your Daddy. He'd probably be jealous."

"I won't. Besides, he's probably got his own friends that he talks to. Maybe that's what he's doing when he sleeps so much."

Mother sat back in bed and looked at me with a deep question in her face.

"Shirl?" she asked. "Tell me again about those spiritual guides you wrote about in your book. Who is this Tom McPherson?"

I cleared my throat and began to explain that one of my great pleasures was having sessions with accredited "mediums" who channeled the soul energy of beings from the spiritual plane who acted as guides and teachers. I knew she was familiar with the material in my book, but hearing about it from me personally was more real to Mother. She needed me to confirm that what I had written *had been* my experience. I explained that a nice young man named Kevin Ryerson had found, some years ago, that he had the talent to attune his body frequencies to spiritual beings who themselves were no longer in the body. These beings used the electromagnetic frequencies of Kevin's body as a channel through which they could communicate with us on the earth plane from the spiritual plane where they resided. Kevin would go into a trance state while the spiritual beings used him as a medium through which to communicate.

Mother listened patiently. "How do you know it's not Kevin talking?" she asked.

"Well," I said, "the soul beings use Kevin's voice to talk through, but they are separate beings from Kevin himself."

"How do you know?" she questioned with an open-minded tone in her voice.

"Well," I said, loving her curiosity, but not certain I could answer to her satisfaction, "I can only say that Tom McPherson, one of the entities that Kevin channels, knew intimate details about me and my life which no other human being on earth knew."

"Really, Shirl?" said Mother. "And did he help you with things?"

"Oh, yes," I answered, "he helped me with a great many things."

"Weren't you frightened that he knew so much about you?"

"No," I answered, remembering my first reactions to the phenomenon of channeling. "No, as a matter of fact it was comforting to feel that I was communicating with a being who apparently could 'see' things I couldn't see. Of course, I was skeptical at first, but not frightened. I had heard about Edgar Cayce and all of his spiritual channeling, so I figured Kevin had the same psychic talent."

"Yes," said Mother, sucking in her breath as she always did when contemplating a new idea.

"Yes, I've heard of Edgar Cayce. He helped many people when they were sick, didn't he?"

"Yes," I answered. "He channeled all kinds of medical and scientific information from spiritual guides, even prescribing medication and various treatments. Doctors couldn't understand it because he had no medical training but was always right."

"So the spiritual entities speak through this young man called Kevin and they help you with things you have questions about?"

"That's right."

Mother nodded. "So maybe my 'friends' are spiritual beings like them?"

"I think they might be, yes."

"Did they live once on earth?"

"Usually they have lived. But not always. Sometimes spiritual beings come through who have never incarnated at all."

"You mean, have never been alive?"

"That's right."

"Well, if they've never been alive, how can they be alive now?"

"By alive I mean they've never been alive in a body. But for the most part, the spiritual entities that come through mediums have had the experience of living in a body on earth."

"And when they die, they go to this spiritual place and live without bodies?"

"Yes," I answered, wondering whether the nurses would mercifully stay out of the room until I finished my explanation. "So," I continued, "when our bodies 'die,' it's really just that the houses for our souls don't work anymore. We are souls who only temporarily reside in our bodies. We pass over to the spiritual dimension where we remain until we decide to reincarnate again. Our souls (the real us) never die. They are eternal."

Oh, yes, I believe that," said Mother.

"Remember what Daddy was saying about leaving his body during the accident?"

"Yes."

"Well, it's the same thing. If he had really 'died,' he wouldn't have come back to his body. He would be up there on the spiritual plane now, just like this Tom McPherson character."

"Oh," said Mother, "I see."

I paused a moment before going on.

"And remember how you've heard about people being visited by their 'dead' relatives?"

"Yes."

"Well, it's probably true. Because the relatives are never really gone. They just live in another dimension after they leave the body."

"Oh, yes," said Mother, "I see." She thought a moment and said, "Well, tell me how this Tom McPherson helped you."

I quickly scanned my memory, looked at my watch, and said, "I'll tell you a story that is really incredible. It actually happened exactly as I'll tell you."

Mother folded her arms across her lap and her eyes lit up.

"First," I said, "let me remind you that Tom McPherson speaks from the sensibility of his favorite incarnation."

"Oh?" said Mother, "and what was that?"

"Well, he was a Scotch-Irish pickpocket who lived about three hundred years ago. I was around at that time, too, and we knew each other."

"Oh, goodness," said Mother. "A pickpocket? And you knew him? Don't get too complicated. Just tell me the story."

I chuckled, remembering how difficult it had been for me to absorb some of the finer points of reincarnation.

"Well, it happened during the Thanksgiving holiday a few years ago. I had been working hard on *Out on a Limb* to meet my deadline.

"The evening before Thanksgiving, I was shopping in Beverly Hills on Rodeo Drive. I was carrying a large purse. Inside, I carried not only my money, credit cards, passport, and tape recorder but also tapes that I had recorded during my sessions with Tom McPherson and some other spiritual guides and teachers. I loved those tapes. In fact, I had become dependent on them because I felt that the language of the spiritual guides was more eloquent than my own. McPherson had warned me about my dependence, claiming that I should learn to trust myself more, but I didn't listen.

"I walked into a shop to try on a suit on sale that I had spotted in the window.

"I put my purse on the floor, took off my jacket, and covered my purse (shopping in Beverly Hills teaches you to conceal your purse). I turned around to the rack and took down a suit jacket. I hadn't turned for longer than five seconds, and *there was no other customer there*."

Mother leaned forward, her eyes wide as saucers, anticipating something dramatic.

"The salesgirl was busy on the telephone behind the counter. As I turned back to my purse, out of the corner of my eye, I saw my jacket gently collapse to the floor as though there was no purse under it! I picked up my jacket. The purse was gone! I freaked out. It was more than my sense of reality could comprehend. I looked up at the salesgirl and said, 'Who took my purse? My purse is gone. I was only turned around for five seconds and somebody stole my purse!' "

"Oh, my," said Mother, "Shirl, what happened?"

"The salesgirl said no one had come in, she'd seen me cover my purse with my jacket, so it must still be under there. Like a crazy woman, I flapped my jacket up and down as though I was beating dust out of a rug. 'My purse is not here,' I said. 'Can't you see that?'

"I ran out of the store. There was hardly anyone on the street. I went back into the store, expecting that the salesgirl had somehow found it. Instead, she was on the phone to the Beverly Hills police, begging them to come over and deal with this crazy movie star.

" 'Look,' I said, 'I'm sorry. I don't care about the money or the credit cards or my passport or anything like that. I care about my spiritual tapes that were in there.'

"She looked at me. 'Your spiritual tapes?' she asked more politely than was necessary.

" 'Yes!' I said. 'My tapes from my guides and teachers on the spiritual plane. They are so important to me.'

"I could feel her thinking that she should have called the boobyhatch instead of the police.

" 'Well,' she said carefully, 'maybe you could consult your spiritual guides to find out what happened to your purse?' "

Mother laughed. "She made me laugh, too," I said, "but she had a point. Well, I met with the police and filled out the reports and all that. But I had this eerie feeling that it really hadn't been a robbery after all. Yet I couldn't imagine what it really was."

"So, then?" Mother said.

"Two days after Thanksgiving, Kevin Ryerson was in town. I called him for a channeling session, thinking I could ask McPherson what had happened. I didn't tell Kevin anything about it. He went into trance and McPherson came through. The first sentence out of his mouth was 'Did you detect the fine hand of my pickpocket capacity the other day?'

"Then it hit me. Of course, it was McPherson."

"McPherson?" said Mother. "Oh my! However did he do it?"

"Well, I asked him just that, and he said he'd miscalculated: he hadn't meant to dematerialize the bag completely—just to move it behind the salesgirl's counter."

"He could have made a lot of trouble for her,"

Mother said. I laughed because that really hadn't occurred to me.

"Well, anyway," I said, "I had quite a fight with him about it. In fact, I yelled, 'What the hell do you mean, you *miscalculated*?'

"'Well,' he said, 'I hadn't realized how much you had actually progressed in your own mediumistic light frequencies. My light frequency mingled with yours and the combination of the two caused the bag to dematerialize rather than simply to move.'"

Mother leaned forward as though she couldn't believe what she was hearing.

"I couldn't believe it either," I told her. "I asked him if he was telling me my purse with all its contents was hanging around somewhere up there on the spiritual plane."

Mother looked confused. I saw I'd better get this over with.

"Well, he said that would be against cosmic law. But since he was responsible for the mistake of dematerialization, it was up to him to find someone who could karmically profit from it. He said I'd get it all back except for the tapes."

"The tapes?" said Mother.

"Yes," I said, "it seems Tom gave the tapes to someone who needed them more than I did."

"Well, what happened with all the other stuff?" Mother said.

"Oh, it all came back, just as Tom had said it would. Including my prescription eyeglasses, which I had been missing."

"How?"

"In a manila envelope, left at the door. No name or return address or anything. The point of the whole thing though, really, was that I had become too dependent on the tapes—they wanted to show me I didn't need them anymore."

"Oh, my goodness, Shirl," said Mother. "And this really happened?"

"It certainly did, every bit of it."

"Well, what do you make of it?" she asked, longing for a "logical" explanation.

"I really don't know," I answered, "but until something better explains it, I just have to believe what McPherson said."

"Oh, my," said Mother, "I don't know whether I'd be frightened or not."

"Well," I said, "I figure, unless something hurts me, there's no reason to be scared. You're not frightened of your 'friends,' are you?"

"Oh, no," she said, "on the contrary. They make me very happy and I love to laugh with them. They're really nice and I feel they are my friends."

"Well, then."

"Yes," she said, laughing. "But I don't know how many friends I'd have left in the neighborhood if I told them about my 'other friends.' "

"Yes," I said, "I know the feeling. But I think you'd be surprised how many other people have 'friends' they don't talk about."

Mother nodded, sucked in another breath, and rolled her eyes.

Just then Daddy walked back into the room. Mother put her fingers to her lips and said, "Sh-h-h," as if this were our secret.

"Well, Monkey," said Daddy, "a cab's waiting. I think you'd better go."

I picked up all my stuff, kissed them both good-bye, winked at Mother, and told Daddy to stay with her. I said I'd call them when I got back to New York, so they wouldn't worry that I had missed my show.

I left the hospital room and closed the door gently. I waited outside for a moment. Then I heard Mother say in a playful voice, "Ira, are you going to take the rest of this chocolate cake home and hide it so Bird Brain won't eat it?"

"Ummm," he said, "maybe I should."

Then, before I walked away, Mother said, "I'm so glad she's taking a cab so you can stay a little longer and talk."

Chapter 5

On the crowded shuttle back to New York, I thought how parental-child roles are reversed when nature runs its inevitable course. The parents become the children and vice versa. They bring us up lovingly, tolerating our moods and mischief. The circle meets itself when we find ourselves becoming their protectors. I loved them more than I could ever express and was realizing more and more how their values had molded me.

I thought of what an integral part they had played in the development of my professional attitudes as a child. I had just accepted that they were always there, supporting me with their love and care. It was not something I appreciated really. It just was. But looking back, I realize that they were the ones who had steered me, not only into my acting career as such, but toward the patterns that that career had assumed—that is, live performing. I had always sensed that this was what they had wanted for themselves. So, in effect, I was doing it for them as well as for myself.

I was born with extremely weak ankles which didn't properly support my weight. So at the age of three my parents searched out and found a ballet school with a fine reputation in Richmond, Virginia. They hoped that ballet would act as therapy for strengthening my ankles. Not only did the therapy work but right from the start I adored the physical expression of dance. It became indispensable to me.

The school was named for its principal teacher, Julia Mildred Harper. I remember Mother being impressed with how Harper taught her students to express themselves with their hands. Mother's hands had always been one of the most expressive outlets for her, and she identified with that outlet for me. Through one's hands came feelings, Mother would say. You can express joy, sorrow, terror, and fun through your hands. I listened to her and even today I can discern another person's character as much through their hands as any other way.

I was not very assertive in school or in dancing class. But Mother continually encouraged me to step up more—to go to the front of the line, to express a new idea for a game or a step. But if I didn't feel I was ready, I didn't want to say or do anything. It frustrated Mother a great deal. I don't think it bothered Daddy very much. Maybe Mother saw herself in me and didn't want me to make her mistake of being too cautious.

I went to dancing school every day. Even though I needed the expression of dance I hung at the back of the classroom because I had a medium-sized birthmark behind my left armpit. I felt it was so ugly, I didn't want anybody else to see it. That birthmark haunted me for years. Today, I have to think twice to remember which arm it graces.

My first performance was singing and tap-dancing to ''An Apple for the Teacher.'' I wore a green cardboard four-leaf clover on my head and I dropped the apple. It was my first laugh. I dropped the apple on purpose every time after that.

As I progressed in school, I regarded my studies as simply what was required; the dancing my parents had begun for me was my life.

I found schoolwork boring. I found the books I *chose* to read an adventure. I loved books about scientists and explorers and philosophers. School, somehow, managed to make these same human beings seem dull. And I loved my telescope. I would gaze from my bedroom window for hours or lie on the steamy summer grass well into the night wondering what could be going on with the stars that twinkled a message I was sure I would decode someday.

Many mornings I would wake up convinced that I had had a particularly advanced and sophisticated dream relating to medicine or to some other civilization that had existed on earth, but I could never remember the dream well enough to write it down.

So dancing and music were my outlets. In the ballet, whenever I heard Russian music, it would bring me to tears because somehow I felt I understood Russian music in my heart. It reminded me of a familiar feeling I couldn't quite remember. But I never mentioned my feelings to anyone because I didn't understand them.

When I was twelve we moved to Arlington, Virginia, and Mom and Dad enrolled me in one of the best ballet schools in the country, The Washington School of the Ballet in Washington, D.C., right across the Potomac River from where we lived. Lisa Gardiner and Mary Day were my teachers.

Every day after school I took the bus to Georgetown, transferred to a streetcar, and danced for five or six hours, returning to Arlington on the bus at night, doing my homework by the light above my seat as I was jostled home in the dark. I didn't realize it at the time, of course, but the habit of this extremely demanding schedule was building a work pattern I hold to to this day. Then it was because I wanted to do it. Now I don't think I could do and be what I am without it.

As I progressed in my dancing, I became very good at character work. Again, it was the Russian influence. My torso assumed the proper posture during a Russian mazurka as though I had been born to do it. I might have had red hair and freckles and looked like the map of Ireland, but I *felt* Russian. Whenever I saw the Russian alphabet, I felt I knew how to read it, but I just couldn't remember how. When my Russian Jewish girlfriends took me home with them after dancing class, I *knew* the food I was eating, even when it was for the first time.

I was confused by how much I responded to anything Russian. I knew I knew nothing about it—yet I knew so much.

I sat starry-eyed when Lisa Gardiner related her days with the Ballet Russe, dancing with Anna Pavlova. Russians were so wildly passionate, allowing their emotions free rein, claiming that control stifled life.

I wanted to be wildly passionate, but as a middle-class WASP American, my upbringing dictated otherwise. Nevertheless, I identified with the Russian soul. I couldn't understand why. I asked my mother and she said it was because I was talented. It was one of those marvelous nonanswers that parents can give and it served very well to make me wonder what talent really was.

Since I was trained in the art of dance, I grew up knowing something about how that process develops. For me, talent never had anything to do with the intellectual processes. It sprang almost entirely from feeling, expressed through the support system of discipline. My interpretation had to be on the mark and identifiable to another human being. If no one understood what I was trying to convey with my movement, then my feeling wasn't communicating.

The combination of Lisa Gardiner and Mary Day was a dynamic source of disciplined inspiration for me. Miss Gardiner (it was as though "Miss" were her first name) was a soft-spoken, intellectually continental woman of high sophistication. It was rumored around the dancing school that she had been married once for one night. No one was able to uncover who her husband had been. It was out of the question to ask Miss Gardiner directly. No one ever knew how old she was either. *That* was definitely unapproachable territory also. But she was deeply kind and wise. She had impeccably erect posture as she sat proudly in her high-backed chair smoking her cigarette from a long silver holder. Her fingernails were polished with a shimmering pink color and sloped as they extended from her fingers. She let the smoke from her cigarette filter through her nose until it curled in the air above her.

Sometimes after class we sat and chatted. She talked about touring and the adventures of the old days in Russia. She talked of the importance of human experience in relation to movement. "So-and-so is not yet a consummate dancer because she hasn't lived enough. She needs to suffer in order to attain wisdom. Such wisdom will then be evident in her movement." I listened with rapt attention. She made inspirational sense to me. I heard her with different ears than I heard anyone else. I didn't want to disappoint her. I felt she understood me and was specifically involved with my progress. I was "special" to her. She didn't exactly disapprove of my boyfriends or my other interests in life, but made it clear that I had better fish to fry, namely dancing. When one of my boyfriends came to collect me for a date, she was polite and gracious, but upon saying good-bye would take a long drag on her filtered cigarette and more slowly than usual let the smoke spiral out of her nose as though counteracting a bad smell. With subtle disdain, she would wave me into the night as though secretly understanding that I would wise up when I was finished with my adolescent years. It was at those times that I was maddened with curiosity about the real story of her one-night marriage.

Mary Day was her opposite. Miss Day (Miss was her first name too) was a direct, down-to-earth, instructional pile driver of a teacher. She had black flashing eyes which she orchestrated to flash on cue under carefully arched eyebrows. She was about five feet six with size four feet which moved like greased lightning when she demonstrated a "combination" which she wished us to execute. Her voice rang with command, and when she didn't like what she saw, she made no attempt to be sensitive in expressing her judgment. She walked with a proud stride, her feet turning out ducklike in opposite directions, her arms churning defiantly at her sides. Her movements were assertive and rapid, giving the impression that she wished to waste no time in her ambition to structure the best ballet school east of the Mississippi and south of New York.

When she was displeased at a student's progress, she never hesitated to denounce them as "ridiculous" and told me once that I would never be able to dance the role of Cinderella because I was too "big" and she just couldn't have Cinderella "clod-hopping" across the stage when the prince was supposed to feel sorry for her. When I told Mother what Miss Day had said, Mother called her up and said, "Fine, Shirley would rather be an actress anyway." That was news to me, but I had to stay away from class for a few weeks until Miss Day apologized for her breach of sensitivity and said I would be really wonderful in the role of the Fairy Godmother because she needed to have size and command. Mother relented and I returned to class. Mother might have been reticent where she herself was concerned, but nobody was going to push her daughter around in an impolite manner. Mother wanted me to be a success and neither Miss Day nor anybody else was going to intimidate me if she had anything to say about it.

Miss Day, on the other hand, admired Mother's spunk and gained new respect for me, too, as a result, so much so that later on when the school was in financial disorganization, she called Mother to solicit Dad's help in "straightening out the mess." Dad complied and the three of them have been friends ever since.

With Miss Day I always knew where I stood. If I could extract a pleased nod or a compliment from her, I knew I was progressing. The summer I returned from an intensive ballet course in New York City, she took one look at my legs and said, "Well, finally you are beginning to develop dancer's muscles. Things are looking good for you." That compliment satisfied me for six months.

So Miss Gardiner and Miss Day were my childhood professional mentors. They were the ones I longed to please and they were my yardstick for accomplishment. I spent more time with them at the school than I did with anyone else. And along with Mother, it was they who planted the seeds of acting in my mind. Miss Gardiner's way of nourishing those seeds was to say, "You are a fine actress when you move. I always know what you're attempting to convey." Miss Day would say, "You know, Shirley, your face moves too much for classical ballet. Why don't you think about going into acting?"

Either way, I got the message. But first I felt I needed to become accomplished at the expression of dance.

I remember the choreography contest. We were allowed complete freedom to choreograph what we wanted. I wasn't interested in "steps" or matching movements. I wanted to express what I was feeling. As I was discussing it with Mother, she revealingly said, "Why don't you choreograph movement that expresses a person willing to die for her art?" At first, that sounded melodramatic to me, but her *feeling* was so intense, I realized it was "acceptable" because that was just where she lived.

I chose some Russian symphonic music. I designed my body movements to express the anguish of the Russian soul in its suffering. I dragged myself across the floor as though being held down by an invisible force and finally convulsed into an outburst of triumph in the last movement.

When I performed my choreography, Mary Day

had me do it twice. The second time, I spontaneously altered the final position. She gave me second prize because she felt I had been more involved with performing than with choreographing. I felt spontaneity was essential to choreography.

Thus began my personal conflict with the classical forms of dancing and consequently the dilemma of whether I wanted to be a dancer or a star. When I graduated from high school I went straight to New York and into the chorus of a Broadway show. I was finally a professional dancer.

Dancers, or gypsies, as we refer to each other, are soldiers with talent, artists who are not allowed freedom, exponents of the living body who are in constant pain.

No one who hasn't done it can possibly understand what the inherent contradictions mean. It is an art that imprints on the soul. It is with you every moment, even after you give it up. It is with you every moment of your day and night. It is an art that expresses itself in how you walk, how you eat, how you make love, and how you do nothing. It is the art of the body, and as long as a dancer possesses a body, he or she feels the call of expression in dancer's terms. Dancers are always aware of how they look physically. Such is the name of the game. I, as a dancer, may move awkwardly, but I am always aware of it. I may profess to be relaxing, but my body speaks to me when the time is up. I may revel in what strength I have, but I always know I could use more. And I always know when I look beautiful, when the line of a crossed leg is exquisitely angled, when my posture denotes certitude, and when a proud bearing commands respect. I, as a dancer, also know that when depression sets in, I cave in in the middle, become slovenly in my movements, and find it very difficult to look in the mirror.

I, as a dancer, may run with graceful strides to catch a cab, but I am intrinsically involved with every crevice of the street because I don't want to become injured. I may adore a certain dress, but I will never wear it if it doesn't enhance the body line. I choose clothes not for style or color or fashion, but for line . . . a dancer's obsession.

When you have observed the progress of your body year after year in the dancing-class mirror, you are aware of each centimeter and bulge. You are aware of how beads of sweat look when they fall glistening from the end of a strand of your hair because you have worked hard.

You know that each slice of chocolate cake you indulge in the night before will have to be lifted in an arabesque the following day.

You learn how to apply your dancer's knowledge to small everyday tasks, how to warm a pot of milk and set a table at the same time. How to talk on the phone and stretch your hamstrings on a tabletop in order to save time. You can deftly change your entire wardrobe in an airplane seat without being noticed because your body is your domain of manipulation and you know you can do anything with it.

Your relationship to pain becomes complex. There is good pain and bad pain. Good pain becomes a sensation you miss. Bad pain becomes a sensation of danger. With age you learn to pace yourself. You learn that breathing is as important to the movement as the physical technique itself. You learn to never breathe *in*. You understand that nature involuntarily takes care of that, as it does when you sleep. You learn to only breathe *out*. By doing that, you release the toxins in the body. Whenever you engage in a high kick, you breathe out toward the kick. With that, you know you can go on kicking indefinitely.

And the personality of a gypsy is volatile. With a solo artist, eruptions of temperament are expected; with gypsies they are misunderstood.

Gypsies and soloists have put in the same amount of time in class, have slogged through their own self-doubt, and have endeavored to touch the soul of their being in similarly confrontational terms. To dance at all is to confront oneself. It is the art of honesty. You are completely exposed when you dance. Your physical health is exposed. Your self-image is exposed. Your psychological health is exposed, and your senses of humor and balance are exposed, to say nothing of how you relate to time, space, and the observer. It is impossible to dance out of the side of your mouth. You tell the truth when you dance. If you lie, you hurt yourself. If you "mark" it and don't go full out, if you don't commit your body totally, you hurt yourself. And if you don't show up for work, it is relatively impossible to live with the guilt. That is why dancers give the impression of being masochistic. Masochism is not a dancer's gimmick. Dancers fear being hurt. They do, however, enjoy the challenge of overcoming. That is, after all, what the art of dancing is all about. Overcoming the limitations of the body.

Dancers know that the mind, body, and spirit are inextricably intertwined.

You know it the first time you face an audience. There is "the big black giant" (as Oscar Hammerstein put it) out there and your task is to make them feel something through your body. You know you have to mean it. You know you have to have faith in your balance, your flexibility, and your strength. You know also that they will readily identify with your physical feats because they all have bodies too. You know that if you trip and fall, you humiliate *them* because that is what they are afraid of in themselves. You know that the easier you make it seem, the more hope you give them for themselves. You know they are rooting for you, otherwise their attendance would be called into question. You represent what they would like to be able to do themselves, because each and every one of them have their own problems with their bodies.

And so you continue day after day to keep yourself in shape, driving each muscle one last mile in order to become a role model for what can be done with the body.

And I have done this for nearly fifty years.

I don't know why I loved dancing so much from the very beginning. As I said, I believe it had something to do with having danced in a prior incarnation. It came "naturally" to me, as they say.

I adored the graceful, lyrical, romantic reward that came after the discipline and perspiration of hard work.

Perhaps the camaraderie of physical pain, accepted and tolerated in the name of dance, binds each of us gypsies together. But when I meet Olympic athletes and the like, I find we all have the same issues and contradictions in common. We love junk food, cigarettes, sugar, and rising to the occasion. We love to complain and set about helping each other with secret techniques to achieve more. Were we overachievers because of deep self-doubt? That's part of it. Yet no one is more seemingly proud than a human being who knows he can do most anything with the body.

Perhaps buried in the art of dance and in the performance of athletes is the human understanding that the body is the temple of our soul's existence, the house in which we live, the instrument of our soul's expression as we determine whether we are part of God or not.

There are always periods when your body is off, out of sync, not responding to your will. It is at those times that we are forced to confront the invisible reasons why. I have gone through many such periods over the years. Certainly food, rest, and mood entered into the picture, but soon I realized that there was a very real correlation between harmonious periods physically and harmonious periods spiritually.

I remembered my mother explaining the law of reversed effect to me. It happened to her once during a swimming contest. It was a contest for the backstroke. She had usually "raced" against the clock in order to win. On this particular day, she glided on her back, somehow feeling in total harmony with the sun above her and the water beneath. She said she exerted herself to the utmost, but she didn't have the sensation of competing. It was more a sensation of harmonizing with the elements involved. She said she just didn't care whether she won or not. She simply wanted to go as fast as possible. She *relaxed* and became "one" with all that surrounded her. The discipline of a trained body took over and, to her astonishment, she won easily.

I began to operate with the same principle, and found that my body hurt less and was capable of doing much more.

Later I studied Oriental approaches to karate, judo, and aikido. Meditation was the mainstay, the discipline of becoming one with mind, body, and spirit. The more I learned to ignore negative emotions, the more positive my body felt. I avoided the intellectualization of movement and allowed my body to respond to itself. I realized my *muscles had memory* if I kept my mind from interfering. If I trusted the muscle memory, I could remember choreography from numbers and combinations I had done when I was twelve years old. The body always *knows* if it is allowed to prevail. The body is a spiritual temple with checks and balances. When the spiritual harmony is not nourished, the body starves too. When the spirit radiates happiness, the body performs miraculously.

Often I look back on the years and years of physical discipline. I can remember nearly every classroom where the beads of sweat fell, where the water fountain was located, the smell of each rancid dressing room during the summer months, the smooth feel of the wooden bar during each warm-up. I remember the dank wetness of woolen tights when the cold night air hit my legs in the winter, seizing my elongated muscles into tight knots until I could reach a warm bath. I remember the tingling of my scalp just prior to breaking a sweat and how the food I had eaten would determine when that would occur.

I remember the bleeding calluses on my long toes as I mercilessly stuffed my feet into toe shoes padded with lamb's wool, how I would measure my height from month to month, shredded with anxiety that I might be growing too tall.

I remember the inflamed lower back pain whenever I had to dance on cement floors in television studios, the incessant mental notes to land with my heels down whenever I performed a jump, in order to prevent ugly calf-bulging, and stinging shin splints.

I remember the nausea doing pirouettes, the stretched splendor of a slow adagio, the joy of defying gravity in a grand jeté, the awkwardness of turns to the left, the strained quivering of the pointed foot at the end of an extension, the burning thighs in a slow grand plié, the certainty that my back must be made of concrete during a backbend.

The mirror is your conscience. You've rehearsed with its definitive image in front of you for weeks. Then the choreographer turns you around, away from the mirror. You are on your own. You're not sure where you are. Your image is no longer there to ratify your existence. Your orientation to space is altered. You become aware of the meaning of movement and your need to communicate to the audience because you can no longer communicate with your own image. The music sounds different. Your spacing is off. You are unable to check out your line, not only in relation to yourself, but also in relation to whomever else you may be dancing with.

Then you begin to soar, you begin to become what you mean. You find a hidden subtext in your movement. You bend and flow and jump to the music when you allow it to carry you aloft. You begin to fill every space with body language; no move is gratuitous. You learn to think ahead, knowing which combination of moves requires the most anticipation. You learn which movements are the most fulfilling and which are defiantly dangerous. You employ shortcuts and pain-saving devices. You know how much breath you'll need to pace yourself.

Your shoes become your support system. If the size varies one centimeter, it throws your balance askew. If there is a clump of harmless dust on the floor, you eye it at every available moment until you dance out of its range because the slightest inconsistency under your moving weight can cause you to lose your footing.

You test the speed of the floor under the rubber soles of your shoes. You know that if the speed is slow, you'll have to exert that much more effort in turns. Yet if it's too fast, you'll lose your control.

Then you begin to need the lights, the costumes, the scenery, and the audience.

You leave everything you learned in the classroom and the rehearsal hall behind you. All of it was only the preparation, the bare bones of expression.

You mold the choreography with additional magic. Your costume feels foreign to you until you learn to work with it, use it, enhance it, make it part of the movement. You complain at first that it inhibits the movement, but you know from experience that it always feels that way at first. You rustle the skirt and toss a scarf, rendering new meaning to the original movement.

Then you have a dress rehearsal with costumes, lights, and a full complement of musicians. Up to that time you have danced to a work light and a piano. Now you feel the complete musical poetry of the composer and orchestrator. There are levels of subtlety to the music that you never dreamed would be there. It is full, rich, awe-inspiring. It confuses you at first because you had been used to dancing only to the melody of one piano. Now there are forty musicians who are as integral a part of the overall illusion as you, the performer, are. You familiarize yourself with the totality of the sound and find that the music kicks your movement to another level and makes you certain you can do anything.

Then come the lights, lovingly painted from the front of the theater. You realize that every nuance of your face and body will be visible. The pink jells leave your skin with a silky glow. The spotlight following you burns through your eyes. The bumper lights stage right and left add dimensional color to your arms and legs. You can see absolutely no one in the audience. It is alienatingly black. Then you realize it is all up to you. You are a performer. You forget everything you ever learned. You forget the intricate processes of technique. You forget your anxieties and your pain. You even forget who you are. You become one with the music, the lights, and the collective spirit of the audience. You know you are there to help uplift them. They want to feel better about themselves and each other.

Then they react. Their generously communal applause means they like you—love you even. They send you energy and you send it back. You participate with each other. And the cycle continues. You leap, soar, turn, extend, and bend. They clap, yell, whistle, stomp, and laugh. You acknowledge their appreciation for what they see and give them more. And so it goes.

The long years were worth it. The miraculous magic of expression overrides everything. It becomes everything. Once again, you realize you are everything you are aware of. You are part of the audience. They are a part of you. You and they are one expressing talent. The talent of giving and receiving, of resonating to a greater spirit by means of the body; the talent of souls appreciating one another, of together creating life on a larger scale. The talent of understanding the shadow awareness that makes us all one, part of a divine perfection which is the essence of sharing. You are dancing with God. You are dancing with yourself. You are dancing in the light.

And my mother and father had been responsible for introducing me to an art form that allowed me to dance with life.

Chapter 6

*S*o much had happened to me in the 1983–1984 time period that some people wondered what I needed the Gershwin run for. As always, I did what I did for personal reasons. If I see no potential for human growth in any of my projects, then I won't do them. I was finally beginning to relinquish my goal-oriented priorities, calculated smart career moves. Personal goals had become more important to me.

I was basking in the success of *Terms of Endearment* and I knew I could rest on my laurels for a year or two, but as my brother, Warren, said to me, "It's probably good to get back into the storm." Besides, I wanted to endeavor to apply my new spiritual awareness to the professional arena. It had brought me so much inner peace in my private life. Would that also work professionally?

First of all, a word about acting and what the process means to me. When I began, I still thought of myself as a dancer. I knew absolutely nothing about the techniques of expressing myself with my voice or how to become another character through written dialogue. I have had maybe four acting lessons in my life, and in my view, it is questionable whether it is even possible to teach someone how to act. One can learn how to dance and how to sing through lessons because those forms of expression require a schooled, scientific, almost mathematical understanding of rhythm, music, tone, body movement, and placement of either the voice or the body. But acting is more ephemeral, more abstract. It is about individualized attitude. Of course, attitude is important in song and dance, but you have to learn how to sing and dance first. Acting is only about attitude and how to achieve it clearly. We act every moment of our everyday lives. So to me, observation was my best teacher. As I have said, my parents were the first objects of my observation. I studied their moods and the orchestration of their personalities. They were clear in their manipulation of characters regardless of how frustrating I sometimes found them.

Later on I began to sit for hours watching people on the street. Sometimes Dad would take us in the car while he did "business," and Warren and I were left to amuse ourselves while we waited for him. We were told to remain in the car and often hours would pass with nothing to do but observe the milling clusters of people passing by, acting out their various dramas while we watched in mesmerized fascination. Those times were among the most effective in educating me about human behavior. To this day I long to be a fly on the wall wherever I am so that I can recall the childhood wonder of observing other people rather than being observed myself.

When it came to acting I never had a trained teacher. Life was my teacher. Concentration was my teacher. The developed capacity to observe another while putting myself in their skin and feeling what they felt became my teacher. In other words, I taught myself how to act by observing life. And from the beginning, it felt "natural" to me. In fact, if I didn't feel "natural" in a given scene, I was usually not very good. If I *believed* what I was saying, it worked. If I watched myself doing it, it didn't.

I never had any acting idols really. I think that was because I believed in the *characters* they were playing. I didn't believe the *acting*. If someone wasn't a good actor, I just didn't like the character they were portraying. I approached acting as a child would, whether I was observing another doing it or whether I was doing it myself. And I still do. I'm not very sophisticated in my demands. I'm a sucker for the movies because I usually believe what I'm watching unless it seems absolutely false. On the stage the proscenium arch dictates that the audience be once removed from reality. On the stage you try to act real. On the screen you try to *be* real.

So acting was a simple process for me. I had just enough childish wonder to be good at it. If *I* believe what I'm doing, the audience will believe it. If I don't, the audience won't. It's making up stories so your friends and your parents will believe you. It never has been a big deal to me. At the same time, I have to admit I didn't take acting seriously enough. It came so naturally to me that I often treated it as a kind of a hobby, a pastime that brought me great pleasure but was nothing to lose any sleep over— and I never did. That is, of course, why I did so many dumb pictures. I usually only looked at my part and if it felt like fun, I'd do it. I could never understand why so many people in the movie business treated a film as though it were their last will and testament.

I'd read a script once, make my decision to do it, and never look at it again until it was time to do a scene. I never studied my lines the night before. And by the way, I never had any trouble remembering them. I *felt* the character as if by osmosis. It never seemed right for me to intellectualize what I was doing. I just, as Humphrey Bogart put it, "got out there and acted and tried not to bump into the furniture or the other people."

I didn't care about the number of close-ups I had or what ended up on the cutting-room floor. I didn't bother much with how I looked, but some- times I turned down parts if I knew I'd have to wear corsets or uncomfortable clothes. Most of my pictures have been shot indoors because, with blue eyes, I have a hard time keeping my eyes open in the sunshine. So I usually turned down Westerns and outdoor epics.

I was vitally interested in the number of days I'd have off, and more than anything, I lobbied to shoot films on French hours, which meant starting at eleven and working till seven without breaking for lunch. I was a night person and loathed getting up early.

It wasn't until my late thirties that I began to take acting in films seriously. Up till then, I had been more interested in traveling, love affairs, political activism, my friends, writing, and living.

I don't know what caused the shift in my attitude. Maybe it was age. Maybe it was the experience of failure (I had done years of bad films in a row). But really, I believe that I was just more interested in the other aspects of my life, until one day I realized that my talent was intensely interesting, too, and I shouldn't slough it off anymore. Also, let me say that I was one of the last to come under the Hollywood star system. I had been brought to Hollywood on a contract which guaranteed me three pictures a year, and Hollywood was churning out three times as many films then as they are today. Audiences were guaranteed. Films were the mainstay of American, European, and Japanese entertainment. People went to the movies. They weren't selective about which movie. It's different today.

So perhaps I began to take my work in films seriously when I realized the audiences were doing the same thing. When they ceased to be casual about it, I did too.

Then one night I saw Marlon Brando being interviewed on television. He wanted to talk about the plight of the American Indian and the interviewer wanted to talk about acting. I agreed with the interviewer. But what got to me was that this was one of the really great actors of our time, and he appeared to have contempt both for his profession and his talent. I didn't want to be like that. So I guess that had something to do with it.

Anyway, with the advent of *Turning Point* and *Being There* and *Terms of Endearment*, I found that I was taking myself more seriously and enjoying it to boot.

At the same time, I had begun my search for the recognition of higher consciousness. Life and acting, then, came together for me. Discovering my identity was a serious undertaking for me. Previously I had searched it out through the development of a socio-political consciousness and by consciousness-raising as a feminist. I had thought that the future salvation of the human race lay in those domains. Concern for my fellow humans seemed to be best served through political and social channels. Yet all the while I knew that within those avenues there was something missing. How could I really help others if I didn't know who *I* was? Organizations lacked individualized understanding. They moved as a group, as a movement. The individual identity was what interested me. And so, although there was still much I agreed with and was attracted to within the sociopolitical activism of the time, I fundamentally understood that the only change I could really effect was the change within myself. *That* was where I would grow and progress to more understanding. So I began to veer away from political and social movements. They seemed to shift within themselves anyway as each individual reached his or her own personal understanding.

The raising of my spiritual consciousness, then, was a natural extension of everything I had previously explored. I had traveled the world, lived among many cultures, been active in political movements: and despite a drive for perfection, I was a happy person, not really agonized by anything much. I was psychologically sophisticated, having had a great deal of therapy as I searched within myself.

But what I was asking was deeper, more profound. I needed an answer—a higher answer to what I intuitively knew was the basis of identity. That, then, became a spiritual question, but one that could only be pursued in terms of continued self-search.

I say all this because it had a profound effect on my acting and my live performing.

I began to work with principles and techniques in relation to recognizing that mind, body, and spirit were intertwined. In fact, I was soon convinced that a healthy state of spirit controlled my mind and body. I realized I was *essentially* a spiritual being, not a mind-body being. My body and my mind flowed from the consciousness of my spiritual capacity.

Negative attitudes, fear and anxiety, were mind sets that resulted from not feeling well in my spirit. When I wasn't easy with something, it didn't flow. It was blocked. I began to realize what dis-ease meant.

I remembered the days when I was often temperamental if I was unhappy with myself. So much negative temperament came from the lack of trust or belief in myself—the fear and anxiety that audiences or fellow workers wouldn't understand what I was endeavoring to communicate. Often the lack of trust in myself caused me to mistrust others. The creative process often feels so lonely, so isolated. Sometimes I wouldn't even follow through on a concept because I didn't give myself half a chance. As a result, others would sense my reluctance and feel unable to respond. That would set up a fear in me that I was not capable of getting across what I desired to and the cyclical pattern of negativity would be set in motion.

All that began to change when I found that trusting my spiritual nature produced a more positive creative flow.

It worked in a remarkably simple manner. I trusted what I can only describe as my higher unlimited self . . . or my "super-consciousness," as Freud would have put it. I knew about the subconscious and the conscious. I was learning about the super-consciousness.

The higher unlimited superconsciousness can best be defined as one's eternal unlimited soul—the soul that is the real "you." The soul that has been through incarnation after incarnation and knows all there is to know about you because it *is* you. It is the repository of your experience. It is the totality of your soul memory and your soul energy. It is also the energy that interfaces with the energy which we refer to as God. It knows and resonates to God because it is a part of God. As in the mind of man there are many thoughts, so in the mind of God there are many souls.

Our higher unlimited self, which has been a child of God from the beginning of time, is with us every instant, silently (and sometimes not so silently) guiding us through events and experiences which we elect to have for ourselves in order to learn more fully who we are *and* what the God energy is. That energy is *totally* aware and the more we listen to it, the more aware each of us can become.

The great spiritual masters such as Christ and Buddha were totally in touch with their higher un-limited selves and were therefore capable of accom-plishing whatever they desired. They were fully realized human beings who understood all of their incarna-tional experiences and were able to incorporate their knowledge and understanding into lives of service for others. While the goal of realizing oneself is basically quite simple it is also awesome. It is to realize that we are part of God . . . which is to say, total love and light.

My personal goals were not so awesome. I just wanted to be as fully realized as I could, both as a person and in my creative expression.

So I began to put into practice techniques I had learned from reading metaphysical literature (meta meaning "beyond"), talking during my travels with people involved in their own self-realization, and ideas that I came up with just by being alone with myself (meditation).

I started to work with these principles and techniques in as earth-plane an environment as there is—a sweaty rehearsal hall.

Putting together new material can be as frightening as it is exhilarating. You're never really sure whether it'll work or not. It may seem wonderful to you, but how will the audience react?

Alan Johnson was my director-choreographer. I had worked with him for years until he finally accused me of not knowing anyone else. He is a wiry, taut-calm overseer who was the dance captain of *West Side Story* and is now the heir apparent to Michael Bennett and Bob Fosse. He has impeccable taste, great steps, and a unique sense of judgment and pacing. He is never flustered, is inordinately patient, and possesses a composed dignity that causes people to want to work with him. He smokes Lark cigarettes, is almost five feet six, wears a small stud earring in his left earlobe, and rehearses in the street clothes he comes to work in, usually either a shirt and jeans or safari pants with T-shirt that blends. His nose twitches when he's about to say something comically absurd and he is never mean and temperamental, as are so many other choreographers who cannot, apparently, help themselves. Alan somehow resolved the pain of being a gypsy and saw no need to inflict the same fate on gypsies who work for him now.

He was also into higher consciousness and claimed that working with Mel Brooks (Alan directed *To Be or Not to Be*) provoked an acceleration of that process or they would have taken him away in a white coat. Alan had gotten in touch with some of his past-life incarnations and many of our rehearsal hours were wasted (nothing is ever really wasted) in discussing our spiritual conjectures. We exchanged metaphysical books and talked about whether it would ever be possible to dramatize a film about reincarnation without its looking tacky, or B-movieish.

Alan understood as well as I did that we both allowed *intelligence* to block our free-flowing creativity. I would watch him grapple with that conflict as he stood smoking one of his Larks, staring at the floor agonizing over which steps he would paint it with. I could see him edit the movement even before he tried it, for fear that the audience would either have seen it before or would not be able to understand its sophistication. He was not a man of facile symmetry, yet movement that individualized itself was not easily identifiable to audiences which were only in the last ten years beginning to fully embrace dance. Alan was basically an intellectual and we both knew what that meant to creativity. It meant *blockage*.

I had the same problem. The mind, with all its potential ramifications, was the great limiter. Our purpose in working together was to unblock the mind's limitations, and just go for it. He winced whenever one of his appreciators complimented him on his "intelligent choreography." He longed to do stuff we could "get off on."

So, sometimes, when he was stuck and I and my gypsy dancers became impatient, we would encourage the rehearsal pianist to play anyway and, catching a kind of madness from one another, outrageously gyrate, undulate, bump, twist, and grind our way to a rousing, vulgar, childish finish because *we* had nothing to lose with our mischief. That's when he'd come alive and say, "Keep it in," and go on to temper our devilment into a number of comic proportions that he had had no intention of doing in the first place. Once again we would then agree that creativity required living in the moment. Too much thinking was simply a handicap.

Alan and I were so linked in understanding that often we choreographed on the telephone. His classic "Tribute to Choreographers," which won him many awards, was done that way. If our mutual concept was clear, our intention without contention, all that was left was to execute the movement.

And now he and I were about to confront Broadway and the New York critics. We had put together my shows for Vegas, which went on to tour in theaters around the world, but New York was another animal—not so much the audiences, because they were usually fairly alike, even in Europe and Asia. It was that bedeviling body of eloquent critical cynics, who took pride in their autocratic roles as *the* pacesetters, who could render you paralytic with fear.

I was going into New York as a variety artist, playing in a Broadway house, doing my little song, dance, acting, comedy numbers, and didn't want to be defined as a Vegas act. I had played Vegas for years, and loved it, by the way, but I wanted this to be a cut above the green velvet jungle. So did Alan . . . which meant that all the surefire, pull-down high kicks had to be adapted. They needed to be there for a reason other than applause, although why applause was beneath critical acclaim I still can't figure out. Obvious "mitt-grabbing" was too honest an intention for the New York critics. They wanted to decide if they would be moved to applaud—they didn't like to be manipulated. Audiences *came* to be manipulated, but critics were too smart for that. Ah, the intricate ramifications of the judging of fantasy. How seriously could you take the exercise of simply giving the audience a good time?

The creative people involved with building a new show work as a team. For me, if a prima donna is involved, I would have to carefully weigh whether his or her talent would be worth the emotional price. It usually isn't. That goes for dancers too. I'd rather have good dancers with stable personalities than a brilliant dancer who was a bad apple. All the other apples live too closely together in the barrel to avoid contamination. Negative attitudes are contagious.

So, attitudes of easement and flexibility were the number-one priority of my company. I couldn't have it any other way. It had been like that for some time, and because so many others around me were working toward their own spiritual enlightenment, we preciously guarded those qualities we had learned to trust and maintain in ourselves and each other.

Many people who came backstage or had intermittent associations with us remarked about the goodwill, the centeredness that prevailed with every member of my company. I was proud of that. We put our spiritual growth to practical use and it literally showed up in the working environment. If there were arguments, we talked them over and worked them out, almost always coming to the conclusion that there had been a karmic lesson to be learned from everyone's point of view.

The star of any company creates the values of that company. If the star is irresponsibly late, the rest will think time doesn't matter. If the star is argumentative, arguments prevail. If the star is unprofessional, rough edges begin to tear away at the internal fabric of the entire production. So, the star is ultimately responsible for what goes on.

During the rehearsal process, the director-choreographer is the helmsman. The star looks to that creative mind for sustenance and support and leadership. But when the show has opened, it becomes the star around whom everything revolves.

And during rehearsals, the lighting and costume designers are as important as the performers because everyone knows "if you don't look good, what point is there in working your buns off?"

Gypsies are famous for overtly expressing their feelings about the costumes their bodies have to move in.

And when the costume designer presents his lovingly painted color drawings to the company, carefully spread out on the dance floor to achieve the utmost effect, he is as nervous as the choreographer, the star, and the performers in front of their first audience. His talent is about to be assessed, judged, critiqued, and, he knows—inevitably—"improved upon."

But you know you have to say it now. If you wait until the costume goes to the beaders, you've possibly blown seventy-five hundred dollars.

Or you might be blessed enough to have a Pete Menefee working with you, who not only was a gypsy himself, but readily and without any inner dialogues understands that physical discomfort inhibits movement.

The lighting designer is the recipient of compliments only from the director or choreographer who sit out front because those of us on the stage never get a chance to see what we look like. We can only feel it.

"Feeling" your way is the process by which stage magic is made.

We felt our way through rehearsals, doing our stuff to the blank wall, capable only of imagining what the final effect would be. Christopher Adler helped me write my lyrics and material. I say "helped" because any good writer knows that the words have to flow from the heart of the performer, especially a performer who not only writes, but has to mean what she says. I am incapable of saying something on the stage that I don't mean. Even when it comes to telling a joke. It's not enough just to get a laugh. It has to spring from my own truth. Or the audience won't laugh anyway. I had learned that by bitter experience—which brings up a vital point where personal live performing is concerned.

Any musical performer who works "live" agonizes over how to communicate with the audience. We may be solidly secure in our singing, dancing, musical ability, but when it comes to "being ourselves" in between numbers, we need "patter." Comedy writers are called in by our agents, and the result is well intentioned, but never really works.

The truth is, you just have to experiment on stage. And experimentation in front of the big black giant is enough to reduce an accomplished and seasoned performer to the rank of blithering idiot. We need to be more secure than that. So we go through the motions of telling jokes stemming from someone else's sensibilities and, depending on the reaction, *that's* where we find our true spontaneous selves. So, knowing who you are on stage is the ultimate goal. The audience never responds to artifice. They can detect sham immediately and just as swiftly respond positively to something you do that comes out of your gut. They want you to be real. That's what they're there for. They want to come away knowing who you are. Well, that means you have to be willing to tell them. No one can really write for you. *You* are the architect of your personal experience. So, if you decide to go into that line of work, you have to be prepared to take personal chances.

None of this applies to proscenium theater, where you inhabit another character and are traditionally forbidden to break the proscenium. Personal-appearance performing *requires* that you crack the formality of that dividing arch, giving the audience a glimpse, even if imperfect, of where you really live. This kind of performing is not about perfection. In fact, it is the opposite. When you break the boundaries of the proscenium, you are saying you are one of *them*. A comfortable performer relishes spontaneous moments that occur with an audience. Because *we* know that the audience knows it's real. What happens between the "big" numbers is generally unrehearsed, and though the overall shape of such a show remains the same, the personal material never comes out exactly the same way twice. But to find your comfortable stage personality takes time and the willingness to relax into spontaneous imperfection.

So, good writers write *with* you, not *for* you. They attempt to ascertain your areas of comfort and ease and bolster those areas with jokes and comments. A good writer never forces you to try something that he believes he needs to prove. Instead he implores you to try to be yourself.

That's what Christopher did. That's what Alan always does. Behind the scenes creative artists know they are there to serve the performer. The performer is, after all is said and done, the person the audience comes to see. They don't want to feel that words have been cleverly fashioned to spill from the performer's mouth, or that movements have been crafted on a body that is unwilling to commit to them.

Even the lyrics of a song need to express either what the performer feels, or what the audience believes you feel. If audiences don't believe what you're saying up there, they just won't come.

But if they do, it's pure joy.

Broadway, the big one-woman show, was rapidly approaching.

To work at one's profession and apply spiritual techniques was an adventure I longed to experience just to determine if it was possible. Yoga had long since become a contributive exercise in my daily life. It helped my dancing as well as my physical well-being. But I wanted to experiment with more detailed spiritual mind techniques.

I began to work with what is known as "affirmations" a few days into the rehearsal period. I found that they were remarkably productive.

Affirmations are spoken resolutions which, when used properly, align the physical, mental, and spiritual energies.

The ancient Hindu vedas claimed that the spoken words *I am*, or *Aum* in Hindi, set up a vibrational frequency in the body and mind which align the individual with his or her higher self and thus with the God-source. The word God in any language carries the highest vibrational frequency of any word in that language. Therefore, if one says audibly *I am God*, the sound vibrations literally align the energies of the body to a higher atunement.

You can use *I am God* or *I am that I am* as Christ often did, or you can extend the affirmations to fit your own needs.

I needed affirmations which would help reduce body pain. So I would affirm to myself (sometimes silently and sometimes audibly, depending on whether I would disturb someone else) a resolution such as: I am God in action. Or, I am God in health. Or, I am God with ease. Whatever came to my mind dictated my creative requirement. Sometimes if I was not feeling as full of fun as I wanted to feel, I would say, I am God in fun. Or, I am God in humor.

What happened was remarkable. I wouldn't have believed it had I not experienced the results myself.

Call it concentration, or call it *believing*, it makes no difference. *I felt no pain.* My perception, and therefore my truth, was altered if I uttered *I am God in happiness* to myself. The result was a feeling that was real. I uttered each affirmation three times. The vedas claim that three times designates mind, body, and spirit. In the middle of the grueling dance number when I wondered, after double days of two shows a day, whether I could finish, I would chant to myself along with the music, *I am God in stamina* and all the pain melted away. One has to try it to believe it. During workout classes when the "burn" was nearly intolerable, I chanted under my breath three times, *I am God in coolness*. The burn was less. Then I would go on to chant gently, *I am God in strength*, or *I am God in light*. The effect is stunning.

If, as happened, there were days when I had either not had enough sleep the night before, or something occurred to jangle my mood, or just the pressure of performing itself caused me to be out of my own center, I would, as soon as I opened my eyes in the morning, begin my affirmations and in five minutes or so I felt better.

Before performing I always did them during the overture and continued right on through my entrance. I felt the alignment occur all through me and I went on to perform with the God Source as my support system.

I began to use this technique in other ways too.

There were many times, over the course of my life, when I was asked to be a public speaker. Either to accept an award or to be a keynote speaker at a political rally. Public speaking terrified me. I always felt the need to have a prepared text to refer to. Either I would write the speech or a professional speech writer would do it for me. I couldn't feel comfortable doing it spontaneously. This discomfort began to ebb away too. I began to work only with an outlined idea in my head. If I carried notes with me, I found that little by little I didn't bother referring to them. I realized that it was what I was feeling that communicated to the audience more than the words anyway. The words, frankly, got in the way if I was in sync with my feelings. A pause or a decision-making moment was infinitely more effective than the studied intellectual twist of a well-planned phrase. Again, I was learning to trust in the moment and with my affirmation. My higher self was my guide.

This process was so self-enlightening that at times I wanted very much to share it, attempting to light a candle for someone rather than tolerate their cursing of the darkness.

I quickly learned that this is where karma comes in. While pursuing my own awakening, *if* I was working with balanced principles, I was aware at all times that everyone else was pursuing their own path, consciously or unconsciously. They had their own perceptions, their own truth, their own pace, and their own version of enlightenment. It was not possible to judge another's truth. I had to simply proceed along my own path, continually reminding myself of the true meaning of "Judge not, that ye be not judged."

The process of self-realization (or even the theories of reincarnation and karma) does not lend itself to proselytization. It is highly personal, ultimately self-responsible. All one can say, really, is: this happened to me. This is how it feels. If it interests someone else, they must do their own learning, their own reading, their own searching.

So, I can only say that this feeling of higher awareness is so personal that it is a matter purely of one's own consciousness. In my life, and in my work, I realized that what I saw in others was that which I did or didn't want to see in myself. I realized that the perceptions I had of myself were, in the main, perceptions I had of others in the world around me. I was, in effect, only living inside of my own reality, and so was everyone else. Therefore, to desecrate another was to desecrate myself. To denigrate another was to denigrate myself. To judge another was to judge myself. And that's what it was all about: SELF. If I was happy with myself, I was happy with others. If I loved myself, I could love others. If I could tolerate myself, I could tolerate others. If I was kind to myself, I was kind to others— and on and on. It was a personal evaluation of self that enabled this enlightenment to work for me. Not the evaluation of others. So when I saw people zealously condemning the "sins" of others in the name of God, I found myself wondering what karma they were setting up for themselves. What ye sow, so shall ye reap. Do unto others as you would have them do unto you. This simple karmic law of cause and effect was predominant in the religious and spiritual teachings of virtually every culture on earth. So many had misinterpreted this law for their own reasons. I "respected" these reasons, whatever they might be, but with the world heading for possible *self*-destruction, I could only say that we are not victims of the world we see. We are victims of the way we see the world.

In truth, there are no victims. There is only self-perception and self-realization. That was the star to which I hitched my wagon. As the etymology of the word disaster suggested: dis—torn asunder from; astrado—the stars. To experience disaster is to be torn asunder from the stars, and from the higher truth.

There were personal events that occurred during my run in New York that provided me with the opportunity of being more aware of how the harmony of the higher dimension works.

I received a call from a psychic trance-channeler, a friend of mine, who didn't want to concern me unnecessarily but wanted me to be aware of something. She didn't know what it meant, but she said, "Do you know someone named Mark?"

I couldn't think of anyone except one of my four dancers, whose name was Mark Reiner.

"Well, I don't know," said my friend J.Z. "Someone named Mark will cause some disruption, not serious, but just be aware."

Every night during the warm-up period before the overture, I would look at Mark and wonder if J.Z. could have tuned in on something concerning him. I never said anything. I didn't want to alarm him.

A few days later, New York went on daylight saving time. It was a matinee day and I was having dinner with friends in between shows. I had forgotten to put my watch ahead an hour. My friends commented that I was unusually casual about lingering over dinner. I glanced at my watch and said, "Oh, I have another hour."

Then our waiter passed and inquired why I was off that night. I said I wasn't off. He pointed to his watch and said, "Then you're on in five minutes!"

I panicked. I raced to my limo, where Dominick,

my driver, stood tapping his foot, wondering. I am religious about performance deadlines.

He drove the getaway car in a way Al Capone would have admired. I arrived at the theater to find Mike Flowers ashen-faced and annoyed. I didn't blame him.

"You don't understand," said Mike. "Mark Reiner has sprained his ankle and can't go on. You have three minutes to rechoreograph."

We used only four dancers. Now there were three. One boy would have to dance two parts!

I rushed to the stage where the other three dancers were perspiringly attempting to work with a fourth person. I couldn't place him. He turned around. It was one of my old dancers. He "happened" to be in the audience, heard the news, and rushed backstage. He knew the "choreographer" number! Mark's clothes fit him perfectly—even his *dance shoes*!

"If you want, I'll go on," said Gary. "But I'd really like to see the show first. I can be ready tomorrow night. Mark is going to be out for several weeks."

The impact of J.Z.'s warning hit me. Yet at the same time, I realized I was protected not only by Gary's "accidental" presence, but by forgetting the time change. I hadn't had time to worry!

We went on without Gary or Mark, rechoreographing as we moved. I explained to the audience what had happened. They loved being in on it. Larry, the dancer now dancing two parts, had the time of his life. The audience wildly applauded him, and when it was all over, I called J.Z. to tell her what had happened.

"Oh, now I understand," she said.

"But how did you know?" I asked.

"When you're tuned in, you're tuned in," she said. "A psychic is just a little more tuned in to the 'knowingness' of his or her higher self than others. That's why they call us psychics. But the knowingness is there for all of us. We are all psychics, we just don't know it. If we each trusted our knowingness, we'd each be totally aware. We are what we're aware of. And that should be our true goal in life.''

I thanked her and hung up. I sat for a long time, thinking again about the limitation of linear time.

I could only perceive events that had either just happened or were immediately about to happen. I felt frustrated that I couldn't view what a past lifetime had been or what a future event would reveal.

I thought of a canoe floating down the river. From the perspective of the canoe, one could only see immediately behind or immediately ahead. Seen from a perspective *above* the canoe, that view became a broader and more elongated perspective. One could see miles behind and miles ahead.

If the river was time, then, and we wished to see the past and the future, all it took was to plug into a higher perspective. Again there was no such thing as reality, only perception. But to plug into that higher perspective required more knowledge of the higher self—our higher selves resided in the spiritual dimension, not in the earth-plane, physical dimension.

The spiritual dimension was real even though we couldn't see it or measure it in linear terms. There is a greater reality than our "perceived" conscious reality. That is what has come to be called the new age of thought. A new age of awareness. An awareness that includes the knowledge that there is indeed a level of dimension that operates in harmony and with perfection, waiting for us to understand that being alive on earth is only a limited aspect of what we truly are.

The sense of knowing that the great unfathomable mystery isn't really such a mystery was a practical, ⌐ontributive, earth-plane support system for me. It was not only out there, it was in fact inside me, waiting to be tapped and realized. As above, so below. The two dimensions were mirrors for each other. I was living on the limited earth-plane dimension, but if I trusted that I was indeed unlimited, then *I* would also be able to tune in and know that Mark Reiner was going to sprain his ankle.

During my years of searching for spiritual understanding in myself and others, my path has led me through some almost unbelievable events and relationships. Some included "regular" people. But other relationships were not of the "home-grown" variety. As I have described, I visited accredited mediums who channeled spirit guides from the spiritual plane. I developed relationships with those "entities." Some were humorous, some purely educational.

He identified himself as Ramtha the Enlightened One. My relationship with Ramtha was deep, seeming to speak to another time and place. He said he had had one incarnation during the Atlantean time period and had achieved total realization in that lifetime. When I was first told about Ramtha, a very strange soul-memory feeling came over me. As a matter of fact, the first time I heard his name I broke down and sobbed. I couldn't understand what was happening to me. I only knew that the mention of his name brought up feelings that I couldn't control and touched me so deeply it almost frightened me.

During our first session, the same thing occurred. He channeled through J.Z. Knight (the same woman who had called me about Mark). J.Z. was a beautiful blonde with a kind of delicate friendliness. Ramtha was a definitive masculine energy of loving forcefulness. When she went into trance and Ramtha came through, everything about J.Z. changed. The soul energy of Ramtha was *in* her. J.Z. is about five feet four inches tall and not particularly strong. When Ramtha came through, he picked me up in his arms and carried me around the room, nearly lifting me over his head. I could feel *his* masculine energy through *her* arms. I am a heavy, muscled woman weighing usually between one hundred thirty and one hundred forty pounds. Using his energy to strengthen J.Z.'s arms, he had no problem with my weight. (Sometime later I watched him lift a two-hundred-pound man.) As soon as he embraced me and lifted me, I began to cry again. I felt some awakened feeling in my heart that I couldn't understand. Then Ramtha put me down. He took my hands in his and kissed them. He stroked my face. Then he gazed intently into my eyes. I could feel him pouring through J.Z.'s face. I *felt* his thoughts. It was unbelievably real. So much so it was disconcerting. I had often experienced the energy of entities from the spiritual dimensions working with Kevin and other mediums. But this was different. Never had it been so profoundly moving to me as with Ramtha. I leaned forward to feel his energy more intensely. I couldn't stop my tears. Ramtha smiled. Then *he* began to cry! I felt that I was in another world. My mind clicked off. I wasn't thinking. I was only feeling. Who was he? Why was I behaving this way? Then something familiar began to well up in my heart. It began first as an abstract intuition. I didn't obstruct the feeling by trying to figure it out with my mind. I let it happen. The feeling expanded until it took the form of an intuitive thought. As I looked into the eyes of Ramtha, I heard myself say, "Were you my brother in your Atlantean incarnation?"

More tears spilled from his eyes. "Yes, my beloved," he said, "and *you* were my brother."

I can only say that what he said *felt* exquisite. I *knew* it was true. That was the reason I had been so moved.

Ramtha and I went on to spend quite a bit of time together. He taught me about light frequencies in relation to the human body. He humorously predicted personal events in my life—that *always* evolved to be true. He was lovingly stern with me when I allowed my intellectual skepticism to block my growing "knowingness." He related story after story of our life together, pointing out other people we knew then who are part of my present incarnation. He examined what was karmically necessary for me to work out with those people. He spoke calmly and evenly of why I had chosen to have conflicts with certain people in order to understand myself and them more fully. He specified the areas of my growth that needed more work. He warned me about my blindness in relation to some of my friends and revealed some of the past-life incarnations we had had together.

He spoke of the vitamins I needed, the kind of exercise I should have, the foods I should stay away from, and even gave me his evaluation of the scripts I was reading.

I asked questions relating to everything from the personal life of Jesus Christ to whether I would ever meet my soul mate in this incarnation. What I learned from Ramtha would fill another book. But no matter how much I learned from him, he continually reminded me that *I* already knew all the answers. I mustn't depend on him or any other spiritual guide for knowledge. I must be my own guide. I should learn to trust and depend on my own capability for awareness. Guru-hopping could be fun, but it only postponed one's own self-truth.

Ramtha was amusing, fun, and loved to have a good time when he was in the body of J.Z. Often he would ask for wine, as he had enjoyed it when *he* was in the body. Several times he got drunk and J.Z. was left with the residue of a hangover.

His was an activating energy. He was not at all laid back and generalized. He could zero in on your personal life until you felt he was invading your privacy. And there was nothing he didn't know about me. He brought up events in my childhood that I had forgotten long ago. He questioned me about my most private inner confusions, which no one could have known. He did this not to prove his credibility, but to help ease my conflicts through discussion. It wasn't possible to conceal anything from him. He knew it all anyway. From the spiritual dimensions there were no secrets, no games, no need for clandestine manipulation. The point of his spiritual education was to impart the truth that *we* were God. We were as capable of knowledge as *he*. There was no pecking order. No one was more advanced or evolved than anyone else. They might be only more *aware*.

That became clear later. I had begun to take exception to some of the techniques Ramtha used when he taught. I still do. I feel that he is often too strong and harsh with his predictions of times to come, unaware of how detrimental fear can be. It is my feeling that warning is not as essential as balance and harmony. I told him so and he agreed that we all learn from each other. That he had as much to learn from us as we had to learn from him.

So Ramtha became a spiritual friend, and he endeavored at every meeting to help me realize that my own higher self was my best spiritual friend. In the meantime he would be there to help me whenever I needed it as long as I didn't become dependent. (The warning about dependency was common with all the spiritual entities I talked with.)

Now in New York a few years later, Ramtha came to help me when I was really in trouble. He often worked with other entities on the spiritual planes whom I had learned to trust. In this case, he worked with Tom McPherson.

I was about three weeks into the run at the Gershwin Theatre. The summer weather hadn't hit full blast until the third week in May. As always in New York when summer is hot outside, air conditioning is like winter inside. The theater was no exception.

During the middle of a performance, the air-conditioning system came on full blast and the change in temperature not only caused my muscles to seize up, but I felt my throat go dry, cold, and finally very raw and sore. The last thing I needed was a summer cold while I was performing. I got a shawl from the wings and finished the performance, but I felt the die had been cast unless I took some preventive measures immediately. I called a doctor I knew, waking him up, and he prescribed an antibiotic which I rushed to have filled at an all-night drugstore. I hadn't taken any medicine for years. Why I made the mistake of doing it then, I don't know.

By the next afternoon I was so weak from the antibiotics that I could hardly stand. My throat felt better, but my legs were gone. How could I perform?

Dominick picked me up at my apartment, but I couldn't walk. He lifted me into the car.

"How're you going to work like this?" he asked.

I sighed, very depressed. "I don't know. Maybe it'll be better when I get there. Don't tell anyone, okay?"

"Okay."

I dragged myself to my dressing room. Maybe if I could get through a warm-up, I'd be all right. It worked in reverse. The more I stretched and jumped to prepare myself, the weaker I became. The rapid blood flow only spread the antibiotics more fully through my system.

The orchestra was tuning up. I put on my opening costume and went to the stage. I did one plié and collapsed behind the curtain off to the side of the stage where no one could see me. I was conscious as I lay there, but I couldn't move my body. It was terrifying. I couldn't even speak.

I heard Michael Flowers calling for me. I couldn't answer. I heard people yell from my dressing room that I wasn't there.

Then, as I lay there, I knew I wouldn't be able to go on unless I had help. What kind of help? I put everything out of my mind and I called on Tom McPherson and Ramtha.

"Come in and help me," I pleaded desperately. "You have my permission to infuse your energies with mine. Please come above me and pick me up."

I waited . . . I tried not to doubt. They would be there if I *allowed* it. Slowly, I felt my arms energize. A permeating glow ran through them. I found I could lift them. Then I felt a current in both of my legs, a kind of mellow, activating current. I moved my right leg. It didn't feel leaden anymore. I lifted it slowly over my head. It stretched easily. Then the left leg. The same ease was there.

I carefully pulled myself to my feet. I felt a dizziness. I looked above me, attempting to *see* what I felt. I visualized the light aura of Ramtha and McPherson mingling with mine. The dizziness left me. I shook myself all over. I felt my energy come into an alignment. I walked to the backstage wings where everyone milled about, trying to locate me. Michael saw me first, walking toward him.

"Are you all right?" he asked. "You look different. Where were you?"

"I collapsed from those damn antibiotics," I explained dreamily. He put his arm around me.

"Well, will you be able to go on?"

"Are you kidding?" I said, almost as though it weren't me talking. "I've never missed a performance in my life and I'm not about to start now."

"Well, good," said Mike. He looked at me closely.

"I may not be doing it alone, though."

"What do you mean?" he asked me expectantly.

"Well," I said, "I've asked Ramtha and Tom McPherson to come in and help me. They are above me right now. I can feel them. As soon as they hovered close to me, I could move again, otherwise I'd still be in a heap behind that curtain over there."

Michael knew all about Ramtha and McPherson.

"Well, okay," said Mike, like a football coach before a game. "So we'll have a little spiritual energizing here, eh? Can Ramtha dance?" he asked with delight.

"I don't know, but I know McPherson can be funny. I think Ramtha will be holding me up and McPherson gets to perform."

Michael kissed me on the cheek as the overture began. I warmed up with pliés and stretching. My energy was fine. With the overture over, I took my place behind the revolving piano and waited for it to turn. My cue came, the piano revealed me, and the spotlight bathed me in number III surprise pink. I stopped a moment. The lights felt different. The sound was off. I couldn't measure the distance from where I was to the front of the stage. I felt like a foreigner in strange territory. I looked above myself as though to reconfirm that my friends were there. I could feel them say, "It's all right. Relax. Let us do this. *Know* that we are here."

I had no other choice.

I began to sing. To me my voice sounded as though it belonged to someone else. The stage under me felt farther away than usual. My familiar reality on the stage I knew so well was being infused with the reality of two other soul energies I knew just as well. It was a remarkably new but "homey" experience.

Apparently we did a good show. I don't remember any of it. In fact, according to others, the show was better than usual, I am unhappy to say. I had always liked to do things myself, regardless of the effort it took. I was learning that to sometimes call on help from my spiritual friends was no reflection on my capabilities. In fact, the sooner I gave up my "I am strong in the face of adversity" streak, the better.

Michael said I took my last bow and then as soon as the curtain came down I collapsed again. The energy of Ramtha and McPherson left me. Michael ran to me and picked me up in his six-feet-four-inch matching arms.

"I see they had another job to go to right away," he said, laughing, knowing that I was all right.

"Were we good together?" I asked.

"Yes," he said, "but I'm glad they won't let you become dependent."

*   *   *

Dominick had watched what happened from the wings. He was a religious man (Catholic) and had been reading my book. Every now and then he would ask me a question about reincarnation or spiritual guidance. He said the Church wasn't answering enough of his questions. So we'd talk after the show. Michael lifted me back into the car so Dominick could drive me home. I was stretched out on the back seat.

"How did you perform like that?" he asked hesitantly, almost as though he didn't want to hear the answer. "I don't understand."

"I had some help," I answered.

"Help? From who?" He swallowed hard.

I sat up and leaned over the back of the front seat. I told him all about Ramtha and McPherson. He didn't flinch. He seemed to almost understand.

"So you're telling me that these Ramtha and McPherson fellas are around all the time if you need them?" There was no sarcasm in his voice.

"Yes," I said. "That's right."

"And they used to have bodies and be alive on the earth." He made a statement instead of asking.

"Yes."

"And they might sometime decide to reincarnate again and have bodies like us."

"Yes."

He hesitated as we pulled up in front of my building. Then he said, "You know why I believe what you're saying?"

"Why."

"Because about one month after my brother died, he came one night to visit me. I *know* he was standing next to my bed explaining that he was all right and I should tell my father not to worry. I asked him why he didn't tell Dad himself. He said, 'Because Dad wouldn't understand. You do.'"

Dominick shook his head with the memory. "And the funny thing is, just that day I was looking at the flowers on our patio and the thought occurred to me, if flowers can come back every time they die, why can't people? Nature does it all the time. So when my brother came to me that night, I guess I was ready to understand it. Maybe he could help me sometimes, like your friends helped you tonight. That's what it's all about, isn't it?"

Dominick's simple eloquence was so much more to the point than all the metaphysical books I had read.

"Where can I read more about this, Shirley?" he asked.

"You don't need to, Dominick. It's all inside of you. Just listen to your feelings and trust them. *You* are unlimited. You just don't *realize* it."

He shook his head again and said, "Wow. You know, I don't think my driving you was an accident. I think I needed to just be around and see how you put this stuff into action."

Dominick helped me upstairs, suggesting that I use vitamin C rather than antibiotics to get rid of my cold. "And don't try to do so much yourself," he chided me. "Let some other people help you, like you did tonight."

I was learning that lesson in more ways than I could keep up with.

I would like to relate two more incidents that occurred with McPherson and Ramtha. First, Mc-Pherson.

Before doing *Terms of Endearment*, I hadn't acted in nearly three years. There might have been good scripts around, but I wasn't getting any.

Then Steven Spielberg wrote a screenplay called *Poltergeist* and asked me to play the mother. My dream had been to work with Spielberg because of his metaphysical proclivities. But to me *Poltergeist* was too violent. It exploited the negative side of the Force and I didn't want to contribute to negative violence in the marketplace. So, after many meetings and discussions, I told Steven I couldn't do it, regardless of what a stupid career move it seemed to be. He understood and said he had a film planned that focused on the positive side of the Force about the love of a small boy and an extraterrestrial. But there was no good part in it for me. When he outlined the story to me, I said I thought *E.T.* would be more successful because it gave people hope and was charming besides. He thanked me and promised we'd work together someday when we could emphasize the positive aspects of spiritual understanding.

Many of my associates and friends thought I was nuts to turn down *Poltergeist*, particularly in view of how my career was going at that time. It was hard for me to explain that it went against the grain of my spiritual beliefs, because *Out on a Limb* hadn't been published yet.

In any case, I had another session with McPherson to discuss whether there was any hope for me to get another good part in the near future.

"First of all," he said, "you made some Brownie points with us up here in turning down *Poltergeist*. It's fine for others to do a film like that, but not for you."

"Great," I said to Tom, "but what about making movies? I mean, when will I get a good part?"

He chuckled and said, "Well, would two weeks be soon enough?"

I, of course, didn't know what he was talking about. There was nothing that I knew of, not even on the horizon.

"You will receive," he said, "a very fine script about a mother-and-daughter relationship and the opening shot of the film will be that of a child's clown."

"A mother and daughter?" I asked.

"Quite right," he said confidently. "It will be very popular and you will win one of those golden statues for your portrayal."

I took what he said with less than a grain of salt.

Two weeks later I received a call from a fireball of an agent named Sue Mengers. She said she had read a script about a mother and daughter written by James L. Brooks, a man from television. She said it was considered a risky art film by most of the studios in town, but she thought it was brilliant and just right for me. Would I read it?

Immediately I thought of Tom McPherson's prediction, read it the next day, met Jim a week later, and the rest is history.

There is an additional twist to this story. When, a few weeks later, I discussed *Terms of Endearment* with Ramtha, he said, "You won't be doing this film for another year and a half. The time is not ripe yet. The financing will not be there and *you* are not yet ready. But it is true that when you do do it, you and the film will be greatly rewarded. Have patience. Do not be afraid."

The timing worked out exactly as Ramtha had said. Studio after studio walked away from the project believing that it was not at all commercial and insisting that they would not allocate the amount of money Jim needed to shoot it on location in Texas.

I waited. I turned down everything else that came up in the ensuing time period so that I would be available, trusting that what McPherson and Ramtha had said would come to pass. Finally Paramount agreed to make it one and a half years later.

And when, at last, we went into production, Ramtha and McPherson were there with me, encouraging me to "become" Aurora Greenway.

Ramtha also spent a good deal of time with me discussing *Out on a Limb.* He was unalterably opposed to my projections of negativism in the original manuscript, even when they seemed logical in the light of what was happening on the world scene. I am enough of a pragmatist to have had some fairly hot arguments with him on this issue. Choosing one's own path in positivity is one thing. Ignoring all common-sense predictions of what one sees around one is another. Ramtha's view, though, was that prophesies are, all too often, self-fulfilling. To project the worst actually contributes to its happening.

I, too, eventually came to this view. This has been one of the most profound lessons for me since beginning my metaphysical searching. Fear and negativity are *not* part of the future. The *erasure* of fear and negativity are the future. And whatever it takes to eliminate those concepts of consciousness, I will address myself to, not only in relation to global conflict but in relation to my everyday life. I had to eliminate a great deal of fear in myself before I could allow *Out on a Limb* to be published. And as my life continues to progress I find that the more I eliminate fear, the happier I am. Fear has become a non-reality to me. It is a perception, not a fact. Fear is only what I perceive it to be. Yes, it is still there sometimes, but in "reality" I know it is only there because I allow it.

Chapter 7

As time passed, my mother's condition improved. She was determined to be well enough to attend my closing night.

True to her prediction, she and Dad arrived at the theater during my next-to-last matinee performance. Sachi came in from California again. Dominick had picked them up at the airport.

I was performing on stage when I looked to stage left and saw three of the most important people in my life seated on folding chairs watching me from the wings. It was a picture I'll always remember. Dad and Mother sitting erect, leaning on their canes in front of them for support, and Sachi with her arms around them from behind.

Their three faces beamed; I could almost hear their thoughts. The grandparents reflecting on what might have been had they not raised a family in traditional fashion and the granddaughter, who sat with stars dancing in her eyes, projecting that being a performer was what she wanted more than anything else.

There was a cast party in between shows, commemorating the end of our run. The tables were decorated with bowls of cherries and there was yet another carrot cake with "Love and Light" spelled out in sugary letters. Many of the stage crew and ushers brought copies of my book to sign and Danny in the box office had me sign the statement of the house record we had broken.

Many of the fans who had waited literally every night at the stage door came again for the last time. They brought me gifts and letters which poured out their feelings of appreciation for my advice on thinking positively.

Danny said ninety percent of the conversations he heard as people left the theater had to do with reminding each other to think positive.

Mom and Dad and Sachi went out front to see the last performance. Mom and Dad were outfitted with the auxiliary hearing devices provided by the theater.

Bella and Martin Abzug were there too.

Before the overture, I did my performing affirmations for the last time. It was true that I was tired from a six-week run, but facing the fact that I would probably never do the show in New York again, I felt an overwhelming sadness that it was over.

In my red sequined pantsuit I walked one last time to my position behind the piano. As the show began, I looked above me. The light rack had become so comfortingly familiar. The scrim hung on a lead pipe waiting for its cue. The face of each musician (not one of them had missed a performance) smiled back at me. The sweep of the music (the orchestra said it was the most intricate they had ever had to play in a Broadway house) lifted to the rafters. I wondered as I gazed around me how much energy from other performers still lingered hauntingly in those rafters. The magic was probably there for always. In a few hours our props would be physically dismantled and crated away in a truck to make way for the next performer, but the magic of our energy would remain. I understood the show business adage of "lucky" and "unlucky" houses. And what was luck? It was nothing more than being aligned with positive energy. Every theater I had played resonated with those energies. I could almost tangibly feel the vibrations of past performers. The communal experience of performance and appreciation, of jokes and laughter, of tears and identification, of depth-plumbing drama and high-soaring comedy, of thundering ovations and stone-silent attention . . . all of it still hung quivering with memories in the unseen ethers of every theater. No wonder theaters were houses of magic, engendering star-struck awe. Theaters were where life was re-created to fulfill the fantasies of dreamers. And without dreams, how could life proceed?

My cue came. The spotlight hit me and I was on for the last time.

I looked down to the fourth row center. Mom and Dad and Sachi expectantly smiled up at me. I smiled back. No one knew who I was smiling at.

I felt content and complete.

I did the show for them.

When it was over, I took the microphone and went to them in the audience. I asked the audience to please respect their privacy and I introduced them. Then I sang songs to each of them. Tears gently slid down their cheeks as they held hands. This was what live performing was all about. It came from the heart and was completely spontaneous, from the spectator's as well as the performer's point of view.

I made my way back to the stage, thanked everyone for six of the most fulfilling weeks of my life, and asked for the curtain to descend.

Backstage, the dancers and I turned and applauded each other. The musicians spilled from the bandstand and embraced us. Stagehands wiped dirty palms on their jeans and slapped us on the back as they began to dismantle. The wardrobe girls said the theater would never be the same as they hung our wet costumes. The lighting-booth guys winked the lights backstage on and off to remind us they were still there and would be again. Pictures and autographs were exchanged and I gave out closing-night presents—small diamond pins in the form of initials of everyone's name.

When I returned to my dressing room, my family was waiting.

Daddy looked up at me. His eyes filled with tears. "Well, Monkey," he said, "I wish I could find the words to describe how beautiful you were on that stage."

"Oh, darling," said Mother, "to realize that something so lovely came from a person who was part of us was thrilling."

I had waited a long time for them to say that. The two people who had been responsible for my formative training, my childhood courage, and the struggle for belief in myself now sat proudly in front of me and said that their dreams for me had been realized.

A few moments later Bella and Martin walked in. I introduced them to Mom and Dad.

"Well, Mr. Beaty, how did you enjoy your daughter?" asked Bella.

Daddy's mischievous twinkle returned to his eyes. "Well," he said, "first of all, I could hear everything she said. Those earphones out there are humdingers."

"Earphones?" asked Bella, not realizing she was walking into one of his traps.

"Certainly," said Daddy, "none of my hearing aids ever work. But this one did. You know why?"

"No, why?" asked Bella.

"Because it is a Republican hearing aid."

"A *Republican* hearing aid?" she said, ready for battle.

"Sure," said Daddy. "If that old cowboy in the White House has one of these, no wonder he always has the right answer."

"The *right* answer?" Bella's voice was slowly rising.

"Why sure," said Daddy, knowing for certain that he had her going.

I winked at Mother. She shrugged her shoulders in mock embarrassment. "Now Ira," she said, "you might think that's funny, but Bella doesn't—"

"Sure she does." Dad wouldn't quit.

Bella looked confused, which is not something I've seen often. I threw up my hands and went into my inner dressing room to change my clothes. There was no doubt about it. Mom and Dad were the leads in any room they played. The rest of us might just as well accept the fact that we were bit players.

We left the theater about three hours after the final curtain. I walked out on my dismantled stage and blessed the empty seats in the house. I knew that our energy would mingle and linger with the energies of everyone who had preceded me, and everyone who would follow. Yet for me, as for most performers, there was an inevitable letdown.

My family watched as, melancholy, I turned away from the work light and into the shadows of the wings for the last time. They sensed that I lived another life when I was out there, a life dreams are made of. Dreams based on hard work and the struggle to overcome the fear of not being accepted. I hadn't realized how deeply embedded the fear had been in me until later that evening and the following day. Or I should say, I had not understood where and how the fear had developed until I was witness to those same fears still alive in my mother.

Live performing has a way of inspiring and provoking immediate emotional reactions in some people. Pent-up, long-suppressed feelings often erupt after having been moved by what you see live on a stage, particularly if it is someone you know and love. It has happened to me many times, so I wasn't all that surprised when it happened to Mother. She had, after all, by her own admission, lived her dreams through me. What brought me closer to her, though, was that she felt safe enough to let herself go completely. In her case, her loss of control probably added years to her life, and it was a compliment that she did it because of me.

Sachi and Dad and Mom and I were back at the apartment after the show, sitting down to a snack of corn muffins and tea. They were still full of their feelings in having seen my show. Sachi was paying close attention to the interplay between my parents and with me. She had never really spent that much time with the three of us. As a fledgling actress, she was riveted by the intense familial emotion, and as my daughter, she was learning more about me and what made me the way I was. The keenness of her interest was second only to mine, as I was beginning to understand more and more *my* chosen karmic reasons for being a part of life with my mother and father.

"These muffins are delicious, Monkey," Dad said, referring to the fact that there was nothing else to eat in the apartment. "I'm thankful for small favors. After Bird Brain's meals, this is a feast."

Mother laughed and there was more conversation relating to Bird Brain's lack of culinary talent.

"But we know she is a good and nice person," he went on. "She entertains us. Since we don't get out much, all I see are your mother's financial-wizard friends."

Mother looked up at him with that "look" in her eyes. "Ira," she said, "I won't have you speak of my friends that way."

I was surprised at the intensity of her reaction, but Dad seemed to understand that he had hit a trigger point and had maybe even done it on purpose. I wondered what this was all about.

"My friends are important to me," said Mother. "You don't understand them at all because you haven't even taken the trouble to know them. You are always too busy humiliating me in front of them."

Sachi and I were astonished at how deeply upset she was, seemingly provoked by nothing. She was reacting far too strongly to his intended humor.

But Dad understood. It was almost as though he had made the remark knowing that the two of them needed a family audience to vent some of their repressed feelings. Yet right now I didn't feel I wanted to cope with one of these familiar scenes. I put my hand on my mother's arm to try to calm her. She pulled it away.

"No," she pressed on. "Your father embarrasses my friends by making bawdry jokes, and I don't like it one bit, not one bit."

Dad smiled, chewed on his muffin, and decided to press *his* point.

"Oh, Scotch," he said, "those old biddies don't care about anything but money. I interject a little humor just to humanize the situation."

He smiled maliciously and waited for her reaction. I remembered so many dinner scenes from my childhood as I watched yet another reenactment of the way they "played" each other.

Mother straightened up in her chair.

"Well, thank goodness *I* am interested in money. *I* have to make out all the checks or the IRS would come and put us in jail."

She wasn't making a melodramatic joke. She was serious. I felt that she was touching on much more than money.

Daddy turned to me. "The boss here gives me twelve dollars and fifty cents a week for allowance. I could drink up that much liquor in half a day. I wouldn't need a week. And any blonde I could keep on that allowance wouldn't be worth keeping."

It was going to be a bumpy ride.

Mother's eyes flashed. I could see her decide not to address the "cheap blonde" remark. She preferred to discuss the money situation. In one minute they had managed to enjoin seven important subjects—adultery, humiliation, friendship, money, liquor, the IRS, and incarceration.

Sachi put down her muffin, listening wide-eyed. This was better than *The Edge of Night.*

Mother raised her voice. "Ira, you don't care enough about us to keep track of the checks you write and what they're for. You have credit cards, like Visa—why don't you use them? No, you leave me with the problem. The bank and the IRS will get us. And you know it."

"I do?" answered Daddy, still smiling.

"Yes, and it drives me wild because I know I'll have to go and apologize to the girls in the bank."

"Oh, Scotch," said Daddy with an intensified emphasis on her name, implying that his nickname for her was more than appropriate. "You know the girls at the bank are your friends too. They *understand* that you don't know anything about how to handle money."

"I *do* know how to handle money," Mother shouted. "I had to learn how because you are so careless."

I thought I should interject. "Mother," I began, "why don't you have an accountant do your checks so you don't have to worry about it?"

"An accountant?" she said, outraged. "No, I like making out the checks. It keeps me alert. Why shouldn't I do something I like to do? But I want your father to pay more attention to the checks he makes out. I want him to keep his records."

"Scotch, if I make out a check a month, it's unusual. I know I'm only supposed to live on twelve dollars and fifty cents a week. You told me. And I do what the boss says."

But Mother was furious now and charged into a marvelous non sequitur. "Your room is filthy," she said. "You sleep all day so I can't get in there to clean it up and the dust goes flying all over the house." She turned to me. "And he can never find his keys. I know he spends his twelve dollars and fifty cents on liquor. That's why I won't give him any more."

I looked over at Sachi. She understood they were deadly serious with each other, but the subject matter and the emotional gymnastics were making it difficult for her to take their quarreling with equal seriousness.

It was Daddy's turn. "I sleep all day so I won't have to hear this. Besides," he went on, "I was born tired, and every morning I have a relapse."

"You sleep all day because you are lazy and you leave everything to me," countered Mother.

"That's right," said Daddy. "In my old age I've thought a lot about ambition and what it can do to your life. It's right nice not to have any more ambition than how the hell you go about puttin' on your shoes. If I came out of my room, I would either hear your opinion of me or I'd hear you and the old biddies talking about their CD's or their investments in the stock market. I'm just lucky I get my twelve dollars and fifty cents a week."

I wondered if Warren had heard this conversation. Considering the money that both of us had made and given to them, it was unreal beyond words.

I felt myself becoming involved now because somehow their conversation was a reflection on us.

"Mother," I said quietly, "why are you so worried about money? You know you have more than enough and there's more where that came from."

She leaned forward and said in all seriousness, "Shirley, I'm just being careful. Anything could happen to you and Warren. I want to be sure we will be all right when we get old."

It was such a stunning remark I could barely respond. Her reasoning was unique.

"But Mother," I said, trying to sound reasonable, "you are eighty-one now. When do you think you'll be old?"

She shrugged. "I don't feel old. I don't want to feel old. Playing with money keeps me young."

Ohhhh, I thought, now we're getting to it.

"Your mother likes to tinker with money," said Daddy. "She likes to play around with the interest that it collects in the bank."

I turned back to Mother. "So you *are* interested in the money."

"It's not the money," she said. "It's what I can do with it if I learn how. Besides, when I'm alert I can argue with your father much better."

Daddy laughed. "So she meets with the old-biddy financial experts and they talk about their checking accounts, and when they leave she argues with me."

"Yes," said Mother, "then you come in the room and humiliate me in front of my friends by saying that I don't know anything about money. He never talks to me unless he's humiliating me. We sit for hours and say nothing until my friends come and then he embarrasses me."

I turned to Daddy, knowing that what Mother said was true.

"Well," said Daddy, "I just try to contribute some information and your mother says I make fun of her."

I turned back to Mother. "Well, maybe you could learn something more from him."

"No"—she shook her head defiantly—"they talk about complicated things I don't understand. Like trusts and things. So I just sit and sit. I'm not interested in that stuff. I don't want to hear about that. I don't want to hear it because I don't have that much money."

"But Mother, you *do* have that much money. And you have a good time playing with it."

She smiled. "Yes, it is fun."

"So don't just sit. Participate in the conversation so you can learn more." Even to myself I sounded too logical to be understood.

"No," she said, "I don't want to get mixed up with them. Your father will just turn to me and say I don't know what I'm talking about and why should I try?"

It was a catch-22 conversation.

Sachi was blinking very fast now.

"So Grandmother," she said, trying to make sense out of it all, "why don't you learn?"

"No, I don't want to learn," she answered.

"Why not?" asked Sachi.

"Because I have some rights of my own," asserted my mother.

Sachi hesitated, looking baffled. So I followed up. "You mean, one of your rights is *not* to learn?" I asked.

"You're darn right," said Mother. "I like to go down to the bank and learn from the girls there. At least it's a place to go."

"Oh," I said, realizing that perhaps we weren't talking about money after all. Mother continued.

"I don't want to learn from your father because the more I know, the more he'll argue with me and I don't like to argue."

Oh, I see, I thought, so this is about competition. Sachi saw no way to contribute anything at this point.

"But Mother," I said, "you've just manufactured a dead-end street for yourself. You're interested in money, but you only want to pursue your interest your own way at the bank with the girls. You say Daddy doesn't talk to you, but you won't participate in the money conversation at home so you have something to talk about."

I lost myself in a jungle of words that made no sense.

Mother sat back in her chair. She was involved with making points and needed to think over her next move. Daddy smiled. He knew just what he was doing and waited for it.

"Your father doesn't want to hear about CD's. But sometimes he goes to the bank to learn about them because he knows that if I die first, he won't know what to do. So I gave him the keys to the safe-deposit box and all the papers. So what have I done wrong?"

This was mind-boggling. Now she had woven

in the subject of death—and Daddy had known she would. It was a kind of game again. Shades of childhood. Mother went on.

"I want to learn to drive again, too, but your father scares the daylights out of me. And I'm not going to let him do it."

"Drive?" I said, astonished and appalled. "Oh no! Mother," I said, trying not to seem alarmist, "don't you think it might be time to *stop* driving and use the car service I gave you?"

"Oh no," she answered proudly, "I like to drive my own car to see my own friends so I can get away from your father's humiliation."

"Listen, Scotch," said Daddy, "I sleep all the time anyway. So what is there to get away from?"

She glared at him with renewed fire in her eyes. "You try to scare me about the Cuisinart that Shirley gave us too. You always say I'll chop up a finger or something. I could save myself so much bother with chopping vegetables but he scares me too much. So I'm just not going to bother with it anymore. I'm not going to bother with any of it anymore. Not your room, or your keys, or your checks. I give up."

I was getting desperate. I really wanted them to stop.

Sachi piped up. "Grandmother," she said, "you know, those Cuisinarts are easy to use. I use them all the time."

Mother ignored her and went on. "You know, we don't use your microwave oven either. Your father is scared to death of that. And he's made me scared of it too."

"But Mother, you *allow* him to scare you, because he's so frightened. Can't you see that? Fear is infectious, even if it's about microwaves and Cuisinarts."

"That's right," said Mother, triumphant. "If his mother didn't teach him anything at all, she taught him to fear better than anything. So I'm going to find another man to come out to our house to help me cut up the vegetables and work the oven."

"Are you going to get the same man to drive you around?" asked Daddy.

Now it was about jealousy.

"You're darned right," said Mother.

"You two are really something," said Sachi.

"Well," said Mother.

I got up and brought more hot tea and diet sodas. Nothing was said while I was out of the room. There wouldn't have been much point. I was supposed to be the referee and add up the points. Daddy, however, seemed to have elected to remain serenely silent. That was unusual, but it was because he realized Mother was more emotional than usual tonight, and it would work to his advantage.

When I returned, Sachi sat waiting for the next round to begin. I was beginning to suspect Daddy was going to "throw" the fight. I handed him a glass of Diet Pepsi.

"Is this brandied Pepsi?" he asked with a twinkle. I gave him a mock glare. "No, of course it isn't," he said. "I'm not old enough to drink." He took a sip and cleared his throat, heralding an announcement.

"You know why I stopped drinking sometimes?" he asked.

"No," I answered, playing straight man.

"Because when I consider that Seagrams can make their liquor faster than I can drink it I realize it's an unfair contest."

Everybody laughed. Then nobody said anything.

"You know," he continued, "the first drink of liquor I ever had was on a hayride." He tossed down some Diet Pepsi and added throatily, "Of course, I did lots of things for the first time on hayrides . . ."

"Oh, Ira," grumbled Mother.

"You know," I began, wanting to say something helpful about how joyous their old age together could be if they would be more tolerant of each other. "I know you two love to fight, but wouldn't it be better just to let go of all your objections to one another and have a good time?"

"Let go?" asked Mother.

"Sure," I said happily. "Just let go and have a good time."

"Let his filthy, messy room go? Let the checks go?"

"Well, maybe you shouldn't just let it go. Maybe you could just stop bugging him. If he wants to sleep in a filthy room, let him. Part of old age is that you *can* just let go and relax."

"Well," she said, "I haven't gotten to that stage yet. But I wouldn't be surprised that soon I wouldn't want to go into an old folks' home. They say they're mean to you there. I haven't heard about one that isn't. But I might like that."

Sachi looked at me, alarmed. I was too pissed off to allay her fears.

"Mother"—my voice was good and loud—"don't you think that's a little extreme? Your capacity for self-flagellation is unlimited, it seems. I wish you could see how you pull the rug out from under yourself. It's awful to watch."

Mother knew what deep water we were in now.

"I don't agree with you," she answered commandingly. "I think I'm doing very well taking care of myself and getting over my operations and all my broken bones."

She was missing the point.

"But *why* are you breaking your bones so much? You're responsible for that happening. It's not an accident."

"Of course it's not an accident," she said with a marvelous mixture of pride and self-pity. "My bones are brittle. I asked the doctor if he could remove the excess calcium, but he said he couldn't. So I keep breaking my bones."

"Jesus," I said. "Listen to you. You fall in the bathroom and—"

Dad interrupted. "She fell off the piss pot."

"I hate your vulgarity," said Mother. "And so does everyone else."

I got a hold of myself. "Well, not everybody hates it," I said a bit more calmly. "But okay, you fell off the toilet and you broke your hip. You fell another time and broke your shoulder. You did something else and broke your wrist. And now you're talking about going to an old folks' home where they'll break your spirit. Can't you see what you're doing to yourself?"

"Well," she said, "if I was in an old folks' home and became completely incapacitated, I'd want them to take away those life-sustaining devices. Ira will have to make up his own mind if it happens to him."

"Thank you, Scotch," said Ira.

"But I'd want them to stop mine," Mother finished.

Oh Jesus. Sachi stared at me. Even though it was ridiculous, the stark picture Mother painted so casually was painful for her granddaughter. It didn't seem to faze Daddy, though. Then Mother turned on an emotional dime again and said, "You know, Dr. Stone said I would have to walk with a cane for the rest of my life. But I say, oh no, I won't. Nobody is going to get me down."

It was clear her survival instincts were intact. What was disturbingly obvious was that she was determined to manufacture adversity so she could hone them even finer.

"Scotch," said Daddy, feeling it was time to participate again, "you just tell me what bone you're going to break next and I'll be right there. We'll put a nice furry rug under the piss pot so we don't have to worry about that anymore."

"I hate your vulgarity," screamed Mother again, "and so does everybody else."

Daddy winked at me so she would see it. His competitive cruelty was one for the books.

"You make a damned fool of yourself in front of people," said Mother, her voice suddenly quiet. "I don't like to see you do that."

"Why?" I asked.

"Because I love him, that's why. And I don't like someone I love to make a fool of themselves."

"I wouldn't call that love exactly," I said. "I'd call that being concerned about appearances."

She waved her hand at me and said, "What would you know about love?"

I felt she hadn't realized what she'd said. It was a line she delivered almost as a throwaway.

"*I* know about love," she stated as though the insistent self-sacrifice of a long stormy marriage proved it.

I could only shake my head.

She went on then, apparently unstoppable, through a catalog of Dad's feelings and her own sufferings.

All of her recalled stories painted a picture of hilarious, bizarre yet intense involvement. She was clearly outraged, yet unable to seriously consider leaving him. For two people who professed to be unable to live peacefully together, they just as obviously could not live peacefully without each other.

When Mother's tirade was finished, I said, "You always told me you loved him." She stared at me.

"I couldn't help *that*," she answered.

I was floored. Sachi was too. After a pause for exhaustion, Sachi said, conversationally, "This is really interesting for me."

"Really, darling?" asked Mother as though it had never occurred to her that Sachi's perceptions were being rather painfully sharpened.

"Yes, Grandmother," Sachi went on. "I've never heard people argue this way before. I can usually follow it better."

"Oh," said Mother.

"Well, Sachi," said Daddy, "why do *you* think we argue so much?"

Sachi looked at him directly and said, "I think you like to argue. I think you think it keeps you alive."

"I argue because I have to save myself," said Mother. "If I didn't, my ego would be destroyed."

"But you fall for his teasing, Grandmother. You *want* him to make you angry."

Sachi's sweet, uninvolved observation seemed to grab Mother's attention.

"I do?" asked Mother.

"Yes," she said, "and if you don't work that problem out, you'll just have to come back again until you do."

Both Mother and Daddy stopped for a moment and thought. Dad spoke first.

"But I thought when you come back everything is changed."

Sachi didn't hesitate. "It won't change to be better in the next lifetime until you work it out in this lifetime. That's what progress is."

I was amazed at Sachi's approach. And they were listening. She continued.

"The way I see it, Grandmother, is that Granddaddy here is providing you with the opportunity to work out your problems of intolerance and judgment. He does so many things that you don't like because you want him to."

"I want him to humiliate me and keep a dirty room?"

"Yes, you draw it to you because you know *you* need to progress along those lines. It's so obvious that you love each other and you chose to be together so you could work out this stuff in *yourselves*."

"But why doesn't he just stop what he's doing that makes me mad?" asked Mother.

"Well," said Sachi, "he probably would if you'd just stop being mad. Until you stop that, he's going to keep on providing you with the opportunity to grow until you do."

Sachi was giving *me* a lesson in objective clarity of thought!

"He's giving you a gift by putting you through all this. And you're giving him a gift by helping him to understand that it hurts you. You each have to change *yourselves*, not each other."

Mom and Dad were halted in their tracks. I had never tried this approach with them.

The living room was blissfully silent for a few minutes. Mother turned to me. "Are you ashamed of me, Shirl?" she asked.

"Ashamed?" I answered. "Why would I be ashamed?"

"Do you think I've said bad things about your daddy?"

"Sure you have," I answered. "I always remember you taking me aside and telling me how difficult it was with Daddy and if it wasn't for Warren and me you'd leave him."

Finally Sachi said, "Boy, you two must have had some very complicated past lives together."

Mother's answer to that was, "Well, it's too late for me to change now. I've been listening to him for over fifty years and I'm just not going to do it anymore."

Now she suddenly started to cry. "I must really be an awful person," she said. My God, where did *this* come from?

I got up and put my arm around her. "C'mon, Mother, why do you say that?"

"Because that's how you're all making me feel."

I hugged her close to me. "*You* are trying to prove you're an awful person."

"It's better that I don't talk. Your daddy can't hear me anyway."

Sachi got up and put her arms around Mother too. I looked over at Daddy, who coolly observed

Mother as though he had seen this a thousand times before.

"Daddy," I said, "why don't you tell Mother why you love her?"

He thumped the pillow beside him and began to talk. As Mother's tears slid down her cheeks, he described how he would be so proud sitting in the car waiting for her to come out of the supermarket. All the other "old biddies" would emerge with their hair messed up, falling unkempt around their faces. Their shoes didn't fit and they were slumped over as they shuffled along with little tiny footsteps. But when Mother walked out, she was a queen, slim and trim, her hair styled and her walk proud and gliding. The other women had "odors." There was never any of that with Mother. She smelled nice, of Emeraude, her favorite perfume. He explained that he appreciated how she had taken care of him, how she kept the house so immaculate, a damn sight cleaner than my apartment, and he told how he loved her cooking and never enjoyed eating out of those damn fool cafeterias where people bumped into him and spilled his coffee. He said he told her he loved her a dozen times a day. When I asked how he did it, he said he touched her shoulder every time he walked past her, and she knew what that meant.

Then he said perhaps she was feeling left out and alienated because each one of the rest of us had had some honor bestowed on us and she was the only one who hadn't. That she should realize that she had been the spark plug responsible for the success of all of us.

Then, out of earshot of Mother as she went to the bathroom, he said, "I think she very much regrets that she didn't become a big-time actress. Hell," he added, "I could say the same thing if I let myself dwell on it. I could have become a big-shot Ph.D. in psychology if it hadn't been for my having to support a wife and children. But that was over when I got married. I never gave it another thought. I wouldn't have had one-tenth of the happiness I've had with you and Warren and your mother if I had become some professional psychologist somewhere or a fine musician at Carnegie Hall. In some ways, your mother is philosophical, but in others she's not."

Mother walked back into the room. When he saw that she had returned, he looked straight at her and said, "As far as the money is concerned, it doesn't mean diddly squat. It's just so many fins on a Cadillac. I don't know why she is so paranoid."

My stomach turned over. I remembered how he used to do the same thing with me. I remembered how maliciously gleeful he had seemed when he told me the story of tying the tails of a dog and cat together so he could watch them fight. I had been horrified. He said it was life. And now he seemed to *want* Mother to continue to fight.

But Mother didn't say anything.

I thought of how she used to recite poetry to me with mellow tones of inflection in her voice.

She sat down carefully in her chair. "You know, Shirl," she said in a completely reasonable tone of voice, "you have no idea what an effect the Depression had on people. It was something. I'll never forget. To this day I can't go in and buy a dress for myself unless it's on sale."

"And," said Daddy, "she looks much prettier when she's dressed up than any of her friends."

"Oh, Ira, they don't even fit me when I buy them. My shoulders are too hunched over."

"Well, you don't have a belly like the financial wizards do. And your legs are beautiful."

"My legs are always breaking."

I stood up. "You know," I said, feeling that the third act was over and I was tired and it was late, "I wish you wouldn't focus on the negative so much."

"Well, you would be frightened, too, if you had a leg like mine."

I began to clear the table. "You're addicted to falling and hurting yourself."

"If I fall again, I think I'd just go to bed for good."

"Mother"—I looked her right in the eye—"do you *want* to die?"

She stopped a moment and thought. "I guess I haven't made up my mind yet," she said conversationally.

I smiled.

Daddy said, "Well, if you decide it's yes, I know where the keys are."

She looked up at him. "The keys you've been making me search for in your filthy room?"

"Yep," he said, smacking his lips, "I just like to have you visit me in my room."

Mother shrugged, suddenly smiling. Then, making one of her swift transitions, she turned to me with a totally serious face and said slowly, thinking it out, "You know, Shirl. One of the things that's held your daddy and me together all these years is the memory of the first night we spent together." She paused. "Our wedding night." And stopped again. "I had never known a man before. To me it was a marvel."

I waited, thinking she might go on, but she simply repeated, "That night was a marvel," her thoughts lost somewhere in her memory. I thought she might be trying to tell me something else. So I asked her, rather hesitantly, "Mother, it must have been a marvel that lasted for more than one night?"

"Oh, of course," she said immediately, and with great conviction, "but when it was new to me it was wonderful."

Daddy was watching her delightedly, his mouth tender and mischief in his eye. Sachi's eyes were glued open. She had certainly never expected to hear her grandmother bring up so intimate a subject. I decided this was a good time to ask something I'd always wondered about and turned to my father.

"Daddy," I said, "had you ever known a woman in bed before Mother?"

His smile broadened and he immediately picked up his pipe. "Had I known a woman in bed before your mother?" he repeated, using an easy joke-stall.

I nodded and Sachi leaned forward.

"Why, no," said Daddy, busily examining his pipe, "but that doesn't count the women I had known on the floor."

Sachi howled along with me. Mother knit her brows at our noise and threw a lofty look at her husband, intent on holding our attention and making her own point. "So," she went on, impervious, "I've known only one man in my life that way. And I'm glad. The memory of that night has always kept me from doing anything foolish."

Daddy tapped his pipe against the ashtray, a familiar maneuver to get the focus on what he was about to say. (Shades of not-so-subtle acting techniques . . .)

"Monkey," he said, in that way which meant we were going to talk about me now—and specifically about my sex life. "Have you heard anything further from that Englishman Gerry that you wrote about? I wondered what his reaction would be when he read that part where you told about his penis floating in the bathtub. That's getting pretty personal, you know." He was referring to a scene from *Out on a Limb* in which I had described Gerry soaking in a tub while we talked and how amused I was by the penis floating gently among the bubbles.

Sachi batted her eyelashes. "Yeah, Mom," she said solemnly, "a girlfriend of mine read that and said she had been *in* the bathtub with lots of men but the penises she knew never floated."

Mother's hand flew to her mouth as she laughed on a large intake of air.

"What did Sachi say?" Daddy asked, knowing perfectly well what she had said.

Very seriously, and somewhat louder, Sachi repeated her remark.

Equally grave, Ira Beaty regarded his granddaughter, and judiciously responded, "I can understand that."

Somewhat bemused, Mother chimed in, "Well. Well, do you think Gerry was proud of your writing about him? An awful lot of men *would* be proud."

"Grandmother," said Sachi, "how could he be proud when Mother wrote that his penis only floated?"

Mother shrieked. When she subsided she said, "Well, I wouldn't know about that. I've only known one." Now she shrugged again. "It was probably stupid of me."

Daddy took a long drag on his pipe. "Well, maybe," he said, "but when people ask me what I do best I always say, 'Look at my children and you'd know the answer to that. Obviously I do my best work in bed.' "

"Oh, Ira," Mother said, "you're really awful." She straightened up as though she had had enough. "I think I'll die if I don't go to bed now."

Sachi and I helped her up and into the guest room, where they would sleep together. I wondered how the double bed would work for them since they had arranged their homemade truce to include not only separate beds but separate bedrooms.

We helped her into her pink filmy nightgown. She had bought it on sale for the trip to New York. As I helped dress her, I remembered that she had given me a nightgown for Christmas every year for as long as I could remember. I have never been able to figure out why.

We helped her into bed. Sachi leaned over to kiss her. Mother hesitated. "I just want to say that after all I've done for your father, I want him to do four things for me."

"What are they, Mother?" I asked.

She moistened her dry lips and formed her words

carefully. "I want him to clean up his room, stop humiliating me in front of my friends with his bawdry humor, stop drinking, and keep a record of the checks he makes out."

"Yes, Mother," I said. "Okay, we got the point. Now please stop fussing."

She sat up in bed and began to cry again.

She looked up at Sachi and me and, incredibly, she said, "Don't let me upset you. You two leave me here to cry. I will be fine. It's not important. You need your rest."

"Grandmother," Sachi said loudly, "you can't do this to us. You're telling us to leave you like this? You're not being fair. You are too manipulative. I'm not going to bed until I see that you are all right."

Sachi shocked Mother, both with her logic and her firmness.

"Oh," she said, and stopped crying. "Then you just go and tell your grandfather what I said. And don't let him have a drink out there in the living room by himself. That's why he wants me to go to bed early, you know."

"Okay, Grandmother," said Sachi, "I think everybody would like some peace and quiet now. You have a good sleep and remember how much we love you. I've got to go back to California early tomorrow morning, but I'll call you when I get there. I love you, Grandmother."

"I love you too," said Mother. "Have a good trip, darling." Then she turned and looked at me. "You were so wonderful tonight, Shirl. It was breathtaking."

"Thank you, Mother," I said. "Did you love the audience when they recognized you?"

"Oh, it was wonderful," she said, "and there was one man in the row in front of us from Canada. He reached back and squeezed my hand. I was so proud to be your mother. Now, you run along. Don't let anything interfere with the work you have to do tomorrow."

I kissed her and Sachi turned out the light by her bed and we left.

I fell asleep marveling at the freedom with which my mother could express her fears, frustrations, and anxieties when she felt comfortable and safe.

Of course my dad's reaction to her behavior was as impressive as she herself had been.

Neither of them could know it, but trying to analyze what she and Dad were to each other and to me would become the "work" I would be most interested in for the rest of the summer.

At breakfast the next morning, Dad decided that Mother's "emotionalism" the night before had been caused by some chocolate she had eaten in the dressing room.

"Chocolate is worse for your mother than strychnine," he said, cheerfully ignoring his contribution of a gooey chocolate cake when she was still in the hospital.

Mother, however, was mortified. "I'm so sorry, Shirl," she said, genuinely upset with herself. As difficult and alarming as it had been, I tried to explain the positive aspects of it.

"Mom," I said, "it was so important for you to get it all out of your system. You made Sachi and me feel very loved because you would expose yourself like that in front of us."

"Oh," she said, "I never thought of it that way. It really was all right?"

"Yes, Mom. It was more than all right. It was necessary and good for all of us. There are more positive aspects to expressing yourself than negative."

"Gosh, Shirl," she said, "I was always taught to control my emotions and not upset anyone with what I was feeling."

"Well," I said, "you don't have to do that anymore."

"Thank you, darling," she said. "Thank you for

understanding. It's a nice feeling to be able to be myself."

She then shot an acerbic glance at Dad.

"So," I continued, "let's forget about it." I looked at both of them for agreement.

They nodded like mischievous, chastised children.

That was that. We dismissed the venom of the previous night and went on to talk about how difficult it was to grow old. How sometimes they felt like children because of their helplessness. Each worried about the other driving a car, and yet each needed their private places to escape from the intensity of being in the house with each other. They agreed that the one who died first had "the better end of the bargain." The bargain, I presumed, was their marriage. Both of them agreed that their own families had conditioned their thinking patterns, and as we explored the values in their backgrounds, we found ourselves drifting into the subject of politics. Both of them had developed political values which were based on resistance to domination. In Dad, this took the form of a violently prejudiced anticommunist stance.

"The Russians are bullies," said Dad, "and I don't like bullies. And I don't believe anyone else does either."

"Well," I said, "a lot of people around the world think the United States is nothing but a big bully."

"Well, at least we can vote for our bullies," he said, chuckling.

"Yes," I said, "and we have the right to be communists here, too, if we want to be. That is what freedom is all about."

"Well," he said, "that freedom is causing our Congress and our courts and our taxes and even our Supreme Court to dictate to us the Russian way of thinking."

I laughed out loud. This was so flagrantly absurd that it wasn't even good for one of our flaming political arguments.

"You must be kidding," I said. "A communist Congress and Supreme Court with *Ronald Reagan?*"

"Well, that's why I agree with the cowboy. Fight Russian force with force. Otherwise we'll be doomed to live like they do."

"You mean on twelve dollars and fifty cents a week?" I asked.

"I'd rather have your mother boss me than some son-of-a-bitch bully. And your news-media friends, why do they portray this country on television like it's some kind of terrible place? Why isn't there ever any good news? That's what I'd like to see. Good news."

"Then maybe you'd be happier in Russia. The news media never tells the truth there." I thought to myself for a moment and said, "Would you accept a socialist or communist society if it was voted in by the people?"

"God, no," said Daddy, "because they would have been battered into it without realizing it."

I sighed, speculating that probably a lot of people in America had the same point of view. "Daddy?" I asked, "why are you *so* disproportionately paranoid about the Soviet Union?"

"I told you," he said staunchly, "I don't like bullies."

"Well, who bullied you so much that you're so resistant to it?"

"My mother."

"That's right," said Mother. "I told you. His mother taught your father how to fear better than anything else. Why, he's so afraid of communists that I couldn't write to my best girlfriend for years just because she *knew* a communist."

"Yeah, and that guy was a damn fool," said Daddy. "A damn fool who was editor of that damn fool magazine. Why, your friend even got conned into going to Moscow."

"What's wrong with going to Moscow?" I asked.

"I've been to Moscow. Lots of people have been to Moscow, but that doesn't make them communists."

"Lordy, I know that," said Daddy. "I got invited to the Russian Embassy in Washington once and I'm sure the FBI has my picture in a file somewhere."

"Oh, Daddy," I said, exasperated, "now, who are you more afraid of, the commies or the FBI?"

"Well, the FBI doesn't intend to do away with the family and the churches and leave life up to the government experts."

"Still, there are a lot of people sitting in the Kremlin who are just as afraid of us."

"Yes," he said, considering what I said, "I've heard that." A smile began to play on his face. "And since we are discussing Russia and what they think over there, you ought to consider the fact that you've been under the influence of a Russian for some time now."

I stared at him, genuinely astonished. "Me? Under the influence of a Russian?" I didn't know what he was talking about. My mind raced to the Russian ballet dancers I knew. "Who do you mean?" I asked. "What Russian?"

"You know who," he said mischievously.

"No I don't," I said. "Honestly."

"Your friend—what's his name, Vassy? We met him when he lived with you in Malibu."

Oh no, I thought. I had wondered what Dad thought about the Russian I was with, but it never came up. Now, four years later, he was prepared to let me have it.

"Daddy," I said, trying to remain calm, "Vassy was under the influence of *me*. He was the one living in America, driving convertible cars in Hollywood and enjoying a free life. Just because a person is Russian doesn't make them a communist."

"Well," said Daddy, his reasoning turning as easily on a dime as Mother's did, "you know that *all* Russians enjoy sadness. They are dedicated to suffering. That's probably why they have the government they do."

Well, I thought, he might have a point there. I got up and looked out the window, down First Avenue. Vassy had loved New York. He said he'd never be able to live in New York City without thinking of me. Memories of our time together flooded back to me. Suffering? Yes, in that respect I guess Daddy was right about Vassy. But my goodness, what a joy his Russian soul could be as well. What a tearing, happy, consuming experience our relationship had been. But none of what went on had anything to do with political ideology. If there was anyone who'd rather be dead than Red, it was Vassy. No, it was his *Russianness* that had fascinated me.

"Daddy," I began, "don't you know that I've been somehow haunted by Russia all my life?"

"Now, what do you mean, Monkey?" he asked.

"I don't know," I said, "it's always been there with me. Their music, their language, their food, their humor—their soul. I somehow understand it. It feels familiar to me. It seemed inevitable that I would meet Vassy. And I can't explain why. And if you want to know, I think *you* have some of the same feelings about Russia or you wouldn't be so involved with your prejudice about the place."

"What are you getting at?" he asked, genuinely interested.

"Well, I think maybe all of us lived there once," I said simply.

"You mean in another life?"

"Yes, I mean in another life."

"Who is all of us?" he asked.

"Our family," I said.

Mother looked on with eyes wide, remembering the conflict about Russia with her girlfriend.

"And," I went on, "look at Warren with his magnificent obsession with John Reed and the hopes for the Russian Revolution. That was such a creative obsession that he produced *Reds*. Now, where do you think all this comes from? I mean, wouldn't you say there might be more to this than meets the eye?"

"Monkey," he said, "Jesus H. Christ, Peter be the Baptist, and George W. God from Goldsborough—when it comes to your mind and your eyes, you can make anything seem possible."

"Well, with the way my mind's eye is working these days, it's possible."

"Yes," he said, lighting one of his pipes, "anything is possible."

"Funny"—I smiled and sighed to myself—"that is exactly what Vassy used to say more than anything else."

"Well, let's hear about him," said Daddy, preparing to be entertained by one of my love affairs.

"Wait a minute," said Mother, "I want to get some tea."

I waited until they were all settled and told them the story.

Part Two

The Dance of Male and Female

Chapter 8

*F*rom the very beginning, Vassy and I both believed we had known each other in at least one previous lifetime. For that reason as well as many others, we were spiritually compatible. The concepts that I was exploring were not foreign to him. In fact, they were quite traditional among many Russians.

Yet our relationship was colorfully embattled because our personalities were diametrically opposed. Dad was right. Vassy's middle name was suffering and creative conflict, while mine was optimism and positive thinking. The combustion of the two of us together made it impossible to believe that our intense relationship was entirely new. We each knew we were involved in a karmic experience. We believed the intensity existed because we were drawn to work out unresolved aspects, not only with each other but also in ourselves, which the other inspired.

We often spoke of literature being abundant in expressing relationships of love, hate, familial conflict, and fundamentally profound feelings of loneliness, jealousy, power, greed, helplessness, and so on. We felt that great literature was epic because it was really about karma. We believed the experience of life itself was only about working out those conflicts within ourselves, using other human souls as the catalyst.

So, for example, we believed each love affair we experience has its purpose—its reasons for occurring. And on a soul level, we *know* that. The chemistry that draws us to someone is really the memory of having experienced them before, and understanding that there are unresolved areas that need to be concluded.

Our love affair validated that truth very clearly in our view. But as we found ourselves caught up in the throes of the joyful conflict of loving male-female embattlement, we often forgot the fundamental mystique of our attraction in the first place. On the other hand, perhaps living completely in the *now* was the only way we could work out our problems together. In the end, the problems were not about each other. They were about *ourselves*, as I believe all conflicts are.

What fascinated each of us more than anything was the undeniable truth that our relationship was analogous to the conflicts that Russians and Americans were experiencing with each other on a global level. Our relationship was a microcosm of those misunderstandings and cultural differences. But more than that, each of us experienced the conflicts of the male and female energy existent in *each* of us.

Let me begin with our initial meeting.

I was frantically winding up making a movie when actor Jon Voight called and insisted that I see a work by a Russian filmmaker, a friend of his whom I will call Vassily Okhlopkhov-Medvedjatnikov (his real name was just as complicated). Jon said the film was long but brilliant.

I pleaded exhaustion and said I wasn't interested in a ponderous Russian film.

Jon said, "I know, but you'll see something deeply moving. Come. I want you to meet Vassy. Please, do it for me."

On that basis, I went.

Driving along the freeway toward the San Fernando Valley, I should have realized what was about to happen as I relaxed my mind after the insanity of the movie set. I tried to picture what this Russian filmmaker could possibly be like. I had known many Russians when I was in the ballet; I was familiar with and amused by the colorful explosiveness that underlined their lives, and attracted to the passion and deeply felt sensitivity they expressed in their creative arts.

A picture of the Russian director swam into my mind as I drove. I was bemused by the clear definition of the image. Outrageous, I thought to myself.

The figure I imagined was very clear. He was a tall, lean, rather tawny-skinned man with high Mongolian cheekbones and deep brown, fawnlike, almost almond-shaped eyes. He was smiling with a broad, full-toothed grin revealing white teeth, an impressive array engineered to present "perfect imperfection." Why such a sophisticated dental allusion occurred to me, I couldn't imagine. This imposing-looking imaginary male wore a brown leather jacket over loose-fitting blue jeans which were not snug because his hips were slim. In my head I saw him standing in front of my car as I was directed to projection room 1. Brown hair crept over the collar of the leather jacket and every so often he swept hair back from his forehead with a circular movement.

All of this flashed in my mind as I negotiated the evening traffic on the freeway.

I pulled up to the gate at Universal and asked where the screening of the Russian film was because I couldn't remember the man's name. The cop at the gate said projection room 1! A coincidence, I thought to myself.

I rounded the alley looking for it when there in the street in front of my car was a tall, lean man in a brown leather jacket and loose-fitting blue jeans. He was obviously standing in wait for someone. He looked exactly like the man I had "imagined." I could see the high-cheekboned structure of his head, although aviator dark glasses concealed the eyes.

Impatiently, with a curved motion, he swept his fingers through his hair. I wondered what the hell was going on while emerging nonchalantly from the car.

He rushed to help me out of it, whipping off his glasses as though he wanted a clearer look at me. I thanked him and looked directly into his eyes. I had the definite feeling that I knew him.

"Mrs. MacLaine?" he asked in that way that foreigners do when they're not really sure how to address one.

"Hello," I answered. "I hope I'm not late, but we shot late."

"No worry," he said. "Thank you for coming. People inside are ready. I am director of movie."

"Yes, I know," I answered, realizing as I spoke that he even *sounded* familiar. "I'm hungry. Is there some food around?"

"Of course," he said, and with a flourish like a general he commanded a gofer to "bring me whatever is available." Jon had told me the man was very Russian, whatever that might mean. I wondered how he had gotten permission to come and work in the U.S.

He ushered me into the projection room as though I were the Queen of England and he the Prince Consort. I was trying to remember his name. No matter. I wouldn't have to introduce him to anyone. *I* was the guest, and I liked him immediately. His flair for commanding tickled me.

Once inside the screening room, he walked back to the chair with the sound controls and waited for me to take a seat somewhere. I, without hesitation, walked back over to him and said, "I want to sit beside you." He seemed clearly delighted. Then he rose and greeted everyone in charmingly halting Russianese English, told us a little about the making of the film (which had taken two and a half years and ran three and a half hours), sat down, and directed the projectionist to begin.

The lights went down. I pulled out my cigarettes and he, without asking, reached over and took one. He smoked it compulsively as people who don't often smoke do. Every once in a while, as the film unfolded, he would smoke and cough and then clear his throat as though it were all a mistake.

The credits told me his name once again. Medvedjatnikov. I said it over in my mind, trying to rehearse it so I wouldn't forget. And the film that unfolded assured me that Jon had been right. It was indeed brilliant. It was grand, personal, sweepingly moving, dramatic, and in parts, funny and strangely mystical.

But what was really weird—and to this day I cannot accurately describe my reaction to it—was that the leading lady, whose name I still can't remember, looked exactly like me. It was more than uncanny. It was downright disturbing. Not only did she repeat the image I had of myself, but she moved as I imagine I move! Her facial expressions and way of cocking her head when she was unsure of herself made me feel as I watched her that I was invading my own privacy. It was more than watching a reflection of myself.

When the lights came up, I turned to face Medvedjatnikov. He had smoked the last of my cigarettes. I tried to find a diplomatic way of asking about my screen image, but he didn't even wait for a question.

"You see, Sheerlee," he began, rolling my name out with his altogether charming accent, "I have been trying to contact you for twelve years. Excuse me, but you have been as an obsession for me. I don't know why. Therefore all my leading women are looking as you. *All.*"

He broke out in a wide, dazzling grin. I was equally flattened and flattered. I had heard of put-ons, come-ons, lead-ons before, but this one headed the list. I shut my mouth.

"Twelve years?" I repeated. Repetition is useful

when you can't find anything to say and need time
to sort things out.

"That is true," said Medvedjatnikov. "Ask any
of my friends who perhaps you will come to know."

Jesus, he didn't waste any time.

"Yes, well," I murmured, "your film is quite
wonderful. What do you plan to do with it?"

"I want American distributor. Is difficult. Who
wants to see Russian film? But I'm told is like Russian *Roots*. Is that not true?"

Yes, he was right. The film traced the life of a
Russian village in Siberia from the turn of the century, through both world wars, and into the 1970s,
exploring the lives and feelings of the village people
as they found themselves thrust into the technologi-
cal future of revolutionary Russia. It was not particularly propagandistic. On the contrary, it was human
and touching in that it expressed the bewilderment
of the villagers as they found themselves pummeled
and shaken by their country's revolution and entry
into the events of the world.

As I talked with Medvedjatnikov about the film,
I realized I was hearing a point of view about Russia
that I had not been exposed to before.

"And," I said, "have you left Russia and brought
your film with you?"

"Left Russia?" He was rather astonished. "Never.
It is my country. I am Russian. I am not defector. I
am not even dissident. I am filmmaker who wants to
be free to make films in West."

I looked at him suspiciously. How could anyone
do that?

"I will meet with immigration people next week
for reapplication of visa—H-1 visa—and soon, God's
willing, all will be in order."

I had the clear impression that whatever needed
to be maneuvered he would accomplish, simply because of the certainty of his boundless, commanding
vitality.

"Well, why are you able to travel in and out of the Soviet Union?" I asked. "Isn't that quite unusual?"

"Unusual maybe, but not illegal. Besides," he went on, "I have French wife and, therefore, half-French daughter. Authorities cannot prevent me from seeing family in France. And I have studied Russian constitution as lawyer and, understanding what you call fine print, I simply follow the possibilities. Maybe not even unusual. Many people who have married foreigners can leave Russia. Of course, for me is more difficult because I am very well known in my country. But I am persistent and, God's willing, I will succeed. I would like to direct you."

He caught me in the middle of a yawn which I was trying to cover up. I was very curious and very tired.

He smiled.

"You are free for dinner?" he asked. "Of course, your shooting schedule is exhausting. But could you make some time for me? It has been a long time for me to finally contact you."

"I'm sorry," I said, "I have an early call in the morning. We are nearly finished. And I have a difficult scene tomorrow. This film has not been the easiest one I've made. So maybe some other time."

"Unfortunately, I am leaving for Paris on the weekend. Perhaps tomorrow night?"

He flashed that full-toothed smile again.

"Tomorrow night?" I considered.

"If you please, yes. Please."

His man-child approach combined with his overweaning confidence amused me.

"Okay," I said, realizing I was already into something unusual up to my ankles. I knew myself well enough to know I was interested in getting in up to my neck. Why not, I thought. So I added, "Where?"

"I am living Chateau Marmont. I will be waiting in lobby at eight o'clock?"

"Okay."

Medvedjatnikov laughed and clapped his hands

with childish joy. Then he announced in a throaty voice, "I am Vassy. Please call me Vassy. Much easier. You make me happy." He gave the impression that he could barely keep both feet on the ground.

My God, I thought. I had had some experience with love affairs, but I could see right away that if I let this develop, it was going to be a whole other order of energy.

I put on my driving glasses to effect a shield between his eyes and mine as he led me to the car.

"Sheerlee," he said, smiling broadly, "you are *won*derful person. I am so *hap*py. And so *hap*py that you loved my film so *much*."

His voice was sincere and husky—not whiskey husky, I thought, but probably vodka husky. And I also had the impression that he was not unused to screaming.

I picked up Vassy in the lobby of the Chateau Marmont the following night. He wore the same blue jeans minus his leather jacket. In its place was a jacket made out of soft blue denim material.

He smiled at my entrance and stood up formally, his torso leaning slightly forward over his hips.

"Thank you, Sheerlee," he said with that well-schooled, boyish charm which I was sure was just as genuine as it was calculated. "You are so sweet because I know you are so busy with your filming."

"Yes," I said, "well, never mind. I am happy to tell you more of what I think of your film and maybe suggest a mode of distribution."

His dazzling smile dissolved to professional seriousness.

"Yes," he said, "may we discuss?"

I nodded.

"And where would you prefer eat?"

"I don't know," I said, "it's up to you."

"I have prepared reservations at a small French restaurant. We take car and then walk."

We slid into my rented car, which he eyed carefully.

"You like Datsun?" he asked.

"I don't even know what make this is, frankly," I answered. "I just know it has four wheels and gets me where I want to go. I gave up owning cars years ago. I travel so much they always ended up going on the blink."

"Blink?" he said. "Excuse me?"

"Never mind," I said. "Let's eat."

He directed me to park near a restaurant on Sunset Boulevard with a sign so small it was hardly visible outside. There was a menu, though, that didn't include prices. He seemed to know his way around Hollywood.

"So, how long have you been here?" I asked, as we walked into the restaurant, which had palm trees swaying over a small fountain.

"I was here for three months," he answered with great assurance, bowing to the waiter who had recognized me and rushed right up.

"I am working with big major studio—Universal. I like very much people at Universal. Very nice and they believe in me."

"Great," I said, meaning it, and wondering at the same time how Universal intended to express their confidence in this startling Russian.

We sat down and looked up at the hovering waiter. Vassy lapsed into French with a Russian accent. I laughed to myself. He ordered a double vodka and I a glass of red wine.

I pulled out my cigarettes and he took one. He didn't seem to own any himself. "I smoke too much last night. First cigarette I smoke this year. Not good."

"Why did you do that?" I asked.

"I am nervous finally meeting you," he answered, "and worry about your opinion of my film. Did you know I am calling you by telephone for twelve years?"

"Oh, come on, Vassy," I said, calling him by his first name for the first time.

"No, is true. You had secretary in New York who protect you very well. She wonders who is this crazy foreign-sounding Russian and always says you are out of country. You have been out of country twelve years?"

I laughed out loud.

"Well, I always tell people to say that, unless it's someone I want to talk to! Most people don't think I'm anywhere anymore. Or, at the very least, that I'm probably in Bucharest for a wine-tasting festival or something."

"So, I called you from Russia many times. Maybe you were in my country when I called you in New York."

"Maybe."

"You were in my country. I remember. You made a scandal. You were with students in Leningrad, yes?"

"Jesus, yes," I said, surprised. "How did you know that?"

"Oh, I know. And you disobeyed authorities by missing train and made scandal."

"Hey, wait a minute," I said, hearing my voice rise. "I had a right to go with the students if they invited me. And if I decided to take another train, that was my business."

"No, no," he said in a way I was to become infuriatingly familiar with. "No. Bureaucratic system unable to change schedules."

"Well, tough," I said, finding myself assuming the persona of a loud-mouthed American.

"But is very funny and amusing," he said soothingly, taking a swig of vodka that would have put away any sailor who wasn't also Russian.

"I wanted to make film of your scandal. You came as plain tourist but you acted as elite American star making scandal. Russian bureaucracy couldn't cope, as you say. Very funny comedy. Big news in gossip in Moscow. Big scandal.''

Vassy smiled to himself and took another belt of vodka. Only the ice was left. He ordered another one. I thought of Khrushchev and how he had told someone the story of Russians coating their stomachs with oil so they could drink each other under the table.

Vassy ordered a complicated French salad with hot lettuce and oysters or something, and I had *rognons* (kidneys).

"I am vegetarian," he said, looking at my meat order with decided disapproval. "Meat not good for muscles," he pronounced. "You must be careful as dancer. Particularly not being twenty-one anymore."

I hooted at the same time I wanted to slug him. He was so unconsciously funny with his dead serious autocratic pronouncements, and, as I was to find out as time went on, he was usually correct.

"I saw you at Palace Theatre in New York," he said suddenly. "I saw your one-man show. Beautiful, brilliant. Did you receive my caviar?"

His caviar? I didn't know he was alive.

"Your caviar? What do you mean?"

"I sent you five pounds caviar backstage. You were brilliant. I wanted you to contact me."

This was all too much.

"I don't remember receiving such an extravagant gift from anyone. No, I'm sorry."

His face fell, but his eye still had a twinkle in it.

"Oh," he said, "I think I make BIG impression. Oh, well. Self-illusion can be happy anyway."

I honestly couldn't decide whether he was putting me on or whether what he was saying about anything was actually true. He was so disarming, so enthusiastic, so total about everything that I guess it didn't really matter to me. His intense vitality was just too colorful to ignore. My feelings and confusions about him during that dinner were the first in a long series of roller-coaster rides provoked by knowing a person, a Russian person, I should say, who really did speak his mind and his perceptions as he saw them. His perceptions were so thoroughly foreign to mine that I was continually delighted, outraged, and amused.

Vassily Okhlopkov-Medvedjatnikov ate his fancy French salad as though the Russians were in Bakersfield. Hunched over his plate, he downed long slurps of vodka in between delicate warm oysters and laughed at how different we were.

It wasn't long before he was obviously just plain drunk. I didn't drink as much because I didn't want to miss anything. He ordered Zoappa Inglese for dessert, which I thought must be some kind of sweet soup. No, it was a rum cake. He finished it in three bites and ordered another one.

"I always eat only appetizers and desserts," he said. "More healthful."

"And vodka instead of water?"

He beckoned the waiter very deferentially. "I would like to have double stinger, please. That's all."

He didn't ask if I wanted anything.

I cleared my throat. "Vassily," I said, "I think I'd better go for an after-dinner drink, too, do you mind?"

"Oh," he said looking genuinely apologetic. "Of course. Sorry. You should have asked."

Jesus, I thought, I wonder how this small social confusion will translate when it comes to a deeper involvement.

In fact, I wasn't really sure whether his "color" was worth a deeper involvement. Minor—and possibly not so minor—cultural differences were glaringly clear already. Before I could pursue that thought any further, he diverted me again with what was apparently a mystical streak in his makeup.

"You know, Sheerlee," he began in his now drunken state. "I have been looking for you all my life, I believe. I believe it. I know it. I saw your face

in my mind here"—he touched his head gently—
"before I ever saw you on the screen. I knew your
face before I knew you were real."

That stopped me in midstinger. He was too
drunk to be consciously making up a sweet Russian-
coated proposition. No, it wasn't like that. Moreover, *I* had seen *his* face—something he did not yet
know.

"Is time," he repeated. "All my actresses are as
copies of you. *All.* I always loved a woman in my
head who had red hair, a nose turning up, long legs,
and blue eyes with small spots on face."

"Small spots? What do you mean?"

He reached over and touched my arm, pointing
to my freckles.

"Small spots. What is name?"

"Freckles," I answered. "I hate my freckles. I've
always tried to cover them up."

"No, no. Never. Beautiful small spots. They are
endearing."

"Endearing?" I said. "For a man who doesn't
speak fluent English, you have some choice words
in your vocabulary."

"I only learn 'endearing' this week. It is a word
I feel is right for what I want to say about these
small spot freckles."

It was sort of like being with a Frenchman who
knows how to sweep an American woman romantically off her feet. But with the exhaustive, concentrated energy of a child. American men never bothered
with that brand of romance. American men were
infinitely more realistic, more down-to-earth, less
motivated by fantasy. They couldn't seem to let themselves become childlike. They seemed slightly embarrassed by sensitive, romantic allusions to childish
associations. Not European men. And apparently
not Russian men either.

Vassy was like some floppy, lean, overgrown
brown Tartar puppy with feet that turned in when
he walked and hair that flopped wildly in his eyes as

he lost more and more control. And there was a reckless quality about him as he enjoyed himself as though he would leap at lightning just to see if it would strike him dead.

Right now, though, he couldn't walk straight. He tried to make it to the men's room in a straight line, but there were too many potted palms around. So he smiled, shrugged, and lurched ahead until he found *hommes* and disappeared inside. I wondered if he could do what he had to do alone and upright.

The waiter brought the check, which I noticed was over a hundred dollars. I felt inclined to pay it because it was simply not possible, in my view, that he could afford such a tab. I left the bill where it was and waited.

Soon he returned, saw the bill, and with a great drunken Russian flourish he pulled out a checkbook from a Beverly Hills bank and made out a check for the required amount of money.

"How can you afford this?" I asked diplomatically.

"I have bank account of money from Universal work, but is almost gone. Why not use it and have pleasure?"

I felt a scribble of guilt pass through me and said nothing.

"Did they pay for your hotel?" I asked.

"Certainly," he answered. "They are major company who pay expenses."

I was sure he was just playing big shot, but even that was "endearing" in my view because he had somehow managed to finagle a freedom for himself that no other Russian I had ever heard of had, without defecting.

"Soon I will be able to travel, God's willing, and make wonderful film here in States and show my minister how American filmmakers want understanding with Soviet Russian filmmakers."

I thought it had to be the vodka talking. Yet, in

a way I couldn't define, I felt that his flagrantly ingenuous attitude might just pull such a thing off.

"Are you saying, Vassy," I asked, "that you believe your minister will allow you to go back and forth between Moscow and Hollywood and make movies and return any time you want to, to make films in Russia afterward?"

"Why not?" he answered. "If I become famous international filmmaker, it will be good for Russia film industry. I will do that. You will see. It will be difficult, but I will accomplish my dream."

I sat up straighter, hoping I could pursue the conversation more specifically.

"And can you make films in France now whenever you want to?"

"Of course," he answered. "I have French wife. We don't live together anymore, not for long time. She prefers live in Russia."

"Are you kidding?" I asked. "Your wife would *rather* live in Russia than Paris?"

"In Moscow, yes. I and my family very well known. She is center of attention and activity when she lives there as a Medvedjatnikov. In Paris she is nothing. Now, so you want to go somewhere and have small drink?"

We stood up and he put his arm gallantly around me as though the evening were just beginning. The waiters and maitre d' smiled and bowed us out, grateful that Vassy would evidently make it to the car.

I must say, I didn't get the impression the guy was a drunk. I got the impression he really needed to get drunk *tonight* and most of that need had to do with me. We lurched back to my car where I could gratefully take off for Malibu, and he said he would rather maneuver back to the Chateau alone.

He put an arm around me as I crawled behind the wheel.

"You will excuse me," he asked, "for being drunk? I'm sorry. But thank you for supporting me.

Will you please see me one more time before I leave for Paris? I want to prove to you this isn't a common thing."

"See you again? When?" I asked.

"I will drive to Malibu tomorrow night and we will have dinner there?"

"You know how to get to Malibu?"

"Of course, I play tennis there often. Please, give me your address. I will behave."

I did, and we said good night.

The next day I didn't shoot, so I sat around in the sun and wondered what would be in store for me that night.

He called late in the afternoon and around eight o'clock showed up promptly at my doorstep carrying a phonograph record and his jogging shoes. He, of course, realized he couldn't have been more obvious and smiled sheepishly, but then nothing ventured, nothing gained.

I cooked him a vegetarian meal over which he "oohed" and "ahhed." And then he expertly eyed my hi-fi set and put on a record of a famous Russian pianist playing (what else?) Rachmaninoff. Vàssy leaned back on one of my sofas, closed his eyes, held out his arms for me. Presumptuous, I thought, and, amused nevertheless, allowed myself to be gathered up in them. Then we just lay back and listened to the crystal sounds of the piano flood the room.

Vassy couldn't listen to anything quietly, of course. Every once in a while he would raise an arm and conduct his invisible orchestra while swaying in ecstasy against the pillows. After the first side played, he got up to turn the record over.

"I was concert pianist," he said. "I graduated Moscow Conservatory of Music. I was in competition in Moscow with Van Cliburn. Then I saw him play with such"—he gesticulated volubly, "freedom, I realized I was working too hard at music and I quit immediately."

"You quit playing the piano when you were in the same league with Van Cliburn?"

"Of course."

"What do you mean, of course? Why would you do such a thing?"

"Because," he said, "in the competition I understood. For him it was easy and freedom and perfect as well. As for me, I had been forced by my parents. I didn't basically want it for myself. So I quit."

"Did you quit right then at the competition?"

"Of course."

"What do you mean, of course?" (This man was making me repeat myself . . .) "That is a very impulsive thing to do, particularly after you had studied music all your life. That's true, isn't it?"

"Yes, of course. We Russians are impulsive. Many times we do things dramatically and perhaps regret it afterward."

A sharp twinge went through me.

"Have you regretted it?" I asked hesitantly.

"I don't know. I don't think about it. I only play now when I am drunk."

That kind of impulsiveness, even *I* hadn't engaged in. It seemed so sweepingly destructive and without consideration of consequence. I was to learn later how right I was. But then, as I also learned, things seemed that way from *my* point of view.

After more music and some discussion of Rachmaninoff, which included how much Vassy wanted to do a film about his, Rachmaninoff's, life, we had some hot coffee and just sat together. He was gentle and self-assured, but I think almost slightly taken aback that I didn't object to any of his further advances.

To make a long story short, he spent the night, thereby establishing that he hadn't been out of line by bringing his jogging shoes. He was a joy to be with and not for a moment did I regret my own impulsiveness.

When he got undressed, I noticed he was wearing a gold cross around his neck.

I didn't have a call the next day, which was Friday, and then came the weekend. Vassy spent the next four days with me in Malibu (he "changed his mind" about his Paris weekend). We jogged along the beach, took walks in the mountains, and talked and made love and talked and made love.

He said he was overwhelmed with happiness, and gratefulness too, because he had finally found me and I was, as he put it, "simply the woman of my life."

For me? I wasn't really sure. I would see. There were so many unanswered questions, but they didn't seem to matter. We were having a glorious time together and apparently we both needed it.

Vassy told me about filmmaking in Russia and how comfortable and supportive his surroundings were at his studio, Mosfilm, where he served as head of the unit for young filmmakers. He spoke of his fellow workers with love and affection and of how they wondered whether he would be successful in the West. He asked me if I would do a film with him in Russia and said how much I would love the Russian people and their sense of passion and joy. He said he wanted me to see the rest of his films someday, and that his final dream would be to work with me. I took some of it with a grain of salt, but a lot of it I felt was genuine.

He told me about his three wives and how marriage was so necessary in Russia because of their conventional attitudes. Divorces were commonplace for the same reason. He loved all of his wives and, for that matter, all of his women. And his lovers apparently had not been insignificant in number. Why not, I thought. One could say the same about me; nor had I married them all.

"I once visited a great psychic in Bulgaria," he said. "I told her nothing about me. She correctly outlined my family's tree and then said to me, 'Why

America?' I said nothing. No one knew I was thinking about America. No one. And then she said, 'You are very dirty with women.' Perhaps I am using wrong wordage here, but she explained to me that I was not fair with women."

I looked at him open-eyed. Vassy visited psychics? And put stock in what they said, and on top of that was totally honest about it? This was an interesting man—a man who seemed to be confessing something to me which he desired to change.

"Well, *are* you dirty with women?" I asked in my subtle way.

"Yes. I think that is true. Yes. But then, I had never met the woman of my life before. Now I have."

"What else did she tell you?" I asked. He laughed.

"She said, 'Don't entangle with politics. Dangerous for you!' "

I tried to say something that made sense. "Well, you don't necessarily believe everything psychics say, do you?"

"No, but I would say they are to be seriously considered," he answered. "She was correct about my family and everyone in it. She knew I had America in my mind before I told anyone. This same Bulgarian woman was consulted by high rank officers. She is guarded by police because she is national treasure. I say she is reliable, but I don't know what she meant in regard to me."

He jumped up and stretched. "I don't know. I will show you now how to make a carrot and apple and beet salad with garlic—Russian style."

Vassy in the kitchen was a culinary expert. He shredded the beets and carrots with sophisticated flurry and whipped up the strange musky concoction, which included apples that he chopped in the blender, before dishing it up on my wooden plates like a lumberjack . . . or peasant, to be more accurate.

Then he began to eat standing up.

"Wait a minute," I said. "You have time. What's the hurry? Let's go outside on the balcony and eat like real people."

Vassy stopped chewing in mid-crunch as though I had just pointed out a basic vulgarity of which he was not aware.

"Yes," he said sheepishly. "That would be nice."

As we sat on the balcony I silently marveled at the strange contradiction of sophisticate and peasant that he seemed to be. He launched into a detailed and knowledgeable discussion of dietary principles and food-combining laced with understanding of what each food did for the human body. Yet, he shoveled the food down indiscriminately as he talked, apparently ignoring the contradiction between what he was saying and what he was doing. He certainly enjoyed himself, savoring the food with total commitment. He was clearly not a man who did things by halves. The food on his plate seemed symbolic of life to him, and if life, or food, or love, presented itself—he partook wholeheartedly. It was a quality I could revel in, because I was that way myself, even if it had drawbacks.

As he finished his salad he looked into his fresh carrot juice and said he had a small problem.

"I was supposed to return to Paris and move in with the woman I've been with. She is leaving her husband for me, but you mentioned, perhaps, being in Paris?"

I gulped because indeed I had it in mind to go to Paris immediately after I finished the picture in order to take a vacation with Vassy. Then we would see what would happen. Play it by ear, I thought. I was not prepared for this earful.

"But now I have met the woman of my life in you and I must be fair with my other woman."

"I see," said I. "I guess you have a slight personal problem. But what has that to do with me?"

He looked up from his glass. "Well, you want to

come to Paris, yes? You proposed coming with me, yes?"

"Yes," I said, "I guess that's what I was driving at, but I don't want to upset anything else that is important to you."

"You are important to me," he said. "You always have been. Although I never expected you to feel this way about me. Therefore I must tell her and explain what has happened."

"All right," I said, once again caught up in the dilemma of man-woman logistics. "Go now. Do what you feel you have to do and I'll be waiting to come when I finish my film, which should be in about ten days."

"You really will come to me in Paris?"

"Yes," I said, thinking of all the other times I had been there and wondering how different this time would be, because of him.

"Good. It's settled then. It will be difficult, but I will tell her."

He stood up, looked out at the sea, and said, "I love very much this Malibu." And then looking straight into my eyes he said, "And you are my real love."

I put my arms around his waist and we held each other.

"Now I must go to the Chateau," he said. "Someone is coming to help me pack and then drive me to the airport. I will call you before I leave."

With organized directorial precision he arranged himself to leave. Then he reached in his bag and, from next to his passport, drew out a small blue medal with a religious figure on it.

"I want you have this," he said. "Put on chain. It was given me by my mummy when I left Russia. Is blessed by archbishop of church."

I held the blue disc in the palm of my hand. In gold mosaic I saw the figures of the Virgin Mary holding Christ, with a halo around each head.

I looked up at Vassy.

"You want me to have this?" I asked.

"Of course," he answered. "You are my love. It will protect you until we are together again. Now what do you have for me that you have worn?"

I took the gold chain from around my neck and fastened it around his. It hung just above the chain of his gold cross.

"Is beautiful," he said. "It has your energy. I feel it. I will wear always. You will see."

We walked through the apartment toward the door. He looked from the window out over the ocean and took one last deep breath. I walked him to his car, his jogging shoes hung over his shoulder. I thought of how sure of himself he was with me.

"Life is a wonderful mystery, yes?" he said.

I nodded.

He drove away down Malibu Road waving at me backward as he went. I wondered what he would be in my life, not realizing then what a marvelously infuriating mystery he really would be.

Chapter 9

Several days later I took the night flight to Paris and waited in customs for my luggage with some anxiety over what it would be like to see Vassy again. I looked through an open door leading to the outside. He was there, all right, a commanding figure in an alpaca coat and a Russian wool hat.

I walked out with my luggage.

Very tentatively he came toward me and eyed my single fairly good sized bag.

"My place is a small cell," he said fearfully. "You will see. A friend of mine, Sasha, and his wife have allowed me to use it because now I have no money for rent."

I remembered the expensive French restaurant in Hollywood and how he threw monetary realism to the winds.

"I don't mind small cells," I said. "I can sleep anywhere."

He quickly recovered from his concern, lifted my bag, and led me outside with proud confidence.

I assured him again that sleeping arrangements or living conditions, for that matter, couldn't have mattered less to me. He stopped and looked at me deeply for a moment as though assessing whether I really meant what I said.

I wondered at this point if I should tell him it

was all still a curious adventure to me that I didn't want to miss because, in some inexplicable way, I felt very familiar with him. I didn't understand him, no, but I felt that I knew him, maybe even better than he knew himself. I said nothing though.

He led me to a car, a Mercedes, which he said he had driven from Moscow.

It might have been Paris in the springtime, but it was also raining. A cold, chilling drizzle.

"The weather all over the world is changing," said Vassy. "Something wrong. Something peculiar. Too much experimenting with nature, I believe. Nature belongs to God. Mankind doesn't understand her mysteries. Nature fights back when she is assaulted."

He opened his window and breathed deeply. Then he sighed. "I love the smells of nature. They are pure and trustworthy."

His English was improving. He pulled the car into an underground garage over which there rose a pleasant apartment building. He bounded out of the car, retrieved my bag from the trunk, and led me, via an elevator, to the apartment. Rattling his large French keys, he opened the door.

Vassy was right. His place *was* a small cell. I followed him inside. He didn't look at me, busying himself with making room for my bag instead. There was just enough room for a mattress on the floor, a table beside the mattress, and in the corner a small refrigerator with a hot plate on top. I looked over at a small kitchen cabinet, which I could see housed garlic and a few jars of spices. Did he really cook here? Maybe that would be my job. How could we eat out now if he didn't even have money for rent? Was I supposed to pay for everything? I could afford it, certainly, but would that embarrass him?

Putting all economic considerations out of my mind, I turned to him and said, "Vassy, I love it. It's cozy and what more do you need with all the traveling you do?" I wasn't just being diplomatic. It was true.

He reached up into a small cluttered closet and began to make room for me. Immediately, I began to unpack to relieve his concern. I took out a few sweaters and slacks and hung them on two hangers. I could feel his relief that I didn't travel like a movie star. I had learned during my own travels how to conserve space very comfortably.

He made some hot tea with lemon, while I walked around behind the closet and found the bathroom. Thank God, I thought. I was afraid I would have to go down the hall, as was the case in so many European living quarters.

The bathroom was as quaint and charmingly minuscule as the "cell." There was a toilet with a chain flush, a sink with a mirror over it, and one of those half-tub-half-showers that the French can somehow get clean in. The shower was a hand shower, which I had never learned to manipulate properly. I usually sprayed the entire room.

I shut the door to the bathroom and washed my face, looking around at his toilet articles on the sink. He used an electric razor, which was plugged into the wall. There was a giant-sized bottle of Jaragan aftershave lotion. I wondered if that was French or Russian. I opened the bottle and smelled it. It smelled how I remembered he smelled. Next to the Jaragan was a white plastic box with a wire attached to it. There were four sticks that looked like toothpicks standing up beside the white box and an electric cord attached to the wall. Was this an electric Water Pik? I had never seen one. Was this what he used to achieve that "perfect imperfection" effect with his teeth?

Feeling the urge, I sat down on the toilet. I looked around the small bathroom more carefully. To my amazement, the door opened. There was no warning knock, no "how are you doing?" Nothing. Vassy simply opened the bathroom door on me, found me sitting on the toilet, and very agreeably inquired, "Are you all right?"

I nodded, attempting to seem undisturbed, and, startled into feeling this was a social occasion, politely asked if the white plastic box was an electric Water Pik.

"Of course," he said. I could feel a pronouncement coming on. "You must use it. Particularly after such a long flight."

I nodded, coming to grips with the dynamics of the situation.

"Come," he said. "Now. We must show you how to use it now."

Too much.

"Out!" I said. And then, with as much dignity as I could muster, "I'll call you when I need you." I was to learn that Vassy had absolutely no sense of privacy—his own or anybody else's. He was even known to follow people into airplane lavatories to make sure they were not sneaking a cigarette.

Presently he proceeded to educate me about my teeth. As always, in matters of health, he was deadly serious. "You must use this every day," he announced. "The water pressure is good for gums. You must be careful of gums and teeth for close-ups. Cameras can be cruel, Sheerlee, you know that. You need to pay more attention."

As he showed me, with insistent determination, how to use the Water Pik, I began to realize I would have to either ignore some of his autocratic dictates, learn to control myself when I felt he got out of line, or just let go and let him have it.

Vassy smiled at me in the bathroom mirror. He could see that I was considering what he said.

"Now," he said proudly, "you don't mind my small cell?"

The association seemed a peculiar one to me, but it was one of the first times I realized that Vassy Medvedjatnikov always needed to be in complete control. On his turf or anybody else's. The combination of the two of us would indeed prove combustible.

His telephone jangled beside the mattress on the floor. He picked it up and launched into a barrage of Russian.

"Mamitchka," he said to someone and then turned to me. "It's my mummy from Moscow." He proceeded to carry on an animated conversation, his husky voice rising higher and higher. I wondered what could possibly be making him so excited. Was something wrong?

The conversation went on for about ten minutes. I really had the impression the KGB must have arrested his mother. Soon he hung up, quite satisfied it seemed.

"What was that all about?" I asked.

"Nothing," he said. "Mummy just wondered if I had arrived back in Paris from States all right. Her flowers are doing well at dacha in country and perhaps she will come to France in summer."

"Jesus," I said. "I thought maybe the Third World War had started."

"It's the way Russians talk," he assured me. "We always scream. You will see."

Vassy went to his small cupboard and pulled out some soft garlic cheese and crackers. Then he uncorked a bottle of red wine and without ceremony began to eat the cheese and crackers and gulp the wine standing up.

"Your flight was fine?" he asked, really more concerned with what he was eating than my inane answer.

"Sure," I replied, absolutely fascinated by his relationship with food. One would have thought he had grown up starving in a hovel in Siberia, but I knew he had come from a very well-to-do family of artists and writers. He had told me that his mother was a poet and linguist and the daughter of one of Russia's great painters. His father was the author of children's books and a big *functionnaire* in the writ-

ers' union in Moscow. I had not pressed the question of individual artistic freedom with Vassy quite
yet. He was clearly not suffering from it.

"I told Mummy I finally met you," he said. "I
believe she is concerned I will go Hollywood. She
admires you very much."

The phone rang again. It was his friend Sasha
who owned the apartment. He was having a party
and wanted us to come.

Vassy shrugged his shoulders and asked me in
Russian if I wanted to go. I knew what he was
talking about anyway. What the hell, I said in Pidgin
Japanese. I figured I couldn't sleep anyway.

So I changed my clothes and out into the cobblestone streets of Paris we walked. In a few minutes we entered a living room crowded with a
confusion of gesticulating Russians and French people. Most everyone spoke English though.

Vassy introduced me to Sasha and his wife,
Mouza. I thanked them for letting us use the apartment. Sasha said I was crazy to stay there. Russians
had a way of being disconcertingly to the point, with
a twinkle of recognition that they were throwing
everybody else off by just being themselves.

Vassy went around joyously greeting people at
the party, not bothering one way or the other with
how I was getting along. Fortunately, everyone knew
who I was and what I did, so conversation was not
difficult, but I could see them eyeing me with a kind
of jaundiced curiosity about why I was in Paris with
Vassily Okhlopkhov-Medvedjatnikov.

Apparently Sasha and Mouza had been born in
France, therefore were not subjected to the restrictions of the Russian-born. But I was learning that
regardless of where a Russian finds himself a citizen,
he still feels he is Russian. As I wandered around
looking at the icon-laden apartment, I noticed a
Frenchwoman eyeing me with more than usual
intensity.

At the first opportunity I mentioned it to Vassy and asked why that would be.

"She is my French woman's sister," he said. "She knows I broke the relationship with her for you."

I felt that sort of paranoid stab you feel sometimes when you know everyone in the room knows more about what you're really involved with than you do.

"Oh," I said quietly, "I see. For some reason I felt *she* was involved with you."

"She was," he admitted, stunning me right up against the wall. "When I was very jealous of her sister, I slept with her out of spite."

I suddenly couldn't keep all his women straight—my heart was thudding away in response to his stupifying directness.

"You mean, you slept with both sisters?"

"Yes," he answered. "I was angry and jealous because Monique was sleeping with her husband."

"Oh my," I said rather helplessly. Then, piqued by curiosity, "What did you expect her to do?"

"Sleep with me," he answered simply.

"I see. So you balled her sister for spite."

"Of course."

Mouza came in with a plate of piroshkis, a Russian pastry filled with ground meat. Vassy took one and swallowed it whole.

"Wait a minute," I said, recovering myself. "Did your Monique know what you were doing?"

"Of course. I am always honest. I never lie."

"No," I said. "I can see that."

"You are having a nice time?" he asked, as though the weather were beautiful.

"Oh yes," I answered. "Wonders never cease. All kinds of wonders."

"This is wonder—ful?"

"Sure."

Vassy pranced like a playful puppy-man into

the living room with the camera he had acquired somewhere on his shoulder.

Mouza sidled up to me at the doorjamb. "Have you ever been involved with a Russian man before?" she asked simply.

"No, Mouza, I haven't. Why?"

"I just wondered, that's all." Then she quickly remembered that she had forgotten to fetch more vodka. I wandered back into the living room, caught somewhere between jet lag and naïveté.

Vassy handed me a glass of vodka and raised it to my eyes. "I am very *fidèle*," he said. "When I am in love, I am *fidèle*."

The roller-coaster ride was well into its first turn.

A few hours later, I needed to sleep. Vassy tenderly took us back to our cell. I undressed as though already asleep, but I was aware enough to notice that he took off his gold cross and placed it carefully beside two small framed pictures. One was a picture of his mother. The other, an icon of the Virgin Mary and Christ. We fell onto the floor mattress and melded into love and sleep.

When I woke in the morning I opened my eyes to find Vassy watching me with an expression of glowing love on his face. He didn't move. His expression didn't waver. He just smiled and smiled and then sighed and touched my nose.

"You are my Nif-Nif," he said playfully.

"I am? What's a Nif-Nif?"

"You know, in Russia we have a children's story about small pigs. You have the same, I think. My favorite small pig was Nif-Nif. You are my small Nif-Nif because you have a face adorable as a small Nif-Nif."

I was overcome with his tenderness.

"Nif-Nif," he said, "I love you. I will always be honest with you. You know that."

"Yes," I said. "I've had some slight experience with that already."

"Do you think," he said, "that we have known each other before?"

I sat up on my arm. He never led up to anything. He just blurted out what he was thinking without hesitation. And he seemed to be asking me something that touched a trigger in me, but I had considered the relationship too fragile—or perhaps too important—to bring the question up myself.

"Do you mean in another lifetime?"

"Yes." He waited for my reaction. Well, I thought, why not? But still I hedged a little.

"I think maybe yes. I don't know what I believe about all that stuff."

"I feel," he went on, "that I have known you all my life. Why is that?"

"I don't know. I feel you are very familiar, too, and yet I don't understand one thing about how you really are."

"We are very different, yes?"

"Very."

"American and Russian. Why have we found each other?"

"You found me, Vassy. You made the initial search. I'm still not sure what's going on. It's crazy."

"You know," he said, "I used to stop women with red hair and faces like yours on the street. I honestly thought I saw you everywhere. It is true. You have seen my film. I lived with that actress for three years because she looked like you. Why?"

"I don't know."

"She knew it too. She had pictures of you on her wall because of it. She loves you very much too. She wants autograph from you."

"Okay. Sure," I said, beginning slowly to comprehend some of the complicated dimensions of his honesty.

"You will come with me to Russian church for Easter service while you are here?"

I glanced at his cross on the bedside table beside

the icon. "Sure," I said. "It means a lot to you, doesn't it?"

"I am Christian. Every Russian is religious whether Communist or not. Maybe these men in Kremlin secretly wear cross themselves when no one around."

Vassy put his arm behind his head. "Russia is very spiritual place," he said. "With system we have, it's necessary. Maybe communist system makes spiritual feeling even deeper. So we don't object."

"You don't object. Why?"

"It's as our strawberries. Because strawberries are buried under the deep Russian snow for six months, they taste so beautiful in the springtime."

"You mean, only strawberries that suffer are sweet to eat?"

"Of course. The same with life and people. Suffering is necessary to art and happiness."

He continued speaking with deep conviction. "Our Russian love of God and spiritual understanding is most important to all Russians. Do you understand?"

"You mean, you're telling me that the group in the Kremlin Marxist government are not atheists and are secret Christians?"

"Not Christian-religious. Even atheists have atheism with passion. Russian peoples have *convictions*. Doubt comes from the West."

I sat up from the mattress and crossed my legs and faced him.

"And you, Vassy? Is that how you feel?"

"I am Russian Orthodox Christian," he stated clearly.

I wondered if *any* of his answers would ever be qualified. He seemed so full of conviction about *everything*.

He went on. "We must fight against satanic forces," he said. "Evil forces will destroy us if we don't recognize God."

"You believe there is such a thing as a satanic force?"

"Of course. And each time we feel it within ourselves, we must look for God."

"Is that why you wear your cross . . . for protection?"

"Yes, yes," he said. "Of course, but you must also understand that we Russians are also Moslem, not in a religious way, but mentally. We are combination of Christian spirituality and Asian Moslem mentality. We are unable to control ourselves and obey order, therefore a big fist government is necessary for us."

I wasn't sure if what he was saying was a contradiction or not. Then I remembered reading what Dostoyevsky wrote: "Russians can be sentimental, but cold and cruel at the same time. A Russian can weep at a piece of poetry one minute, and kill an enemy on that same spot a few minutes later. A Russian is half saint, half savage."

"My Nif-Nif," Vassy went on. "We Russians have no sense of respect to personality, it's more emotional—love and hate. Since the time of the czars, and now too. Russians respect only mightiness, power. This respect is mixed with fear and sometime admiration. That's why Russians admire Stalin. He was the real iron fist. See, therefore we don't expect to be respected unless we have power, muscles."

I was distressed by what he said. How was it possible to carry on a relationship either personally or on an international level, if, in fact, such a chasm of mistrust and human values separated us? What would happen with the SALT talks or nuclear disarmament or even the exploration of space if what he was saying was true?

He went on to speak of the dichotomy in the Russian character, a kind of duality in their temperament and approach to life, formed by their climate and geography as well as their history.

"Can you imagine," he said, "what it is like to

live in small village for seven months under twenty feet of snow, with five days of travel to nearest railroad or neighbor? That, for centuries, was life of a Russian. Sometimes the news they got, if they got it at all, was a year old."

He went on to say that a Russian could be scientifically disciplined for a period, and then fall apart with self-indulgence. He could be privately unassuming and publicly pompous. He could be kind and compassionate and uncaring and cruel.

I remembered Hedrick Smith had said the same thing in *The Russians*, his Pulitzer Prize–winning book. Half savage, half saint, as Dostoyevsky had said.

I had to admit, my Vassy fit the description to a T. Oh, my God, now I understood why Mouza had asked me if I'd ever been involved with a Russian before. Again, I felt that same haunting tap of familiarity somewhere deep in my mind, as though I had known this man from hundreds of years ago.

Vassy took my hand in his. "You are my sunshine," he said. I felt myself blush. "You have beautiful fingers," he said. "So sweet and graceful." He gently squeezed the tips of them. "I love your soft finger pillows here," he said. "My padded pillows. You must cut your nails so I can see them more."

He startled me back to reality with yet another personal directive. I kept my nails long because if I didn't, I unconsciously picked at my cuticles, sometimes even until they bled. Someone had told me once that I did that because I was attempting to peel away the outer layers of myself in a desperate unconscious attempt to reach the core of myself. Pop psychology maybe, but probably some truth to it.

"Will you jog with me, Nif-Nif?" he asked like a small child requesting a big personal favor from his mother. "I never knew a woman who would jog with me before."

"Sure," I said, feeling jostled between his childlike charm and his adult assertiveness.

"But first Water Pik," he directed. "You must

make Water Pik. You were too tired last night. Now you must make Water Pik properly."

I got up, cursing, because I knew he was right.

In jogging togs we bounded into the crisp Parisian sunshine and headed for the Luxembourg Gardens. We talked of where we would eat brunch as we jogged.

Vassy jogged with a straight-backed stride, his head proudly peering straight ahead, his brown hair bouncing over his ears as we moved. Vassy's face took on a gleam of determination.

"I will now jog five miles," he announced.

"Of course," I agreed. I knew he meant it. I wasn't about to do that. Two or three miles, okay, but while he was doing the remainder, I would do some stretching exercises.

Vassy did not jog correctly. He used the outside of his heels too much and pounded his monstrous size eleven feet severely into the ground, causing much too much trauma to his back.

"You know, Vassy," I began hesitantly, "you are planting your feet wrong with your stride. It's too hard on your back that way."

He looked over at me with disdain. "For me it is fine," was his answer. No more discussion.

Shit. Fine. What do I care? It's not my back.

His loping turned-in feet continued to punish him. After a while I peeled off from our stride, stopped, and put one leg after the other up on the back of a park bench and stretched. After the plane flight, I needed it. Vassy didn't even acknowledge that I was gone.

For another hour I did some standing yoga positions and deep breathing. The thought crossed my mind then that perhaps Vassy thought physical pain was necessary to good health. If it didn't hurt, it wasn't doing any good, that sort of thing. I knew that feeling myself and was beginning to realize its folly.

Rounding his last turn of the gardens, Vassy

gestured that he would now jog home without breaking his stride. Jesus, I thought, this man is a glutton
for discipline. He'll probably pig out at lunch.

That's just what happened. We showered, changed,
and charged to a small bistro he knew close by. True
to form, he ordered several hors d'œuvres, a bottle
of red wine, lots of bread spread thick with butter,
and a few desserts. I went along with him. Who
needed a heavy, ponderous entrée when you could
get the same effect with variety? Privately I prepared
to allow myself to gain ten pounds on this trip.

Over the meal Vassy brought up the project he
was interested in for the two of us—a book called
The Doctor's Wife by Brian Moore.

"Isn't that funny?" I said. "That very book was
suggested to me sometime back by a writer friend of
mine."

We discussed it at length. He spoke with great
passion about each character. He understood their
conflicts, their sorrows, their compulsions. He became each character as he spoke. He was larger than
life, broadly stroked and impossible to take casually
as he outlined in his passionate, husky voice, what
he would do with the film.

I wondered how it would affect our relationship
to work together. I knew he was watching me closely,
editing in his head which of my habits and manner-
isms he would use and which he would discard. I
didn't feel in the least invaded because I was doing
the same thing with him.

We were adoringly fascinated with observing
each other. Two professionals using life as grist for
the creative mill.

"Vassy," I said, "how would you feel if you
ended up in one of my books?"

He smiled proudly. "I have been in several
books," he announced. "We are all in each other's
lives for many reasons," he said. "Creativity is
everything. And creativity comes from experience.

I love all of my characters. I know you will love all of yours."

Back at the cell, when I came out of the bathroom, thoroughly waterpiked, Vassy was sitting on the mattress, munching on a carrot, smiling up at me like a floppy bear.

I remembered a present I had forgotten to give him and, rummaging through my suitcase, I pulled out two adorable pink rabbits with their arms entwined around each other. I dumped them on his flat tummy. Immediately he placed the rabbits on the pillow and talked to them, scolding them in rabbit language. He stood them on their heads and spanked them in Russian. He covered them up and purred a little children's song to them. He teased them for sleeping too long with their arms around each other. With his long arms he retrieved them from under the covers and rocked them against his shoulder. Then he bounced them over to me. I lofted them back carefully, half convinced they were real. He patted their heads and got up to sit with them in his lap on the one kitchen stool the cell boasted, cradling them in his arms while I took a picture of him with my Polaroid.

I was entranced by his ability to have such childish fun. He said he loved my enchantment, that I could make a game out of anything. He said he had learned a new meaning to the word "fun." Then we fell on the bed and made love, the pink rabbits tumbling to the floor.

Lovemaking with Vassy was one of the most pleasant shared experiences of my life. We laughed, cried, shouted, and nibbled at each other. Every now and then when abandonment seized him completely, a surging rush of Russian passion flowed forth. He was never rough, but he wasn't delicately gentle either. He certainly knew what he was doing, but I sensed a deep-seated conventional Christian morality in him.

I asked him if he got involved with his actresses during filming. He said during filming he was never interested in sex. His work was his life. He had no time to concentrate on anything else. But yes, his actresses usually fell in love with him. Humility was not his strong suit.

Our days in Paris revolved around the small "cell"—sharing stories of life experiences, laughing until our sides ached, making a mess of cooking in the Pullman kitchenette, sleeping with garlic and onions lying unattended next to the floor mattress, and fantasizing about working together. He directed me to use the Water Pik every night until, not to my surprise, my gums were fine. I asked him when he expected to get his medical degree.

He never laughed when I teased him. He took himself extremely seriously, which, of course, was grounds for my teasing him even more.

Sometimes he'd pout when he saw that he couldn't really dominate me, but our childlike play and kidding saved us every time. I had never before encountered a man who could joyously throw himself into such wondrous and magical games. Maybe it was because he was Russian or maybe it was just Vassy. It doesn't matter. His capacity to give himself totally to zany make-believe was the source of much tenderness and loving laughter between us.

He told me a story from his childhood, of how he had overturned a beehive and gotten plastered with honey.

"My honeybear," I said, laughing as he finished his story. "You are my Russian honeybear."

"And you are my sunshine Nif-Nif."

We rolled over in each other's arms. I couldn't remember when I had been so happy.

We played at everything. I lived delightedly from day to day, reveling in my Honeybear's capacity for laughter. We made the ancient city our playground, the pink rabbits going everywhere with us. The world looked on, smiling. But we were oblivious. Eventually, Honeybear took me away to a small island in Bretagne.

When we arrived, it was dark. But Honeybear had made reservations at a small hotel whose proprietor had waited up for us. With each new night and each new place, life was an adventure for us. An adventure maybe more real than the reality we would experience later.

We unpacked our bags in the small hotel room. There was one tiny closet, two twin beds which we promptly pushed together, and a small shuttered window through which the wind howled.

There was no shower in the cold bathroom, but the tub was sufficient. We each took a quick hot bath, because the heated water was scarce, and crawled into the quilt-covered beds. As we began to make love, I found myself relating to him in a maternal frame of mind. Words came to my mouth that expressed how I felt.

"My honeybear, my baby honeybear," I heard myself murmuring as I curled my fingers in his hair. "Yes, you are my baby, my baby, aren't you?"

Vassy sat up in bed, his face like stone. He took his arms away from me.

"I am not your son," he announced, and there was real anger in his voice.

I sat up too. "My son?" I asked. "Of course you're not my son. I was just fantasizing because I felt so maternal with you and I wanted to express myself and maybe make love with that expression. What's wrong with that?"

"Sometimes you are a radio in bed," he said. "You talk too much."

I stared at him, stunned. His hostility was so total, so sudden, I couldn't take it in.

"A radio in bed?" I repeated.

"Of course," he answered.

Oh my God, I thought, now feeling crushed with humiliation. Obviously I had said or done something that threatened him in a deep-seated way. My hand flew to my throat, where I wore the religious medal, blessed by the Russian archbishop, that had belonged to his mother.

"Vassy, wait a minute," I said. "What's upsetting you so much? What is wrong with some maternal fantasy in bed? It's not real incest, you know."

His eyes blazed. He got up and walked around the room.

"Such a thing is not necessary to you, is it?" he demanded.

"No," I answered confusedly. "Not necessary. Of course not. It just occurred to me, that's all. I was just feeling that way, so that's what came out of my mouth."

He sat down on the bed. "You talk too much. Talk not necessary."

He was hurting me deeply. I felt completely humiliated. The trust implicit in my free expression of fantasy had been thrown in my teeth.

"But all the games are play, Vassy. They're not necessary or real either. You love to do that, don't you?"

"Yes," he answered, "because you love it."

The roller coaster started.

"Because *I* love it? What do you mean? You love those games, too, and you know it."

"I play them because you love them."

I began to cry. He had shattered our playful, fragile fantasies, apparently without a thought and clearly without caring at all.

"You are really mean," I heard myself say, tears choking my throat. "You are mean and uncaring and insensitive in hurting the feelings of others. How could you be so mean?"

I was crying hard now.

Vassy blanched slightly but I could see him decide to refuse to give any emotional ground.

"I am not mean," he answered finally. "You are being influenced by evil."

"*Evil?*" I choked on the word. It was from so far

out in left field that it stopped my crying. "What the *hell* has evil got to do with this?"

"That was evil thought you spoke of in bed. I cannot go along with that."

"Well, fuck you," I shouted. "Who gives a fuck? I'm glad I'm not your goddamned mother. She's really raised some cruel character in you, hasn't she?"

His eyes flashed. I thought I saw a hint of violence as he raised his hand to his hair and pulled his fingers through it.

"You are the evil one," I yelled and cried at the same time. "I didn't mean to hurt you. I was only pretending. Why are you doing this?"

He sat down on the side of the bed, flushed with anger. Then, very quietly, he said, "Stop it, Sheerlee. You are feeling satanic forces. They are evil."

I couldn't seem to break through to him, and the frustration triggered something in me that was primitive and fundamental.

"Vassy!!" I shouted. "There is no such thing as evil. Evil is fear and uncertainty. Evil is what you *think* it is. *Listen* to me, goddammit!"

He leaned over me and with gentle strength held me by my shoulders.

"Sheerlee, stop it," he said strongly. "Stop the evil."

My brain tumbled over in confusion. What was he talking about? I had simply wanted to fantasize about being his mother while making love and to him this was some kind of fundamental evil? I cried and cried.

Vassy put his arms around me. I didn't resist. I wasn't angry at him anymore, or even insulted. This business of "evil" and "satan" was a ridiculous concept to me. I couldn't really understand why such images would be evoked by my simple fantasy, but what he had done was thoroughly shocking and sad to me.

Something snapped shut in my head. I remembered the intuition I had had that he might be restrictively, conventionally Christian. Could that be the nerve I had just struck? Had I triggered some unconscious incestual fantasy that had actually attracted me to him in the first place? Was that what had been going on with him for twelve years? Or was Vassy, the boy-man, more involved with "Mummy" than he knew, to the point where the actual verbalization of such a fantasy was totally unacceptable to him?

Then, as I was sorting out my tumbled confusion, I had another flash. If we really had had a past-life experience together, could it have been as mother and son? *That thought*, I knew, I shouldn't raise with him.

I stopped crying. "I'm sorry I said what I did about your mother," I apologized.

Vassy said nothing. He neither acknowledged my apology nor rejected it. He just crawled back into bed. He turned out the light. In the quiet darkness, punctuated only by my residual sniffles, he said, "Nif-Nif, there is evil in the world. I don't like to see it touch you."

My mind went white-blank. There was nothing more for me to say. How could one argue good and evil where sexual fantasies that hurt no one were concerned? But I think I began to understand a little bit more about Vassy's relationship to his own sexuality. And it was disturbing to me that his personal hang-ups could succeed in getting me so upset.

When, oh when, I thought, will I ever learn to be mature enough not to allow the problems of others to become an even bigger problem for me? I rolled over toward Vassy and fell into an exhausted sleep. I wasn't sure what had really happened. But one thing was certain. I would no longer be a "radio" in bed.

Chapter 10

I suppose when one is in the throes of a newly developing relationship, it is necessary to overlook accumulating obstacles, putting them on the back burner of the mind, until they can be examined in the clear, objective light of a later day. That, I believe, is what Vassy and I did. Or maybe he never felt those obstacles were necessarily serious. I couldn't have either, not then, because after our "evil-incest" night, the subject never came up again. Why would it though? We had so many other areas to explore in one another.

Vassy loved his wild island. He led me along the jagged cliffs overlooking the churning waters beneath. He took his camera everywhere. And I took my Polaroid. He instructed me in light exposures, framing, and attitudes to assume in front of the camera. He was alternately delighted and harsh depending on the moods that seemed to surge through him.

Vassy jogged every morning. He seemed to need the insistent pain of runner's strain in order to feel the reward of the rest of the day. Sometimes when he jogged, I would run with him so we could discuss whatever was interesting us at the moment. I would go as far as I could, then stop and walk fast, whereupon Vassy would jog in circles around me so we could continue talking. For a while there I thought

maybe he was training for some secret Olympics.
But no, he really needed some kind of basic regimen
to allow himself the reckless wonder of what he was
feeling.

We walked and ran and talked through island
fields of wheat, barley, and flowers. He even jogged
in the muddy rain one morning.

Vassy was more and more certain that *Doctor's
Wife* would make a good film. I loved to watch him
contemplate aloud the visual images he wished to
achieve. His eyes were double cameras. They regis-
tered multidimensional images in one flash. And he
never forgot a face. He never missed much of anything that went on around him. But he didn't really
perceive the subtleties and emotional depth in people around him unless it was a feeling he himself
could identify with. Either that, or he couldn't afford
to heap more emotional entrées on his plate than
were already there.

Eventually Vassy and I returned to Paris and
our small cell. He arranged for me to see more of his
films. He tried to translate the French subtitles and
give me a quick rundown on the Russian nuances,
but I found myself becoming more and more frustrated because I was realizing that a great deal of his
artistic motivation had to do with rather complex
intellectual symbolism. He wrote and directed his
pictures, and, given the Soviet restrictions, most of
them made a deep spiritual point. I couldn't decipher the difference, though, between what he regarded as spiritual and what he regarded as religious.
I wondered if he saw any significant difference.

As Vassy ran his films for me one after the
other, I was struck by the purity of his romanticism.
The relationships that he painted on the screen were
storybook, yet etched with a tragedy that smacked
of the old classics. The heroines were childishly playful and wistfully patient as they accepted the fate of
adverse circumstances. The heroes were buffeted by
events while gamely attempting to contribute to the

personalization of their own lives. Vassy seemed to be allergic to happy endings—as though each of his artful depictions of life was to remind the observer that destiny is cruel.

I didn't really analyze his work in such a way as it unfolded before me, but I was conscious of two things. One, he had been deeply influenced by classic tragedies, and two, he seemed compelled to express a belief that, in the end, life was so romantically tragic that smiling through tears was not only attractively appealing to the audience, but *because* of that appeal, a positive workable solution to any given problem was not only not inspiring but could never be achieved. I wondered if Vassy's "Russian" soul, which showed so clearly in his work, would be transmuted to his life. It bothered me, but I brushed it away from my mind because there was so much more to enjoy.

Easter came on a sparkling Sunday morning in Paris, and for me it was a Russian Easter. Vassy took me to a Russian Orthodox church where we stood, mingling and respectful, with hundreds of others as they lit candles and said silent prayers to the altar of Mary and Jesus.

As I stood in the midst of the reverent Russian throng, I saw eyes glance at me, then up at Vassy. What were they thinking to themselves? Some of them nodded to him, some smiled, some looked totally blank.

Periodically Vassy would lean down and whisper in my ear that so-and-so was a famous gypsy singer or someone else the ringleader of the dissident writers in Paris. There were old women who were friends of his mother's, and colleagues with whom he had developed screenplays which, not surprisingly, had never been made. It seemed that the entire Russian community in Paris had come to the Easter service, which was somehow not really a service but more of a religious observance.

A boys' choir sang continuously, accompanied

by an organ. No one sat. There were no pews. We
stood and milled and stood and milled, each of us
holding a candle and directing our attention to a
gigantic altar dripping with lit and quivering candles. There seemed to be no organization or planned
program. Instead, individuals participated in prayer-
ful reverence as they saw fit.

I watched, fascinated by the uncontrolled yet
peacefully milling throng. I remembered that Vassy
had said the Russian people needed order, otherwise there would be chaos. Was this not true in a
church? Was this the one place where all recognized
the higher authority as God?

The ceremony continued. Vassy took my hand.
Very tenderly he held it, gently entwining his fingers through mine. The choir and organ music
reached a crescendo. I looked up at him. His moist
eyes closed as though he were making a deep promise to himself. Somehow, that promise included me
in the presence of what he called God. His eyes
remained closed for a long while. When they opened,
he leaned to my ear and said, "I have never taken a
woman to church before."

After a while, Vassy guided us out. His smile
dazzling, he spoke in Russian to those who came to
pay subtle homage to him on the steps of the church.
He introduced me casually, as though the world
should already know we were together. He stood
tall with his hands in his pockets as he enjoyed the
attention, until finally he said, "Now we have Russian meal in place near here."

When we entered the small restaurant, a blast of
emotional Russian voices flooded my ears . . . just
casual conversation over piroshkis, caviar, and vodka.
The smell of pickles hung pungently in the air. Waiters shouted in French and Russian across tables
packed with people and laughing children.

Vassy asked for a table for two. The waiter
shouted something in Russian which obviously meant,

"Can't you see there are no tables?" The waiter then recognized me and with a great flurry escorted us to a quickly evacuated table while Vassy straightened his shoulders into a preen again.

We sat down. Vassy surveyed the position of the table. Satisfied, he ordered half the menu. Immediately we were served iced vodka as the chef came out to pay his respects to me. Three waiters produced menus for me to autograph, which I cheerfully proceeded to do, asking Vassy how to write certain words in Russian. When I looked up into his face, his smile seemed a little forced. He became quiet while the flurry of activity continued and food arrived.

"You like Russian Easter?" said Vassy finally, stuffing his face as usual, which seemed always to be a cure for his woes.

"Yes, my honeybear," I answered. "It was beautiful. I was marveling at how everybody seemed to know what to do in that church, how to obey a kind of respectful order with each other."

"It is real democracy," he said with a certitude that he wanted me to be sure not to miss.

"And were there many dissidents there? All those writers and people, are they dissidents or defectors or what?"

"They are friends and they spend their lives discussing what to do about everything. No Russian wants to be defector or dissident. Sometimes they are forced."

I sipped on my vodka while he chuggalugged his.

"And you? Will you be a defector one day?"

"Myself? Never!" he said spiritedly. "It would be stupid thing for them to force me to defect. But I don't believe that would happen. I try my best to stay as I am. I will work in West and prove that Soviet can be recognized everywhere in world. You will see."

"Yes, Honeybear," I said, feeling my heart turn

over at the impossible task Vassy had set for himself. Did he realize how hard-nosed and competitive movie making was in the West, whether it was Europe or America? Was he as hard-nosed and competitive himself?

That he was a brilliant filmmaker, there was no doubt. But there were brilliant *Western* filmmakers who couldn't get work, much less an unknown Russian. I admired his undaunted courage even though I was very well aware of his probably unbridled ambition.

I suppose it was sometime during that Easter day that I felt myself decide to support the idea of working and living with Vassy in California. I liked the challenge of helping a Russian who I knew was a fine artist and with whom I also enjoyed loving and learning. As with most of my life, it was to be another adventure, and more—there was still the matter of our previous lives to explore.

So, sometime after the gargantuan meal had been consumed, I said, "Well, Honeybear, I'll be leaving to return to California in a few days. Why don't you come with me and stay in Malibu for a while? Maybe we can get something going with *Doctor's Wife* and we could work together."

He straightened up in his chair. "You are proposing that I live in your place in Malibu?"

"Why not?" I said. "See how you like it. You like the ocean?"

His sun-lit smile flooded his face. "Nif-Nif," he said, "you are my sunshine. You are crazy. I am crazy. The world is crazy. I returned to Paris to live and find work here. Now I will return to States and find work there. I will fulfill my dream, God's willing, with your help. You will see."

The thing about Vassy was he told you exactly what he was doing, ambition and all. I began to wonder then what the difference was between hard ambition and glorified, intense dreaming. Weren't all of us propelled and motivated by visions and desires that best fulfilled avenues for our own self-expression? If he was using me, so what? Didn't each of us use the people in our lives to insure, through friendship, our own personal growth?

Vassy proceeded to get very drunk, drunker by far than the first night we had had dinner. I poured him into the front seat of his Mercedes and, through the complicated Parisian streets, somehow navigated us back to the cell. The Easter rabbits were waiting up for us, and I fell asleep wondering if the spiritual dimension we shared was the glue that actually held us together despite our obviously glaring differences.

Vassy woke with liver trouble, a bad headache, congested lungs, and a fierce determination to jog in the gardens despite it all. If the Russian army was built of men like him, it would be better to settle SALT II.

I jogged with him while he gave me a rundown of the paperwork involved in arranging for his U.S. visa and settling his affairs in Paris. He would have to see his lawyer and he wanted us to visit his Yugoslav friend Milanka, who had traced him to my house in Malibu the day after I met him.

"She knows me," he said by way of a warning. "You will enjoy. I leave you there while I make business."

That seemed fair enough. I could ask her lots of questions about him.

He jogged his five miles while I stretched on a park bench for three of them. Like a brass ring, Vassy grabbed me up at the end of his last mile and we jogged back to the cell, his liver, headache, and lungs either cleared up or shoved under, I couldn't decide which.

We gobbled some garlic cheese and crackers and then splashed around with the Water Pik in the shower. He nuzzled the rabbits while I took another Polaroid picture of him. We dressed and left the cell looking as though Napoleon had just ransacked it.

Vassy ushered me into the spacious apartment

of his friend Milanka. She had a glint in her eye
which meant our relationship was the most colorful
subject of Slavic gossip she had had to talk about in
a long time.

"I am not surprised at all," she said in her deep,
well-used voice. "You two are combustible combination. Much fire, much trouble. You are nice with
her?" she demanded of Vassy in an accusatory manner, indicating that she had watched his behavior
through many women.

Vassy stretched out on her couch, the daylight
playing across his face. "Milanka," he announced,
"I have finally met the woman of my life. I do not
know anything else. I will be myself."

"And you?" said Milanka, not wasting a moment with small talk or tea before getting right to the
point. "You love this man knowing what he is?"

Oh, my God, I thought. His checkered past has
certainly been no secret. "Is he that bad, Milanka?" I
asked.

"He is Russian," she answered.

There it was again. Not because he was Vassy
with his past trailing him like a grade-Z movie, but
simply because he was Russian. What were all these
people trying to tell me?

"You have been involved with a Russian before?" she demanded to know, with her hands
squarely on her hips. "In love have you been involved with a Russian?"

"No," I answered meekly, as though she had a
right to know. "But I did have a short affair with a
Yugoslav like you. It was fine, but he was too rough
in bed."

Milanka threw back her head and laughed. "She
is good," she said to Vassy. "She is good for you.
No bullshit. She will not be one of your slaves. That
will be your problem." She turned to me. "All of his
women have been slaves. He insists. You will see."

I sat down beside Vassy. "Is that true?" I asked
like Alice in Wonderland.

"That is correct," he answered with no hesitation. "I like slaves. Women are slaves because they want to be. You are my equal. You will not be slave."

"And you," said Milanka to Vassy, "will have big trouble this time . . . big trouble . . . I am very happy. Now you would like a coffee?"

I nodded. Vassy nodded. A small boy of about two years toddled into the living room. He walked directly over to me and looked into my face. With no shyness or reluctance he climbed directly onto my lap, stood up, and laid his head on my shoulder. Milanka stared at him.

"This is my son," she said in astonishment. "My smallest son. He doesn't like strangers. He never is friendly. I don't understand what he has just done." She stopped a moment, looking at him closely.

"Dimitri," she said, addressing him gently in Serbian, "what are you doing?"

I felt Dimitri lift his head and look at his mother. She smiled. He replaced his head on my shoulder and put one of his arms around my neck.

"I don't understand," said Milanka.

Vassy sat up on the couch, having witnessed the young toddler too. "It is clear," he said. "Dimitri knows Sheerlee from a previous life. That is all."

I looked over at Milanka.

"Is true," she said. "Is the only explanation. He is speaking to you from deep memory."

I lifted Dimitri's head gently from my shoulder, turned his face toward me, and looked deep into his round open eyes. They were blue-green and trusting and wise. He gazed into my eyes with that unnerving, unblinking stare that babies bestow on objects of curiosity. Then he smiled as though he understood something I did not. But I felt as if I were looking into the eyes of a small human thousands of years old, and with each passing minute in his life he would forget where he came from and become as unknowing as I was.

He blinked at last, his eyelids screening off that moment of knowingness in order to cope with the world of now. He returned his head to my shoulder and refused to move.

Milanka sat openmouthed. Vassy just smiled.

"We must respect the young," he said. "They remember more than we do. We are corrupted with age. They are pure truth."

Milanka looked at Vassy as though she were seeing him for the first time. Vassy stood up.

"This," he said, "is why Sheerlee is the woman of my life. She recognizes me. And her face and soul is the reason I came to the West. I have been looking for her all my life. Now I have found her and we shall see."

Milanka stood still. She had apparently not heard Vassy speak in such terms before. I had never heard a man I was involved with speak in such terms either. He was touching on dimensions I had only speculated upon and never experienced with love in another human being. Friendship, yes. Love, not until now.

The level of the conversation obviously curtailed Milanka's intended interrogation. Nothing she had planned to ask made sense. Instead she talked about herself.

"As for me," she began, "I have three sons. Each son has different father. I don't agree with marriage, only children. I have son twenty-one years. You will meet him. He can be father for middle son, eleven, and Dimitri, two years. Men are nuisance to have around. I will never marry unless I meet millionaire to start new business. You know nice millionaire?"

She was perfectly serious. If I thought my life was unconventional, it was archaic compared to Milanka's.

Vassy took his leave, smiling at Dimitri, who

still rested on my shoulder. He said he would come for me in a few hours, then we would have dinner at La Coupole.

Milanka made coffee while her housekeeper collected Dimitri to dress him for a ride in his pram. I told him I would be there when he returned, not to worry. He seemed to understand my emotional meaning even though he spoke no English, and willingly went with the buxom housekeeper.

Milanka served coffee, lit a cigarette, and delved more into the saga of Vassily Okhlopkhov-Medvedjatnikov's life. She mentioned a few other actresses he had been with, particularly one who was extremely accomplished and famous, but who had had a difficult time letting herself go sexually unless she was plied with booze. Milanka didn't mince words when gossiping or at any other time. She got right to the nitty-gritty. She said Vassy and the actress had had screaming shouting matches which left both of them exhausted and unhappy, and she, Milanka, couldn't understand what either one of them was doing with the other. The actress had obvious intelligence and fine judgment. She was not Russian and according to Milanka had the same trouble with Vassy's "Russianness" that I would soon encounter. I asked her exactly what she meant.

"Is difficult to explain," she said. "Being Russian is a state of mind. Is different than any other Slavic person."

"Well, is it because of the repression of the society, or what?" I asked.

"No, not what you think. Russians as individuals are free in the degree of their anarchy, that's why they needed to be restricted by the state. They are crazy, cruel, wonderful, passionate, impossible. What can I say? You will see. You are not a slave. You will survive it. For that reason I don't understand why he wants you. He loves your talent. That is clear. But he really loves you. He has never had experience of equal woman before. Will be interesting. He has instructed you how to eat yet?"

So, I wasn't the only one. "Yes," I answered, wondering what else in the way of duplicate behavior patterns I was experiencing with Vassy.

"And your smoking?"

"He doesn't approve."

"Of course. He is crazy when he has something in his mind. He nags and nags because he cares. I think he nags because he likes to give orders. You have met his mother?"

His mother? How would I meet his mother? I had only heard him scream inconsequentialities to her during a casual international telephone tête-à-tête.

"No," I said to Milanka. "Isn't she in Moscow?"

"Correct. You will meet her soon. He will insist. Take care with the mother. Wants her son for herself. You have met brother?"

"No, what's he like?"

"They are same. Impossible with women, but talented as men."

I sipped my coffee, wanting to know more, but not wanting to invade Vassy's privacy, although privacy did not seem to be a matter of consideration among the Slavs. On the contrary, everyone's business cheerfully belonged to everyone else. The Westerners were the ones obsessed with privacy.

The doorbell rang.

"It is my gypsy singer friend," said Milanka. "She will play for us and sing. She will sing with her heart. You are feeling with your heart now, my dear. Never forget to feel with your brain also."

Milanka walked to the door, clad in her white overalls, and ushered in a raven-haired woman who entered and went immediately to the piano as though music was fresh air in a clogged, polluted world. She nodded to me with a smile of greeting and began to play, singing in a voice that rose from her toes. I felt I was watching a three-dimensional performer in a movie that I could reach out and touch.

The rhythm and passion of her song took hold of me immediately, arresting my coffee cup in midair. I didn't know what she was singing about but it was all so dramatic, so intense, so urgent, a self-expression of such immediacy that it held me entranced.

The intensity of her rhythm and emotion began to grow. I put my cup down carefully, afraid that it might clatter. The gypsy woman smiled, realizing that she had me now. Her voice was whiskey-velvet and her huge right foot began pounding the floor as the theatrical Slav in her came pouring out across the piano, spilling into Milanka's living room.

I found myself rising from the couch and beginning to move involuntarily with the urgency of her escalating rhythm. My feet dug into the wooden floor one foot at a time like a challenged Flamenco dancer. I stamped in time with the compelling music and before I knew it, I was whirling and bending with gyrations that accompanied the feeling that surged through me. I felt Slavic myself, like the music. I remembered my mother telling me, thirty-five years before, that one's origins didn't prevent one from experiencing the emotions of another culture. Emotions, she said, were everything. Understand the emotions and you can become whomever you wish. But how was it possible to understand the emotional depth of a passionate Russian Slav when you were a white-bread American Protestant?

Then again it flashed in my mind . . . something that was to occur to me many times for the duration of my relationship with Vassy. Had we *both* experienced a previous life together in Russia? Had I once been Russian *myself* and was that why I had felt so familiar with him from the first moment I laid eyes on him? I stamped and shouted words that I didn't understand. Maybe they were just conglomerated sounds, I don't know. Maybe that's all words were anyway. My arms rose into positions I felt best depicted what I was feeling from the music. I crossed them in peasant fashion and made up steps that

jarred through the rest of my body. I felt I had
danced those steps many times before. Perhaps every role I had played was a role I had somehow lived
before. Maybe acting was the art form of remembered identities.

We sang and shouted and danced together
throughout the afternoon, until Vassy returned to
pick me up. When he walked in on our multicultural
Russian spectacle, he sat watching and smiling for a
while.

"My Nif-Nif," he said finally, "you will do that
in the film we will make together, and Milanka will
be a character. You will find a Russian community in
Paris during the scenes of your second honeymoon
and we will show how your leading character responds to cultures that are buried in her past. I think
we will call the film *Dancing in the Dark* and we will
have Cole Porter's song as the theme song."

As Vassy outlined his creative plans he seemed
to be watching me as though he were looking through
a camera, slightly detached. I felt like a piece of
putty which he intended to mold according to his
theatrical desires. And if my emotional desires were
different, would I say so, or would I accept his
written and directorial concepts as an actress responding professionally to her director's wishes? Simply put, could I work with him in good faith when I
knew that I was being manipulated by his intimate
knowledge of me? Would I feel that he was forcing
the character I would play into a mold that was
familiar to him rather than familiar to her?

We said good-bye to our gypsy afternoon. Milanka poked Vassy in the chest and warned him she
would be monitoring his behavior and he had better
not insist on being too Russian.

When we returned to dress for dinner, I cleaned
up the cell, removing the wilted lettuce and the
hard-crusted garlic cheese, the smell of which now
permeated the room. I hoped it would all blow out
before we got back from dinner.

It didn't.

Before we went to bed Vassy began to pack his bags for America. Sasha would be renting the place to someone else and Vassy would store his remaining belongings in a box which Sasha would keep for him. He put the rabbits on top of the box, saying they would take care of everything until we returned someday. Then he went to his big table on which lay a huge and ancient Russian Bible.

"Nif-Nif," he said, "I want you to have this Bible. It has belonged in my family for hundreds of years. It is for you now with my love. I love you and want you to carry it with us always. It will return with us to California."

I lifted the Bible. It weighed about twenty pounds. I opened it. It was extraordinary. In ancient Russian script was the story of mankind from the Russian Orthodox point of view. It was illustrated with colored drawings and the thick leather-bound covering was worn with age. It was clearly a museum piece. It was obviously very valuable and meant as much to Vassy as anything he owned.

"Thank you, Honeybear," I said. "I will take good care of it and it will be with you anyway."

I didn't want to think of what he would do with this Bible if our relationship didn't work out.

Vassy and I left for California. He obtained a multiple visa to travel to the U.S. and was full of ideas and surprises he would delight his Hollywood friends with when he returned. Flying over the ocean, we played games with each other which only new lovers can concoct to make magic out of being with each other. It was a delight. We watched a comedy film about CIA spies in South America that made us laugh so loud the stewardess complained that we were keeping other passengers awake. We ate whatever the economy class offered, which, because we were together, tasted gourmet. Then we fell into a high-altitude sleep and when we landed in L.A., we were both aware that a new and unorthodox life lay ahead of us.

Chapter 11

I was glad Vassy had an acquaintance with my place in Malibu. He had already decided which bathroom he would use, where the Water Pik would go, and which side of the bed he would sleep on. He knew just what food he would buy at the health-food store, and tested the blender to ensure that it was in good running order. He stacked his records beside the hi-fi system and unloaded his Russian books into the bookcase across from the bed. He cleared out two of my drawers and made room for his shirts and two sweaters. He hung his trousers (three pair) and his two jackets in an empty closet which he assumed was for him. He placed his two pairs of street shoes and a pair of dress shoes out of the seventeenth century neatly next to his tennis racket. He unpacked his hair tonic, Jaragan cologne, and electric razor and stacked them neatly on the sink. He placed his scripts and notepaper beside the bed and hid his passport in a drawer that didn't look like a drawer. I was amused by that piece of intrigue because he had left the valuable passport on the airport bus before we left Paris. I had noticed it was gone and retrieved it in time. Now, as though my house could be broken into at any time, he was insuring the safety of the document that allowed him freedom. He gently placed the heavy Russian Bible on my Bombay chest across from the bed where we would sleep. After he had arranged his new life, he put on his sneakers and went out to jog. I looked around my place at his swift directorial takeover, and laughed at what I had gotten myself into.

In between writing (I was finishing one of the several drafts of *Out on a Limb*), I began rehearsals for a new television special. Vassy had meetings with producers. It was as though we had begun a life together respecting immediately that each of us had schedules to keep.

I had never lived with anyone in my apartment in Malibu. It had always been a place where I went to think and write. Now it came alive with communication between myself and another human being. I loved the feeling. It was a delight.

When I wasn't writing or rehearsing, Vassy and I took long walks in the Calabasas Mountains and we found a special fire trail that was painful enough for him to negotiate so that he felt he was really getting some good out of it. He was as strong as a bull and had the stamina to match. I had never been with a man who had as much physical stamina as I did and also liked to test it daily. So we enjoyed testing our stamina against each other. Vassy was just as enthusiastic on our walks as he was on the set or with food or his famous Water Pik. As we trekked he gave me pointers on how to hold my posture, which way to bend my legs, and of course, how to breathe. If he had seen me smoke a cigarette the night before, he scolded me and blamed any slowness I might be exhibiting on the smoking. If I had had only two hours sleep and was exhausted climbing the trails, he blamed it on a cigarette I had had a few days before. Walking with Vassy was not only a loving experience, it was also an athletic event to be endured for one's own good. It also kept me in shape and opened my eyes to the nature of the mountains around me. Whenever I walked alone, my mind crackled with thoughts and ideas and solutions. When I trekked with Vassy, I was aware of every wild flower and vibrant green bush. He would stop and inhale long breaths of fresh mountain air and was able to isolate and identify every smell of nature that passed through his nose. He was an expert on flora, and fauna too; exclaiming over this or that plant, greeting another like an old friend. He'd crinkle up the eucalyptus leaves and pass them under my nose like smelling salts and watch me for appreciation. If I failed to react with passionate pleasure, he'd quickly draw them away from me as though I had had my chance and chances never lasted long. "Nature is the province of God," he said. "Mankind doesn't understand her delicate mysteries."

We'd talk, as we walked, about pictures and music and the history of a certain composer or artist that his mother knew. Vassy seemed to be deeply involved with the individual's relationship to nature. In his view a person's recognition of the laws of nature were in direct ratio to their understanding of life. He obviously had a sophisticated appreciation for food combining and herbal medicines, but he also respected the spiritual knowledge of the seven chakkra energy centers along the spinal column in relation to cosmic harmony. And soon after we were together, I brought my yoga instructor out to Malibu to give us a lesson.

Vassy took to it immediately except for one thing. Hatha yoga is, of course, physically painful at first, but it is to be approached with gentle discipline, never with force. Vassy would stand in front of the mirror as though he were revving himself up for the Chinese torture chamber, setting his face in an expression of such determined misery that I'd burst out laughing and lose my balance in a posture. He didn't find my laughter amusing. He'd say I had no sensitivity to his need for pain, making me laugh even more. Vassy would lie on the floor in front of the mirror and lift himself in the cobra position until he nearly broke his back. Then, of course, I would have to stop laughing long enough to try and help him extricate himself from permanent curvature of the spine. He was then even more determined to prove that he was correct, that force was the best approach. Was this Russian, or simply Vassy? I was afraid to speculate on the implications for the world if the need to suffer was true of an entire nation.

The sessions with my yoga instructor were less maniacal because my teacher, Bikram, wouldn't allow such determined self-torture.

"It is unnecessary, Vassy," he would say. "Yoga can be painful but only because you are gently realigning the body in relation to its energy. And your body will react to the expression on your face. Relax your expression. It will determine how you approach your body."

Vassy would listen because Bikram was an expert, but I saw him looking for a way to avoid curing his misery and soon he found one. Through conversations after yoga class, he discovered that Bikram was a lover of Rolls-Royces. It wasn't long before Vassy was concentrating on cars instead of relaxing into health. I continued with the yoga and Vassy got into cars.

During this time, my rehearsals progressed nicely on my television special and Vassy would pick me up after meetings at the offices of the producers who were producing the special with me. I began to understand the invisible power of a commanding personality—even when people had no idea whether that personality was anybody or not.

I didn't say much to my friends about my new Russian friend, but I suppose the word got around anyway. Perhaps it was the fact that he was a real Russian which precipitated some of the reactions, but whenever Vassy walked into a room, the conversation would come to a grinding halt because everyone there sensed they were now in the presence of a "somebody." It was hard to define how that worked exactly. They didn't stop the flow of concentration and conversation because they didn't want him to hear. It was more that his energy was so commanding that he simply could not be ignored. His need to command attention was so strong that he achieved his purpose with very little effort. The spiritualists would attribute it to his aura. An inaudible language emanated from his aura which said "Notice me." His physical appearance was certainly striking enough to cause such reactions regardless, but then after my co-workers became acquainted with how he looked, his arresting quality still continued to function—at least on social occasions.

Vassy's intrinsic need to be the center of attention was important to his work as a director, not only because the director is the helmsman on any movie set but also because he personally adored individualism and insisted that in the creative process it be respected. So intense was his respect for individual "presence" that sometimes it seemed outrageously "Russian" to me.

One evening, as I was rehearsing the dance numbers for my special in a big gymnasium in downtown Hollywood, Vassy dropped by to watch me work. I knew he was coming and had invited him, although he knew he was free to watch anytime he wanted to.

When we dancers were rung out and ready to call it quits, I walked over to him, greeted him, and asked him how he liked what he saw. He nodded fine, but didn't go into any detail. I let the low-key response go by; I was tired and wanted to get to food.

At dinner, however, he was morose.

"You not pay enough attention when I visit you at rehearsal," he said.

"I what?" I asked, genuinely perplexed.

"When I enter room, you continue to work. You don't acknowledge me at all."

Oh brother, I thought. There is trouble here. In

America nothing interfered with the concentration of people at work. But perhaps in Russia one was supposed to make a big deal out of a fellow artist walking into a room.

"Are you serious?" I asked.

"Of course," he answered. "I am not insignificant. You continue your work. You don't care whether I am there."

"No, Honeybear," I said, "I do care that you are there. I love that you are there. I love that you are interested in what I'm doing. I'd love it if you would give me constructive criticism, too, as long as you don't suggest that you rechoreograph. But I'm a professional dancer and in America we don't interrupt all the other dancers in order to greet a friend."

He didn't smile. He didn't acknowledge my point of view. We were silent through most of the rest of dinner because I think we both realized there would be an explosive argument otherwise.

Then, a few weeks later, I began the four-day marathon of taping my special. Taping a special is not recommended to people with limited stamina. It is cruel and punishing because taping costs are astronomical. Time is money. It's as simple as that.

I had a monologue-in-song to do which ran about nine minutes. Television directors don't work as intricately with performers as film directors do. There is no time. Vassy had seen me rehearsing my monologue-in-song alone at home and asked to read the script of it. I gave it to him.

"This is soap opera," he said with finesse.

"Well," I said, "it's television. I think it will work."

"Maybe," he answered, "however, I have some ideas."

Well, I thought to myself, this would be a good trial run to experience in a small way what it would be like to work with him.

"Sure," I said excitedly. "Let's do. I'd love it."

We sat down together while he broke down the

emotional requirements of the acting. Then we began to work.

With each line of either prose or lyric, he had an idea of how it should be done. He would stop me and explain what was in his mind. I listened and to my delight it was imaginative and charming. He suggested pieces of business and emphasis on emotional attitude. Nearly every suggestion was magical, although all were reminiscent of what I had seen his actresses do in his films—the same playful, child-like quality. But it worked for what I was doing. We worked together for an hour or so and I enjoyed every minute of it, particularly pleased that he seemed so able to identify with what the woman I was singing about was going through.

"I am partially female, you know," he said interestingly. "I identify with the female sensibility often. It is from several lifetimes I spent as a woman long ago."

I didn't think that was ridiculous. I had considered the possibility of myself having been a man long ago, since so many people who dealt with me today found me ballsy as well as feminine. I had made a kind of study of male and female energy. The female energy was the yin energy, residing in the right hemisphere of the brain. It controlled mystical, receptive, intuitive, artistic characteristics. The left hemisphere of the brain (the yang side) controlled assertive, logical, active, and linear characteristics.

Both Vassy and I seemed to exemplify the characteristics of each. Each of us had male and female qualities in our personalities. The combustion between us occurred when each of us expressed ourselves identically at the same time.

"I know how women feel," Vassy went on. "That is why I am good woman's director."

I wanted to ask him why he couldn't seem to extend the same sensitivity to women in real life but instead I thanked him for his help and said I thought the director of the special would appreciate what I would bring to the scene the next day, and of course Vassy and I would both consider the help he had given me a private matter so as not to tread on the director's territory. Vassy nodded but said nothing.

The next day the stage and lighting was set for the scene. Vassy was there to observe my exhibition of what he had suggested to me the night before. The TV director was working from the "booth," as we call it, and directed me by voice.

We went for a take. I could see Vassy in the shadows at the back of the set. I appreciated his control in not feeling that the sound stage was his, particularly with his new-found personal involvement in the show. However, his control didn't last long.

The minute I finished the take, Vassy walked from the shadows directly into the lit set, where he proceeded to loudly praise my work and also to explain to me what I had done wrong.

I headed for the ladies' room, motioning Vassy to follow me. In private I thanked him, but said I preferred not to have his direction obvious to all the technicians and most particularly not to the real director.

"Of course," he said, understanding completely because he would not have liked it if another director had done the same thing to him. Vassy could always understand something if he could identify with it.

The third day of taping fell on my birthday. Some of my close friends knew it, but I didn't like to broadcast it. First of all, any celebration would interfere with our tight schedule, and second of all, frankly I was shy and didn't like the attention.

Bella Abzug and her husband, Martin, were in town and staying with Vassy and me. They found Vassy colorfully and amusingly Russian, intrigued because of their own Russian ancestry. But as time went on they also found themselves learning how profound our differences actually were. They came to the taping and arranged for a cake and champagne to be wheeled out during a break. I finished the song I was taping. The assistant director beckoned for the "surprise" cake and champagne and the crew sang "Happy Birthday." We stopped taping for a brief period to enjoy ourselves, but I noticed Vassy was nowhere to be seen. I asked for him and Bella said she had seen him in my dressing room, where she had informed him to hurry up to the set for the surprise party. There wasn't much time for conjecture, so we finished our partying and went back to work. Still no Vassy. An hour or so later, we finished the third day's taping and I stumbled into my dressing room exhausted. As I walked in, there was Vassy seated on the Sears Roebuck couch, staring at nothing across the room.

"There you are," I said, so happy to see that he hadn't gotten lost in the labyrinth of CBS hallways. "Where were you when they brought out my cake? We missed you, Honeybear."

His face was frowning and hard-set.

"Where were *you*?" he asked harshly, yet with a touch of petulance born out of something I didn't understand.

"Where was *I*? What do you mean? I was taping on the set, but we stopped for a few minutes for cake and champagne."

"You should have come for me," said Vassy with a face like granite. Except for the look on his face I really thought he was kidding. Putting me on.

"Are you serious?" I laughed. "It was great cake and I was embarrassed when they made a fuss over me, but if nobody had done anything it would have been worse."

"You should have come for me," Vassy repeated.

Jesus, I thought, he's really not kidding. But what did he mean?

Still in my costume, with the makeup man and hairdresser in tow (as they usually are with performers who can't afford to mess themselves up because it takes too long to repair), I rounded the coffee table, my sequins scraping the wood, and put my arm around Vassy, who clearly felt left out.

"What's wrong, my honeybear?" I asked. "I wish you had come to my makeshift party. I wondered where you were, but I couldn't leave all those people to come and get you. You knew it was happening, didn't you? Bella told you, didn't she?"

His expression became even grimmer. "Of course," he answered, leaving me somewhat perplexed as to what was going on.

"Well, why didn't you come to the set, then, and be a part of it all?" I asked.

Vassy turned to me, not at all concerned that my professional retinue was watching. "I was waiting for you to invite me," he said.

"Invite you?" I said. "You don't need to be invited, Honeybear. You know that."

"That is not correct," he went on.

"*What* is not correct?" I asked, feeling angry now and at the same time stupid, thinking that I must be missing something. Maybe his choice of English words was really the problem. The makeup man and hairdresser discreetly excused themselves into the hallway for a while.

"Please, Vassy, explain to me what is bothering you."

"You should understand."

"Well, I *don't*." My voice was distinctly impatient. "I was working against the clock and when we had the surprise party we couldn't take much time to do that either. I'm sure *you* understand all that."

"I understand," he continued with steamroller persistence, "that I was waiting in this room to be invited to your party, and you did not invite me. You were insensitive and not concerned with my feelings—not at all."

I was floored. He was dead serious. He continued.

"You must have someone come to me, at least. But *you* should come to me."

I controlled, with an effort, the anger welling up in me. What did he think shooting a TV special was—a ceremonial picnic?

"Just a moment," I said. "Let me get out of these sequins and let my people take me apart so they can go home, okay?"

Vassy sat in the middle of the couch with his feet planted firmly in front of him, not moving. He didn't acknowledge that he was upsetting everyone . . . people who already felt uncomfortable around him because they sensed in some primitive way that they did not do things the way he expected things to be done. I called my people in from the hallway. With their customary, but touching, professional discretion, they took the hair ornaments out of my wig and wiped the painted makeup from my face. They spoke swiftly and professionally about the requirements for the following day's shooting and left.

By that time Bella and Martin had come to the dressing room to prepare for all of us to leave. As soon as they walked in, they could feel that trouble was brewing. I had had enough time to work up an anger born out of confused frustration and couldn't control myself.

Vassy had not relented one iota and in fact had entrenched himself into his attitude even further. I could tell by his feet and his rigid posture. Flashes of the rehearsal hall and the "respected Russian artist" attitude crossed my mind. I wondered how I could have prevented what was happening, but I was growing more angry by the moment. It was one thing to accuse me of not exhibiting proper respect, but it was another to demand it in a "time is money" circumstance. Where the hell was his professionalism, or even common consideration for that matter? Whose birthday was it, anyway?

Bella, wanting to be friendly and communicative, said, "Vassy, why didn't you come and enjoy the champagne and birthday cake? We told you it was being wheeled in.''

He blazed a look across the room at her that could have started a Russian village fire. "I was not invited,'' he stated.

"Invited?'' she asked. "You know you were invited. We all knew about it.''

"Never mind,'' he said. "Sheerlee must collect me herself. I sat alone and uninvited in this dressing room—as an outsider.'' Bella's eyebrows went up. Vassy continued, "Sheerlee is insensitive and cruel.''

That did it. Maybe it was because the thought *had* crossed my mind that I should see where he was when I was cutting the cake and had promptly decided I couldn't leave because the dressing room was too far away. It had seemed the sensible decision at the time because I honestly thought he had gotten waylaid. For him to accuse me of being insensitive when I was exhausted and frankly confused by his demands was more than I could take.

I took a breath to blast him but Vassy had more to say. "*She* was not concerned at all with my feelings,'' he said to Bella, who looked uncharacteristically helpless, "she behaved as big star.''

I sprang to my feet and leaned down toward the coffee table. Cupping my arms under the table, I felt myself lift it and turn the whole thing over in the middle of the room.

Bella and Martin eased out the door.

Vassy's expression didn't change. He didn't register shock, dismay, surprise . . . nothing. He maintained his emotional posture, which was just as surprising to me as what I had just done.

"*You* are an elitist shit,'' I shouted.

"And you are violent,'' he stated calmly as if he had had nothing to do with it.

"You're so goddamned provocative. I feel like turning over this whole building.''

"You see?'' he said. "You have no respect.''

I turned my back on him, leaned my hands

heavily on the dressing table, and rested a moment, head down. What energy I had left from shooting I knew I should conserve. I did not want an escalated shouting match because I knew I had only six hours to sleep anyway before reporting for the final day's taping in the morning.

I collected the strewn objects from the coffee table. Bella and Martin came back in and helped me get together my dancing shoes and tights and leotards. Vassy calmly sustained his no-break expression throughout the whole proceedings and, when we were ready, climbed behind the wheel. We drove to Malibu in silence, with the Abzugs following in their car.

When we got home I said good night to everyone and went directly to bed, trying to secure my emotions in a neat compartment in my head, which would enable me to sleep. Fortunately, except for circumstances which were actually frightening to me, I had the capacity to shut off when I knew I simply had to. (I could always rely on my left-brain, yang, male approach to things!)

Apparently Vassy hung around in the kitchen with Bella and Martin for a while and they were honest enough to communicate their feelings about what had gone on. They said they felt he had been excessive in his demands and that the pressure of taping had really been the reason for my behavior. He said he had felt unwanted and "unspecial" to me.

The next morning neither of us said anything about the night before. Bella, though, took me aside and said, "Was that about male chauvinism or about being Russian?"

"I don't know," I answered. "You're Russian. You tell me. I'm only a beginner with you people."

Vassy and Bella and Martin all accompanied me when I reported to CBS and began the final day of the marathon taping. Vassy, in a good mood, was fascinated with the advanced equipment used in American television.

The final taping included a twenty-two-minute dance number and, not unpredictably, we got to it at two o'clock the next morning. Exhausted would be an understatement in describing how I felt. I hadn't been eating properly, mostly because there was no time. And I had been suffering from fainting spells due to what the doctors described as hypoglycemia. So, when the big number rolled around, I was not exactly in marathon shape.

The number was shot in sections, with long waits in between while the technicians changed the scenery and the lighting. During one long wait I sat beside Vassy, parceling my energy to get through the rest of the night. Bella and Martin had, of course, long since departed.

"You are a horse," said Vassy. "You are as a well-trained horse that has had many races and can operate automatically. A real monument of strength."

He said it with such admiration it made me proud. I was coping reasonably with everything, until we finally finished the last section. I had some orange juice and cottage cheese, which usually worked for me during taping days (to eat a whole meal would have been disastrous to dance on). We finished the number and I sat down next to Vassy again for a well-deserved collapse. The director and technicians went on to shoot the final pickups I wasn't needed for.

Vassy patted my knee and congratulated me again on my stamina. I breathed deeply. I began to feel dizzy. Oh no, I thought, am I having a low-blood-sugar attack now because it's safe? It wouldn't be costing any time to do so.

My lips and hands began to lose their mobility, familiar signs of what was happening to me. A low-blood-sugar attack was not really serious, but it could be frightening to people who had never seen it before. Vassy had never seen it. All I needed was for someone to get me some orange juice—quickly. But predictably, Vassy reacted as though he were dealing with a four-alarm fire, at the top of his not inconsiderable lungs.

"Sheerlee is dying! Sheerlee is dying!" he shouted huskily.

The whole place was astonished as he roared for help, gathering me in his arms as though I were at death's door.

"Sheerlee, my Sheerlee, don't die!" he shouted again.

Someone got the orange juice. I didn't know whether to laugh or cry. The crew confusedly returned to their work as I tried to calm Vassy and sip the juice at the same time.

Whenever I finished taping a television special, the entire experience, in retrospect, dimmed like a bubble lost in time. The intensity of the grueling work tended to make me separate the marathon days from real life. Of course, the work involved was inhuman. I knew that as I was doing it, but the sense of isolation also made me tend to relate to events that occurred during the same period as a bubble lost in time too. Such was the case with Vassy. The drama that had occurred on my birthday, along with the passionate theatrics of the low-blood-sugar attack, receded from my memory as theatrical everyday living took precedence instead.

Vassy subsequently apologized for his birthday-party demands, explaining that upon reflection he thought he understood what he had done wrong. I apologized for turning over the table. I said I understood that living with the demands of my being a "star" couldn't be easy for him, and he said that his frustrations from being an unemployed director contributed to his behavior.

Where my low blood sugar was concerned, however, he had decided I should go on a strict diet—to put it bluntly, a fast. I refused, and that became the

new source of conflict. He said fasting cured everything from arthritis to hypoglycemia. I said it would
kill me—a Mexican standoff.

He proceeded to comment about every morsel
of food I put in my mouth, on occasion literally
pulling the food out of my hand and throwing it
down the garbage disposal, or if we happened to be
in a restaurant, he would simply return the food to
the kitchen. Sometimes I laughed, sometimes I was
outraged. The roller-coaster ride was in full swing.

His deeply felt convictions about my health
stemmed from real fear for me and because he cared
so much. In principle, he was often right, but I felt
that he conducted himself autocratically, as if he
were an expert in absolutely everything, and I responded by being in a constant state of very vocal
protest. Nothing either of us did eased the situation.

Even as I was living through it, I found myself
standing outside of my own personality observing
the scenes unfold, richly endowed, as they were,
with valleys and peaks of passion, floods of feeling,
and hilarious humor. Smooth it was not. Confusing
and bewildering it was . . . for both of us, I'm sure.
Perhaps we continued through the melodramatic maze
of it all because we were both involved in profes-
sions that used such emotional tumult as grist for
the mill. Certainly we were attempting to coexist as
man and woman. Therefore whatever occurred as
we worked through our crossed cues was productive
and contributive. Perhaps the lives we led were indeed scenarios we had mapped out for ourselves to
experience long before we had been born.

Living with Vassy made me think that way.
Maybe we really had chosen these circumstances
with each other in order to work through values and
points of view we hadn't completed in previous lives
together. Karma—cause and effect—whatever it was,
I was more and more aware of the precognition that
everything was happening for a reason. That Vassy
and I were destined to spend time together was a

predetermination I felt more and more. Whether it would resolve anything was up to us . . . how well or badly we handled our problems. He recognized the meaning of what we were experiencing too. Some of it was harsh and heartbreaking, some of it was delirious delight. One evening as we lay together in the twilight zone just before sleep took over, I felt a strong urge to prop myself on my elbow and look into his face. I was not surprised to see tears welling in his eyes. I didn't need to ask what was wrong. Without acknowledging in any way that he was crying, and totally without self-pity, he said, "I was thinking of how long it took for me to find you again."

He said no more than that. It was so simple, so unadorned, so completely self-revealing.

"How many times do you think we have been together?" I asked gently.

Vassy sighed with the breath of ages and said, "I don't know. I am only sure that I was a woman and you were a man more than once. Of that, I am certain. Don't you feel it?"

"Yes," I said, playfully kicking him in the side of the leg. "I feel it because this time around you act so macho, like you're making up for lost time."

"I am not macho. I am Russian," he answered, tickling me in the ribs. I pulled his hair—an off-limits indiscretion, as I was fully aware.

He sat bolt upright in the bed, a grin of pure joy announcing his intentions.

"Now," he said, mock-grim, "now you will have big troubles."

With no more dialogue he proceeded to tickle me unmercifully. I laughed and screamed and laughed and screamed. At last, thoroughly frazzled, I fell off the bed and called for a truce. Flushed with playful power, Vassy affected a stern look of mock agreement and released me from his bearlike grasp. We crawled under the covers, curled up together, and hibernated for the night.

*   *   *

The next day I was driving in Beverly Hills and through a large, spacious store window I spotted a big, almost life-size furry toy bear. I slammed on the brakes, parked close by, and went in to look at it. The store sold electronic equipment, but the owner collected big toy animals. The bear was brown and cuddly with a white face and saucer-sized, Bambi-like eyes with long lashes and furry brown ears. His expression made me chuckle inside when I looked into his face. He had a pudgy stomach and out-stretched furry arms. I wanted to hug the creature.

Next to the bear, sitting on the floor, was a comical lion. Vassy prided himself on being a Leo (born in August), therefore king of the jungle. I knew I had to buy both animals. I would give the bear to him right away, and save the lion for his birthday. The owner agreed to sell them to me and we wrapped them in two monstrous plastic bags.

That night I gave Vassy the bear, which of course we named Honeybear, Jr.

Honeybear, Jr., became the source of delight that alleviated our most seriously destructive moments. Whenever we reached a low point of unresolvable difference, either I or Vassy would use Honeybear, Jr., as token of humorous apology. Rather than waving a white flag of truce, we would place Honeybear, Jr., in a comical position somewhere in the house, either on his head in the sink with a towel hanging from one leg, or maybe on top of a half-opened door, which one of us knew the other would walk through, so that Honeybear, Jr., would fall on our heads and remind us to laugh. We used him as a humorous intermediary since neither of us would ever admit we were wrong. I wondered if the Russians and the Americans should bring furry toys to the SALT talks.

After my television special I went to work on my live show because I had a Vegas and Tahoe date

to play. Vassy began work on a project for us to do
together. Perhaps all artists feel the need to work for
their own experience and creative interests. I don't
know. But we did. I had concluded that working
with Vassy would be difficult but worth it. Besides, I
admired his overall plan to bring Russian and American artists together with film, using our respective
countries as locations. We talked about many subjects, including *The Doctor's Wife*. The subject that
surfaced more often than any other was reincarnation. We wanted to do a love story based on the
recognition that the two characters involved had lived
and loved together in previous lives. We searched
through old films and found that no one had suc-
cessfully done that before. So we began to consider
writing an original screenplay and hiring another
writer, who was also conversant with the subject, to
work with Vassy. Vassy was anxious to express some
of his spiritual beliefs on the screen and felt he
would be very good at a spiritual love story. I agreed
with him. There were several American and English
writers he was anxious to work with. He put his
agent to investigating their availability. And so did I.

In the meantime, Vassy was working with an
English writer on his screenplay about whales, which
he had outlined to me during our first dinner together. It was a fascinating romantic and metaphysical adventure story, and he had financing to develop
it.

While I played Tahoe and Vegas his co-writer,
Marc Peplow, would come with us and work with
him so we could all be together.

We all piled into the performers' house in Tahoe, a set and a setting straight out of an old Betty
Grable movie.

It wasn't long before Vassy and I both complained bitterly about the night hours we had to
adjust to because of my schedule. He was a man
who liked to rise just after the sun. He felt turned
around and "out of order with nature" when he

went to bed when most people get up. He tried to sleep before I got home, but said that that wasn't possible for him, either, because he couldn't really relax unless he knew I was there. I understood completely. I would have had the same trouble.

Perhaps the day-night reversal was responsible for some of what began to happen. But I think perhaps it had more to do with his own emotional work habits.

Whatever the reason, as Vassy began to work on his script with Marc, I noticed that he became more and more tortured. They would decide on a scene and read me the outline of it, happily sure that they were working in the right direction. Then Vassy would begin to emotionally writhe around in agony. He really suffered the pangs of insecurity to an extent greater than anything I had observed in the American writers I knew. He stared at the ceiling, and instead of analyzing the scene he was involved with, he verbalized about how much he was suffering . . . how difficult and painful the creative process was. I knew something about that, but I somehow just accepted it as part of the process. He went into long detail about how excruciating it was. We tried to discuss the problems of creative work where original ideas were concerned, but he really didn't want to acknowledge that creativity could also be joyful. He simply *could* not countenance such a concept, claiming instead that in order to be creative one *needed* to suffer. I had been having that discussion for years with artists I knew. It was a favorite topic among creative artists who were good and knew it. Some came down on the side of creative happiness, some came down on the side of creative torture. Did one need internal emotional conflict, pressure, in order to produce great work, or was greater work forthcoming when neurosis was unblocked? To Vassy, though, there was no discussion. Creativity that flamed easily was suspect, and whenever he felt it in himself, he was certain his creative expression was faulty. I saw his theory in action. Marc seemed able to roll with the tortured punches of creative pain, yet I could see an aspect of him wonder also if all the pain was actually necessary. But Vassy had institutionalized his suffering and without it he felt he was literally incapable of creating.

I remembered my years in film, working under all kinds of circumstances. Every time I was happy, I was better. When I was miserable or blocked, nothing worked. That seemed to apply to those I had worked with, as well, or maybe that had been because I usually walked away from self-imposed suffering, figuring it just wasn't worth it. With an artist like Vassy, though, it wasn't possible to walk away because, first, he was brilliant, and second, he *needed* everyone involved with him to be involved also with his *grande torture* in order to plumb the depths of *their* potential.

I watched and observed as the weeks bumped by. Great shouts of gut-wrenching excitement followed by sinking silences emanated from the room where Vassy and Marc worked. During the day I brought them coffee and mounds of cheeses and salads prepared by the cook hired to take care of the entertainers. Then around six o'clock every afternoon, we would all sit down to a family meal of rice and vegetables, homemade bread, and a lusty meat dish which Vassy usually had had a hand in preparing. He loved to preside at the head of the table, where he would pour glasses of chilled vodka flavored with raspberry leaves he had plucked from the bushes surrounding the house. He could identify each flower, bush, and tree on the property and told us just where the corresponding flora grew in Russia. He stuffed the raspberry leaves into the vodka and let it marinate until it was permeated with the fruit flavor.

While presiding over the head of the table, Vassy held forth on many subjects. He loved to hear himself talk as much as we did. But it wasn't so much *what* he was saying as much as it was the *fact* that he was. I felt that he needed to be the commanding head of the household, the master orator, the initiator of conversations. It was a charming need because he took such pleasure in our being there. It was clear he missed the family environment of his country house in Russia. He would lift his chilled raspberry vodka glass, look into it, and while watching its contents gradually disappear, he would launch into one of his favorite topics—Love versus Respect. Vassy had the conviction that one could not love and respect another human being at the same time.

"When one loves another," he would say, "one is so involved with that emotion that it is impossible to respect the integrity of another."

"But Honeybear," I would counter, "you can't have real love without respect."

"That is not true in Russia. You either love or you respect. You cannot do both."

"How do you mean?"

"With love you have jealousy, possessiveness, and many other emotions and passions which make respect impossible. We know that in Russia, therefore we accept it."

I had heard him espouse this theory many times, usually profoundly shocking everyone within earshot. It was a theory which we in America might have subscribed to in the nineteenth century, but since the evolution of human rights—civil, female, and otherwise—we had come to comprehend that it was not only possible to have both, but actually necessary, otherwise democracy couldn't work. But then it was becoming clear to me that Vassy, in his "Russianness," wanted his own freedom, yet didn't understand the democratic principle of respecting the freedom of others *while* you loved them.

"Sometimes I think that Russians don't know respect," he would say. "They know only love. Therefore their actions are motivated by feelings when they love. In Russia my neighbor can knock at my door at 3:00 a.m. and ask for five rubles, or a cup of hot tea. And if I don't help him, he is surprised. And I expect the same from him. Here, you respect privacy. You Americans know only respect. You don't understand love. You don't know how to love. You know only how to respect. You think you are doing both, but you're not."

His was a one-sided theory that nevertheless bore examination. It seemed outrageously judgmental on the surface. But the more I observed the outrage he precipitated, the more I began to wonder if he didn't have a point.

"For example," he would say, "you have your muggings and your crime on the streets. People complain. But we in Russia do not have such crime. Because the people would lynch muggers. Your people here prefer not to be involved. They permit others to be hurt. We have community love. We don't permit."

"No," I'd say, "you have drunks."

"Perhaps, but no drunkard would freeze to death in the snow. Everyone protects drunkards. That is love. You respect the rights of someone to die if he is not your problem. You see?"

I could see his point. But to me his logic was faulty. It was neither respectful nor loving to let a drunk freeze to death. Far more likely, it was apathy or worse . . . a desire not to be "involved." Yet the stories I had heard of Russians who, overnight, turned their backs on any individual attacked by the state were truly terrible examples of "not becoming involved," even though involvement might put one at real risk. I had to conclude it was much too easy to be simplistic about such matters.

But the subject that haunted Vassy most of all was the issue of good and evil. He saw it as a black and white dilemma. And he saw both good and evil as forces outside of man—as God and Satan. Sometimes when we argued and his intractability versus my stubborn analysis became frustratingly heated, I would scream and shout at him, and he would feign calmness, which enraged me even further. During such times, he would grasp my shoulders and say, "Don't allow yourself this. It is Satan getting the better hand." He spoke with genuine belief and conviction. It wasn't pious or self-righteous. An anguished expression reflecting his unhappiness at my inability to cope with my "evil" would flood his eyes. He actually seemed to fear that I had been overtaken by Satan during my more explosively frustrated moments.

I remembered how, upon entering my Malibu place from Paris, his first act was to unpack the beautiful Bible and place it in an honored position on the bureau in the bedroom. "Where we will always be aware of it," he said.

I used to walk by that Bible, open its leather-bound cover, and wish I could read the Russian writing. Maybe somewhere in its contents lay the keys to understanding Vassy's fundamental values, which were sometimes so foreign to me.

He would often talk about how spiritually in tune we were, that I always could feel everything he was feeling, physically and mentally. He said it would be impossible to lie to me because not only would I know it immediately, but he would be lying to himself. I said I felt him the way one sees colors, clearly, very sure and always right about his innermost moods and fears.

As his work process became more and more tortured for him, I tried to help alleviate the emotional conflict by talking about it. He didn't like that approach. He never believed anything could be solved by talking—only by feeling. Wouldn't open discussion help alleviate the problem and help open the lines of communication again? "No," he said, "Russians don't talk. They *feel* their passion. You Americans analyze your passion until there is no passion left."

"But how do you resolve your differences that way?" I asked.

"We don't. We accept them until we cannot accept them anymore."

"Then what?"

"Then change happens. All things have their time. Nothing should be permanent except struggle with the dark side within ourselves."

There it was again. The concept that happiness and resolution were not possible because it was one's destiny to suffer was beginning to seriously get me down. It wasn't an ever-present emotional cloud, exactly, but it certainly lurked under the surface of every projected idea Vassy and I contemplated in working together. Yet he really did enjoy being happy—unlike many people I knew who felt they didn't deserve happiness. No, he *loved* happiness. He brought explosive passion to joy, to sex, to laughter, but always I was conscious now that our relationship was tinged with an anticipation that the happiness not only would end, but *should* end in order to make room for predestined struggle.

So Vassy and I launched into a permanent argument about good and evil. Neither of us questioned the concept of reincarnation. Neither of us questioned the existence of God or that God was total love. Neither of us questioned the struggle toward the realization of God. Where we came apart at the seams was in the *process* of the realization of God. I wished, if possible, to come to a resolution of this difference.

When we left Tahoe and returned to Los Angeles, I called Kevin Ryerson, the medium through whom I had had my first personal encounter with channeling. Vassy was accustomed to consulting with "seers," so one more would just add to his knowledge. He had full respect for spiritual entities who spoke through human channels.

Chapter 12

I had long since shared with Vassy my experiences with John and McPherson. Indeed, one of the ties that bound me to Vassy was the knowledge that I could freely discuss my new awareness and beliefs with him. Vassy had had an acquaintance with trance mediums in Russia. He said many people there visited psychics and mediums these days, because most of the personal information gleaned from them eventually checked out.

So Vassy, well acquainted with trance mediumship, accepted Kevin as an individual who simply had a talent for acting as an instrument of communication with spiritual entities, who only differed from us because they were not physically incarnate. That spiritual entities existed in the spiritual realm was not a question for Vassy. That they had lived before on the earth plane was not a question either. Vassy's problem was whether or not some of them might be evil. So the thrust of Vassy's interest and inquiry on this particular evening was the dichotomy between good and evil. It was an issue that plagued him and he was genuinely attempting to resolve it in some way.

When Kevin arrived at the house, Vassy and I were eating Russian kasha (a kind of roasted buckwheat) with garlic and onions. Kevin was wearing one of his immaculate, all-beige outfits, but was not deterred in the least by the prospect of spotting or staining it. He joined in the consumption of the kasha with verve and enthusiasm and Vassy didn't wait for Kevin to trance out and bring through John and McPherson. He engaged Kevin immediately in a discussion of his favorite value-confusing topic—the forces of evil.

Between mouthfuls of food Vassy, the Russian Christian, questioned Kevin, the nonreligious but God-loving American trance medium, about what he thought of the whole matter of good and evil, and as I watched and listened I was impressed by how well thought out the specifics of Vassy's point of view were.

"Don't you think," asked Vassy of Kevin, "that if humans, and the earth plane itself, are the result of having fallen from the grace of God, then evil is a part of the supernatural Divine Force? Therefore evil itself is a part of God?"

Kevin calmly chewed his kasha. This was clearly not the first heavyweight "good and evil" discussion that he had ever encountered.

"I don't believe," said Kevin, "that there is any such thing as evil."

"No, no," Vassy went on, "this is philosophically extremely important to me. Don't you think that evil was created for us to overcome?"

"I think," said Kevin, "that what you are calling evil is really only the lack of consciousness of God. The question is lack of spiritual knowledge, not whether or not there is evil."

"No, no," said Vassy, "if evil is ignorance of God, then how to explain those people who consciously rebel against God? They consciously destroy God inside themselves with conscious knowledge. Therefore they are not ignorant of God."

"It is impossible to destroy the God in oneself. It is immortal," answered Kevin. "That is why people, primitives, who have never in this life encountered even the concept of God, cannot be condemned

as evil." Kevin seemed to enjoy the novelty of someone seeking his point of view rather than using him
simply as a human telephone.

"But," continued Vassy, "there are very intelligent, knowledgeable people who are against God."

"No," said Kevin, "then they don't really know
God. Whatever your *concept* of God might be is what
you yourself will end up being. If an intelligent
person rebels against God, he is only rebelling against
what his *concept* of God is. Ultimately, then, that
person is rebelling against himself."

Vassy chewed and thought for a while. I made a
small salad with lemon and mustard dressing as the
discussion continued.

"We are all *under* the law of God, is that not
correct?" asked Vassy.

"No, wait a minute," said Kevin. "We are not
under the law of God. We are *as* the law of God. We
are God. We have to totally accept ourselves—to
accept the laws of self which are divine. Then we
become God. And God and self are one—therefore
we are basically total love. You do agree that God is
total love?"

"Of course. But where is the place of evil in this
scheme then?"

"It doesn't exist. That's the point. Everything in
life is the result of either illumination or ignorance.
Those are the two polarities. Not good and evil. And
when you are totally illuminated, such as Jesus Christ
or Buddha or some of those people, there is no
struggle any longer."

Vassy rose and began to pace around the kitchen.
"No," he said, "we are created to have struggle on
this earth. There is no life without conflict."

Kevin smiled. "Oh," he said, "I can very easily
picture a life without struggle. Very easily."

"But no," protested Vassy. "Even the body alone
is such a struggle. For example, just to eat involves
struggle. This discussion is struggle."

"Sure," said Kevin, "but that's not what we were created *for*."

"No, but struggle *is* some sort of conflict between two polarities. For example, I believe that nature was created to be undisturbed. I believe that an apple has some sort of pain when we eat it. And flowers have pain when we cut them."

Kevin put down his fork. "Well," he said, "if you can believe that, then it's just as easy to believe that the apple is pleased to be eaten because it knows that it exists for the nourishment of other conscious beings. It is in perfect harmony with God and therefore understands that its purpose is to nurture life. Eating, therefore, isn't necessarily a struggle because everyone benefits—the humans who eat it and the apple which fulfilled its purpose."

I stood in my kitchen, munching on a carrot, entranced with the conversation, which sounded like a home-grown version of *My Dinner with André*. My thoughts were like a tennis ball, bouncing back and forth as I identified with each player's point of view.

"I am stubborn," said Vassy. "Everything you say is okay until there are three persons on a desert island and only one apple. The struggle and conflict is who will survive."

"Depends upon the people," said Kevin. "If you had three Buddhist monks faced with the conflict of survival through one apple, they would probably meditate and not eat it at all until they lost consciousness from starvation and simply passed from the earth plane. They would know because of their spiritual education that they were only losing their bodies and not their souls anyway. Therefore their higher knowledge would absolve them of having to engage in any conflict with each other. If you had three pirates faced with the same conflict, they would probably massacre each other, which would only manifest their ignorance of the immortality of the soul. My point is that this would be an example of the ignorance of higher knowledge, not evil per se.

Struggle and conflict is in direct ratio to the knowledge of God. The more knowledge one has of God and one's own immortality, the less struggle there is. Therefore there is no evil—only the lack of knowledge."

Vassy thought. Then he said, "Yes, but for me, I am only interested in this lifetime, in this short-term struggle with its mistakes and ignorance. I am not trying to change or understand the cosmos. I am only trying to overcome my ignorance in my struggle *now*—not in future lives, but *now*. So to me the short term is more important."

"Well," said Kevin, "I don't see how you can approach the deeper truth in the short term without understanding the nature of the long term."

"Of course the knowledge of God relates to the long term, but the real practice of life is *now*—in short terms. My karmic investment is according to my life *now*."

"Okay, but if you think in terms of God being both good and evil, you will end up manifesting both of those polarities in your life because you believe it is true. You are the result of your own thought. We all are. What we think is what we are. If you believe you are good and God is total love and God is in you, then your personal behavior patterns will express that belief."

"So it is endless, yes?"

"Yes."

Both men sat down on the couch while I brought them cinnamon coffee. Then Kevin asked Vassy a question that never would have occurred to me.

"Have you ever had an out-of-body experience?" he asked.

Vassy looked suddenly frightened. "You mean, have I experienced an astral projection?"

"Yes."

"Yes, I have. Once. I was in a state of total peace. A state of nirvana during a period when I was practicing yoga and fasting. Suddenly I felt myself rise out of my body. I saw myself sitting meditating on the floor. It was extremely frightening to me."

"Why?" asked Kevin.

Vassy leaned back against the pillows, trying to frame his words to his recalled thought.

"I lost control," he said. "I didn't know where it would be going. I had no ground under me. No earth, no restrictions. I was very frightened. It was very strong experience, very fantastic. Since that time, I have been more cautious with my spiritual searching."

Vassy took a long sip of coffee, seeming to brush away the memory of what he had just described. I thought it interesting that he felt a need for restriction. Kevin continued.

"Do you think you would feel less frightened if you experienced it with another person?"

Vassy looked over at me with an involuntary expression of longing on his face.

"I believe I could have that experience with Sheerlee. She feels every thought of mine. I can't lie to her. She feels everything I feel."

I reached across and touched his hand. What he said was true.

"I feel," he continued, "the connection with my mother. I feel her prayers. I always know when she is praying, particularly when she is praying for me. And when I check with her, I have always been correct. Sometimes when she is praying during nighttime in Russia, I can feel it during odd times of the day here."

Kevin was silent.

Vassy stood up. "Listen," he said, "we Russian Christians are sure that anyone who is not Russian Orthodox Christian is possessed by the Devil—in one way or another."

Kevin put some sugar in his coffee. "I try to educate people, but I don't try to change people. If they find higher spiritual knowledge too difficult to cope with because they don't want to give up their concepts of good and evil, then they usually join the Church. Within the Church they get the confirmation that good and evil do exist and they still get a touch of God. But it's too bad that they give evil equal credence with good. Eventually everyone stumbles across some aspect of higher knowledge and they change of their own accord."

Vassy put his hands squarely on the coffee table in front of him. "You are saying that the absence of struggle puts you closer to God?"

"Yes," answered Kevin, "because you already *are* God. The discrepancy comes in not believing that. Human beings believe they are part evil—so they act accordingly. We are a product of what we believe, what we think."

Vassy punched his head. "I have real difficulty with this," he said exasperatedly. "Real difficulty. It's very far from Christian understanding of God. It is difficult for me to be a part of this world where *I know* struggle with evil is required and believe that if I gave up that struggle I would be closer to realizing God."

"That *is* the struggle," said Kevin. "Struggle is the struggle. We are on this earth, in my opinion, to learn that we don't need to struggle. That is the real enlightenment. The process of learning that there is no struggle takes struggle, but life itself is *not* struggle."

Vassy punched his head again. "But I am trying to write a script and it is a struggle. Or when I make a movie it is a permanent struggle."

"Yes," said Kevin, "but if you relaxed more and just let the creativity flow, you would find your need to struggle decrease. But if you believe that creative struggle is necessary to a good script then you will create *struggle* instead of a good script. Or maybe you will create struggle *and* a good script—but you will never know whether it could have been better if you had not struggled. . . ."

I laughed out loud.

"Sheerlee doesn't like me to explain my philosophy about good and evil."

"Yes, I do," I said. "As a matter of fact, I've learned a great deal from this discussion."

"Yes?" said Vassy. "What have you learned?"

"I have learned that it has been a struggle for me to watch the struggle you two have gone through in struggling to prove that struggle to understand only produces more struggle that is the most struggling struggle of struggles."

"My dear," said Vassy triumphantly, "may I have some vodka?"

Vassy and Kevin and I cleared the table. Kevin prepared to go into trance.

"Kevin," Vassy asked. "Do you get ridiculed for this trance channeling you do?"

Kevin smiled patiently. "Oh, sometimes," he said, "but usually the people who come to me are interested in higher spiritual knowledge or they wouldn't be with me in the first place."

"But," I asked, "do they think you are only acting when the spiritual entities come through?"

"My dear Sheerlee," announced Vassy, "I can tell you that spiritual entities exist. We know that in Russia. And as a director I can also tell you that they are not acting. No, they are not acting."

"All right," I said, "but I have been reading lots of literature on the subject and perhaps the channeler is picking up what Carl Jung called the collective unconscious. Maybe it isn't really spiritual entities you are channeling, but more what your subconscious perceives."

"Perhaps," said Vassy, "but the information is usually the same wherever the channeling occurs. For example, reincarnation is the basic truth and everything else stems from that."

Kevin calmly listened to Vassy and me discuss the authenticity of what he, Kevin, had devoted his life to. He nodded with each point of view and each question. He didn't feel called upon to defend himself but he was interested in how each of us related to the phenomenon.

Vassy leaned forward. "Can I ask about evil tonight from your guides?"

"Sure," said Kevin. "Ask anything you want. That's what I'm here for. Shall we begin?"

Vassy asked Kevin if he was comfortable and puffed up a pillow for him to rest his back against. I retrieved a glass mug from the kitchen and filled it with water, remembering that McPherson appreciated the pub feeling.

Kevin placed his arms gently on the armrest of the chair and quietly began to breathe deeply. I turned off the telephone and turned on the tape recorder.

The following is a slightly edited version of what transpired.

Kevin's head fell to his shoulders as he went into trance. His breathing changed. In about five minutes there was a sudden shudder through his body. His head bobbed up again. His eyes were shut. His mouth opened and in a few moments these words came:

"Hail. State purpose of gathering."

It was the John entity that had come through.

"We are two people here," I said. "We would like to ask some questions. We don't really have them organized. Is that all right?"

"Yes," came the voice. "Proceed with questioning."

I gestured to Vassy. He indicated I should go first.

"John?" I asked. "Is that you?"

"Yes," came the answer. Very sparse, with no frills or further greeting.

"Well, it's nice to speak with you again. I have a friend here whom I've met since we last talked and he is as interested in this stuff as I am."

"Very well," said John.

"So, I guess my first question is, is there a real need on our earth for spiritual enlightenment? I mean, would it decrease human suffering and pain if more people understood the spiritual dimensions of themselves?"

"That is correct," answered John. "The collective consciousness of the entire human race manifests the reality of your earth plane. The influence of the mind of man creates disturbances in nature and of course your human activities."

"You mean," I said, "that the mind of man can influence nature, like earthquakes and flooding and things?"

"That is correct. Gravitational influences and planetary harmony are affected by the minds of beings on every planet. You are experiencing natural disturbances on your planet because the consciousness of the human race needs raising."

"Is that why spiritual enlightenment is necessary?"

"Yes, the mind of man is more powerful than nature. You are suffering from your state of mind, which is influencing the patterns of nature on your plane."

Vassy sat watching. I gestured to him to ask a question. He indicated he preferred to wait.

"Okay," I said. "With all the bad stuff that's happening in the world today, would you say there is a negative force operating here that is equal to the God-force? I mean, is evil a part of God also?"

"You are speaking of satanic influences?" asked John.

"Yes."

"The concept of Satan as interpreted in your Bible had its origin as follows: Adam and Eve stood symbolically for the creation of the souls. They were created originally as pure spiritual soul energy, as everyone was. When they became captivated by the material plane, or the earth plane as you know it, they found themselves incarnated in the bodies of the lower primates because they were seduced by the attractions of physical existence. Because of their fall from grace, they activated the law of karma. Their spiritual and divine origins were only dimly remembered because of the confined restrictions of their physical bodies. The struggle back toward original divinity is what your Bible terms Satan. The Hebrew meaning of the word "Satan", as the instrument Kevin has told you, is struggle, or that which is not *well* for you. What you term as Satan is merely the force of your lower consciousness as you engage in your struggle to return and know God, which was your origin. The feeling of what you term evil is the struggle with self."

John stopped talking as though to engage our response. Vassy still didn't want to talk.

"Well," I said, "how could we have gone so far wrong about this subject?"

"The struggle for self-knowledge would not be a struggle if one loved God with all one's heart and soul and one's neighbor as oneself. For one's neighbor is one's self. But mankind set up the dualities of good and evil in order to judge others rather than to discover self. Therefore, it was even possible to make war on one another. Out of lack of knowledge of God came the concept of evil. But when mankind understands that it itself is a collective being representing the God-force, it is impossible to make war on the self. Is this to your understanding?"

"Yes," I answered. "May I ask you a more specific modern question?"

"Indeed."

"Is the Soviet Union aware of the need for spiritual enlightenment?"

"Not so much in the realm of the government, but very much so in the realms of psychic researchers. These individuals have spiritualized the intellect. They have come to realize that perhaps there is one universal mind."

Vassy raised his hand.

"You want to ask something now, sweetheart?" I asked.

"Yes," he said. "Should I represent myself?"

"If you wish," said John.

Vassy cleared his throat. "I am Vassily Okhłopkhov-Medvedjatnikov. I am from the Soviet Union and I am now in United States and I would like to work here. My first question is, how can I be effective in my private and social life in the fight against evil or satanic forces?"

There was silence for a moment. Then John said, "Do you consider yourself a soul?"

"Yes."

"Do you consider yourself born of God?"

"Yes."

"You are all sons and daughters of God?"

"Yes."

"Therefore you, in your personal life and personal adventures, acknowledge yourself as a son of God and as a soul. With this, you will educate others, through your own personal acknowledgment."

"Yes, I will."

"You must not resist what you call evil. If you seek to struggle against evil, you will find that it has engaged you. You will be lost within the battle. Allow yourself to be fully illumined. Seek to give love and knowledge so that others around you can progress. For if ignorance is destroyed by the example of your life, the satanic force, as you term it, will also be destroyed. For the light is always present, the darkness, which is ignorance, sees the light and does not comprehend. It is better to light a single candle than to curse the darkness. Darkness is that which you determine as the satanic force. Discover the love and the light within you as well as the love and the light within others. Nurture it. Be patient. Be long suffering. Then in turn you will serve others. Is this to your understanding?"

Vassy leaned forward. "So, you mean," he said, "that suffering is necessary in this struggle?"

"The Hebrew definition of experience is the knowledge of suffering. Suffering is therefore only experience. Suffering is what you would term long experience. Because there is no time or space. There is only experience. For instance, if an individual comes to you and strikes at you and does you wrong, what would you do? Would you strike back at the individual or would you suffer-experience those things and deal with him with patience? I would hope you would speak peacefully with that individual, that you would bring him to a greater illumination. So great would be his shock, his surprise. For the expected reaction according to his own behavior would be that you would strike him back. Therefore, by experiencing his strike with gentleness, you would give him greater food for thought and overcome his personal ignorance. Then he will have learned, from your personal suffering-experience, how to overcome his own ignorance. Then perhaps he also will come home to God. That is what we mean by suffering. Is this to your understanding?"

Vassy turned John's words over in his mind. He made no further reference to the question of evil. Instead he said, "I would like to ask a more private question."

"Please do."

"Did Sheerlee and I meet by accident or was it somehow ordained and planned?"

There was a moment of silence. Then John said, "Pause please. There is another entity desiring to speak."

There was another pause. Then Tom McPherson came through.

"Hello. Tip of the hat to you. How are you doing out there?" He spoke with his familiar, funny Scotch-Irish accent. Vassy and I laughed. Neither of us said anything.

"You are there, are you not?" said McPherson.

We laughed again.

"Yes, we are here," I said. "You are just so startlingly funny, that's all."

"Quite right," he said. "Now, I understand I have been brought in to answer a question about past lives?"

"Yes," said Vassy.

"Yes, one moment. Allow me to collect myself."

There was another pause. "Excuse me," he said, "I wasn't quite here. There was a question directed about two persons meeting. Could you redirect the question to myself?"

"Vassy wants to know if he and I met as an accident or part of a plan."

"One moment please. Allow me to check into this."

Vassy and I waited while looking at each other. McPherson came through again.

"Hello, again. I was just in consultation with another entity over here who keeps track of past-life information. According to his records, your meeting *was* a bit planned, in the sense that both of you had a past-life incarnation during a time period in Greece. You were both studying to be oracles. Both of you developed psychic faculties as well as theatrical and drama talents. Therefore you had a full bag of studies. Of course, drama in those days was considered quite sacred, which is not the case these days. Actors and actresses in those days were considered demigods. Therefore both of you during that time period wished to spiritualize your art form even more and you began studying and practicing an esoteric form of the theatrical arts whereby you actually threw yourselves into an altered state of consciousness and channeled great actors from the past. In that lifetime, you were very close friends and stayed close during the entire lifetime. However, during that time your genders were reversed. In other words, the current female was a male and the current male was a female, which might be reflecting in your personality struggle today."

Vassy and I laughed. "You see?" he said. "I told you how I identified with the female, didn't I?" I nodded.

"Then why does he get upset with my ballsy-ness?" I questioned.

"You are currently engaged," Tom interrupted, "with understanding your yin and yang and passive and nonpassive tendencies. You are learning about male and female energies in one another, as are most of the human beings on the earth plane at this time. But anyway, in answer to your question about this particular lifetime, no, you did not meet by accident. It was definitely mapped out."

"By whom was it mapped out?" I asked.

"By yourselves, as souls, before this incarnation. We all plan out our own lifetimes before we incarnate so that we can work through particular conflicts and experiences."

Vassy and I nodded to each other.

"So what are we supposed to do together?" I asked.

"Well, right now we would say you are sort of enjoying each other's company. In a very intimate sort of way, we would say."

I laughed and Vassy blushed a bit and smiled.

"But both of you are creative in your art forms. And we believe you are a good polarity for each other. One is rough-and-ready. The other is more meticulous and is developing degrees of sensitivity. Therefore we feel the combination of both your intellects is going to produce similar forms of creativity, concerned with putting spiritual understanding into the art forms of drama, films, and theater, such as you are already manifesting in your technologies. Do you understand all that?"

I laughed and said, "Yes. Do you?"

McPherson hesitated and then laughed too. "Not

exactly, as this information is coming from other sources."

Vassy spoke up again. "May I ask you another personal question?"

"Please do," said McPherson. "But understand that you have had many incarnations together. I have addressed myself to only one. In time you will recognize others yourself."

"I would like to ask a medical question," said Vassy.

"Please do."

"Sheerlee has hypoglycemia. How can we treat it?"

"You mean to throw it into complete remission?"

"Yes, please," said Vassy, probably remembering that it would be easier to cure my blood sugar than his theatrics.

"Very well," said McPherson, "describe your current diet."

I thought a moment and outlined that I ate mostly raw vegetables, fruit, grains, some protein but no red meat.

"Do you seek a high-protein diet?"

"High protein?"

"Yes."

"Well, I like nuts and things like that."

"Have you ever tried fasting?"

"That's correct," said Vassy. "She must fast."

"But Tom, I can't fast or I'll faint."

"It doesn't matter," said Vassy.

"All right," said Tom, interrupting the argument. "We have a fast that you might find successful."

"Really?"

"Quite right. We will see. One moment. Allow me to check with another entity who specializes in these things."

A moment passed.

"Yes, I have help on the question now."

Tom proceeded to give me a detailed rundown on an overall apple fast, followed by high protein (in the form of tofu) and raw vegetables to bring about, as he said, "a complete remission of the toxins in your system."

Vassy then asked about his own health. He described what he ate, but left out the desserts, particularly his love of chocolate sauce. Tom called him on it. Vassy looked sheepish. We both laughed as Tom gave him specific and detailed advice. Tom told him what minerals and vitamins were missing in his body, while Vassy made notes.

Both of us had questions about arthritis for which Tom recommended peanut-oil and olive-oil massage, plus more calcium and copper. . . . The health session went on for about an hour until Tom and Kevin was tiring.

"Are there any other questions? Because we must be careful not to tire the body of the young man."

"Oh, yes. We're sorry."

"One more question," said Vassy. "Please."

"Very well."

"You told us that Sheerlee and I did not meet by accident, that we had had a life experience during the time of ancient Greece."

"That's correct."

"Well, what shall we do together now?"

"Both of you have talents in coordination of certain art forms. You could be sponsors of certain metaphysical and spiritual art forms."

"We came into this life to emphasize the metaphysical aspects of art?" I asked.

"We would say so, yes."

"Well, how can we do that if the response to those sorts of things is ridicule?"

"We disagree. There have been successful milestones already. Your *2001: A Space Odyssey*, your *Star Wars* with 'the Force.' And there will be much more."

"Well, were people relating to the metaphysical aspects of *Star Wars* or were they mostly drawn to it because it was an adventurous space opera?"

"Let's put it this way, the artists got the attention of the people and then the public was ready for more subtle messages. Yes, much of the public reacted to 'the Force' as an activity of God."

"So you mean," I asked, "that buried somewhere in the public mind is an appreciation of this stuff we're talking about?"

"Most definitely. For instance, the art form of *2001: A Space Odyssey* is a magnificent expression of metaphysical potency. The symbolism is incredible. Stanley Kubrick is a master metaphysician."

"What has that to do with us?" asked Vassy.

"You are now ready to begin such projects," said McPherson, and paused. "Will there be any more questions then?"

"No," I said. "Thank you, Tom. Thank you again."

"Very well. We'll be going now. Saints be lookin' after you. And God bless you."

Tom left the body, and John came in again to pronounce the benediction.

Vassy and I held hands as Kevin regained consciousness.

"Hello?" said Kevin with a question, as though he were lost in time and space. "Hello. Are you there?"

"Yes, Kevin. We're here," I said.

He blinked and stretched. "How long have I been gone?" he asked.

"About one and a half hours," I said.

"Yes, my time frame gets mixed up sometimes when I'm not conscious." He yawned and rubbed his eyes.

"Let's make some coffee," I said, getting up and reminding myself that I still lived in the real world. "I think we could all use some caffeine."

Chapter 13

*A*fter the channeling session, Vassy and I took more long walks in the mountains, discussing possible structures for a film which would dramatize the spiritual story of a human being in a personalized form. We had more sessions in which both John and Tom offered advice on what we might do and how we might work together.

Vassy accepted the information that John and Tom channeled through, but the more interested I became in what they had to say, the more guarded he became. I thought I could understand his position. I believe he was concerned that I would give more weight to their creative input than to his, as though he feared that I regarded the truth from "above" as more knowledgeable and expert than his. I tried to be sensitive to his creative concerns, but couldn't find a way to reassure him. So I just let it slide.

Kevin came over several times during the next few weeks and we continued to have more sessions. Sometimes Vassy was busy with outside meetings and would come home in the midst of a session I was either having alone or with other friends who were interested. We usually used a room which was out of the flow of traffic in the front of the house, and which was quiet. Vassy joined us when he had time, but sometimes he gave me the impression that he actually *wanted* me to feel that he was interfering. He would poke his head in the door to find out what was going on, then leave without coming in. I wanted him to participate and learn with the rest of us. I was too much involved then to realize that Vassy actually felt his relationship with me was threatened by the relationship I was having with the spiritual entities in my life. Meanwhile I didn't know how to handle his behavior without provoking an argument— which I feared would be explosive.

One evening Vassy came home while my friends and I were talking with Tom and John. I didn't know he was back. The session continued until our guides said we were tiring Kevin's body and should stop.

Very casually we broke up our spiritual teaching session and I went into the kitchen. Vassy was cutting up beets and apples, making one of his blender specialties and cooking one of his superb soups on the stove. He had long since taken over the cooking because he was better at it than I—not only in his opinion but also in mine.

"Hi, Honeybear," I said, surprised. "I didn't know you were here."

"I am here," he answered gruffly. "There is no dinner," he went on. "I am preparing."

"Oh, great," I said. "Just let me say good-bye to everyone."

I ushered everyone out, not wanting to burden Vassy with dinner for five. When I returned to the kitchen, he was staring into the vegetables with a face of stone. He didn't look up. He stirred his soup grimly. I was confused.

"What's wrong, sweetheart?" I asked.

"Don't come near the stove, please," he said as he fried some onions in olive oil and spices. It smelled delicious.

I didn't say anything.

"You shouldn't act ignorant of what is wrong," he said.

I was really confused now. If I am confused
enough, I usually get angry.

"What do you mean?" I said with a shrill sharp-
ness in my voice that hurt even my ears.

"You are too busy with your spiritual guides.
You have not prepared my dinner."

Astonishment vied with the anger flooding
through me.

"*Prepared your dinner*?" I said. "You must be
kidding. We usually cook dinner together. I didn't
even know you were home."

"Yes, you knew it," he insisted.

"I'm sorry," I said. "That's a bunch of shit. You
didn't come in and let me know. How could I possibly tell you were home? What's more, you know
damn well you always do the cooking. Why are you
saying all this?"

"I am saying nothing," he said. "You are doing
something."

That did it. I fell into an immediate and plum-
meting depression. His certainty was so outrageous
that I actually found myself racking my brain for
what I could possibly have done wrong. I was so
confused by the unreasonableness of his hostility
that my only recourse was rage. I wanted desperately to hang on to my own identity, to at least try to
be reasonably adult, but I could feel myself losing
control.

"You are a real shit," I screamed. "You are
overbearing and totally self-centered and I don't know
what the fuck you expect from me!"

"That is because you are not sensitive," he said
calmly.

I slammed the soup spoon onto the kitchen floor,
shocked at the violence he brought out in me. I ran
from the kitchen into the bedroom. Vassy followed.

"You drive me crazy," I yelled. "I never know
when you will go into one of those elitist expecta-
tions of yours and it always throws me off balance."

"*You* are elitist," he said, his voice rising now.

"You care only for what you are learning. You care nothing for what you promise me."

"What did I promise you?" I yelled.

"You would have dinner waiting for me."

"Now that, by God, is a flat lie!"

What he had just said was so totally alien to our habits and custom that I was doubly outraged. I wanted to leap from the balcony and run from him. I felt he would drive me completely crazy if I couldn't somehow comprehend not only what was happening between us but specifically to me. He always seemed so certain of his point of view, without even a hint of acknowledging anyone else's right to differ. I couldn't deal with it. It didn't matter to him that I might be confused, enraged, or just flatly opposed to his evaluation of the circumstances we were *each* responsible for.

So I blew. I ran to the balcony and climbed onto the railing, feeling that I *had* to get away from him, but that I also wanted him to stop me. I wanted to force him to somehow *equally* engage himself in the responsibility for the turmoil that was occurring. I couldn't seem to get him to a point of even exchange with me by talk or discussion. I felt I had to resort to dramatics. Yet, at the same time, I really was feeling desperate. Vassy rushed after me.

"What you are doing, Nif-Nif!!" he screamed. He took my arm and wrenched me away from the balcony. I tore away from him and lurched to the other side.

"You drive me nuts!!" I screamed back at him, aware that it had only taken a few moments for such an explosion to occur. "I don't know how you come to the conclusions you reach that I am insensitive and unattentive!! *You* are so demanding without ever letting me know what it is you want. And I hate what you turn me into. I hate it when I'm like this! I just simply *hate* it!"

Vassy seemed genuinely stunned, as though the possibility of my exploding had never occurred to him. His eyes had a bewildered look. "What you are doing?" he pleaded.

"What do you mean, what am *I* doing?" I yelled. "Isn't it obvious? You drive me bananas! I'm telling you I will *run*! I will *leave*. I can't stand this stuff, and I'm afraid I will really leave you if you keep doing this, whether you do it by design or not."

"You will leave me?" he said as though that hadn't occurred to him either.

"Yes. Yes. Yes!" I said. "Because I can't stand this tower of rage that you seem capable of turning me into."

"Nif-Nif," he cajoled, "it is satanic forces again. Please recognize. It is not you."

I sat down abruptly, in tears. I was shaking, trying to get some measure of control. "It is not satanic forces, you stupid shit. This is *me*, Vassy. This is *me* allowing myself to become this. And *you* provoke it. But what I can't take is that we somehow never talk about it. I'm not able to control it when you do this to me because we can't talk. We cannot seem to ever come to terms. This Satan shit has nothing to do with it!"

"Pray," said Vassy. "Pray to God and you will release yourself."

Oh my, oh my, oh my, I thought. What have I got here? He was probably right that I should pray— but not to exorcise the Devil. I should pray to the best I could muster up in myself.

I stood up and wiped my cheeks.

"My Nif-Nif," he chided gently.

I looked up into his face. He was confused.

"Vassy," I said haltingly, "don't you understand that we are two human beings involved with trying to work out a relationship here? The Devil doesn't have anything to do with it. Please, take *some* responsibility for your role in it. Don't blame it on satanic forces."

He sat down on a canvas chair. "My role and

your role is to approach God and overcome negative forces when they seize us."

"But Vassy," I tried again, "*we* are responsible for our actions. *We* are supposed to be mature adults who are aware of what we do to ourselves and each other. I believe that I am as spiritually evolved as you, but I can't go around saying God and the Devil are having open conflict within my being. *I* live in there too." I pounded my chest, visualizing that my real self was somehow within my solar plexus.

"No," announced Vassy. "And how can you allow this satanic violence to overtake you? Is not good."

"You bet your ass is not good." I heard the weariness in my voice. "That's what I mean. If I was negotiating at SALT II, I think I'd throw in the towel."

"Towel?" asked Vassy.

"Never mind. I'm gonna take a shower."

Vassy went to the freezer for vodka. I poured myself a glass of red wine and carried it away. Again, we hadn't talked. I wondered why Russians drank so much vodka. Was it the system? The system that somehow repressed open discussion? From what I'd read, Russians had been drinking excessively for centuries. Why? Was it the weather? It was just as cold in many places. So was it confusion? Confusion about identity, about God, about reality. What was reality? It was relative. What he was experiencing was his truth, his reality. I couldn't seem to cope with his demands, but maybe he was having the same problem with me.

"If I am stubborn," he had said once, "or how you call 'obstinate,' then you must hit me. Hit me hard. Russians need to be hit. We only understand to be hit. We need big fist, I can tell you."

I couldn't hit. I needed to understand. I took a shower and we silently ate dinner and went to bed.

For days after that I thought about our relationship. Something had shifted. He said he couldn't respect my sense of equality. I said I couldn't live without respect *and* equality. He said there was no such thing as equality in love . . . only possession, jealousy, passion, and total fidelity. I would argue for the equality of identity. He said in love equality was a fantasy. Democracy did not exist in the state of love, only possession and passion—true, direct, honest passion. And the love would last as long as the passion was there. When respect emerged, there was no longer love, no longer passion. When I accused him of believing in a blueprint for disaster, he said it was man's destiny to suffer, that to suffer was to know God.

At last it dawned on me that the differences between us were not really and simply because he was Russian and I American. Sure, we were having trouble with our cultural differences. But it was our versions of evil that really differed—evil in relation to God and man, not evil in relation to sociology or socialism. Russians and Americans couldn't have been more diametrically opposed in relation to hope and the future. And the Bolshevik Revolution hadn't that much to do with it. But it was just too easy to say the Russian soul was imprinted with the need to suffer. Nor was it true that the American soul was imprinted with an adolescent naïveté causing enthusiasm and optimism to spring eternal. Maybe Vassy was correct when he said we would never understand each other. Perhaps his objection to my so-called Freudian questioning was a valid position because the questions only related to a limited point of view anyway. He seemed to be saying that what might be true for him one day would not necessarily be true for him the next. And I couldn't keep up because I was *questioning* too much. I should just accept.

We declared a diplomatic truce for a time, trying to relate to each other on a surface level. For him it would have worked. For me and my nature, it didn't. If I had been capable of continuing to laugh off his structured orders about the way I should eat, dress, work out, sing, dance, do yoga, and breathe, I suppose life would have gone more swimmingly. But I couldn't, even though he was usually right. When he rejected my protests with the perfectly reasonable argument that he was only ordering me around for my own good, I often stopped and conjured up the validity of that point of view. But as I told him equally often, I had done okay without his orders up till now. He didn't seem to think so.

Weeks and months blended combustibly together. Sometimes the harmony took my breath away. Other times we were so discordant together I needed to cover my ears, eyes, and heart.

I read many books on Russian artists, writers, philosophers, and musicians in an attempt to understand. I seemed to be concluding that the Russian himself was saying, "We are not to be understood." It was maddeningly challenging to me. I didn't like not understanding . . . at least to my satisfaction. Half savage, half saint. That seemed to be the consensus of opinion among the Russians themselves. The communist government appeared to be irrelevant, merely a continuation, in a different form, of a system which basically denied the importance of the individual. Vassy had told me in the beginning that the Russian people had the government they needed and understood, and in many respects he even claimed they would want Joe Stalin back because he would, in effect, protect them from themselves.

"We would have anarchy without our severe rulers," he would say. "I can tell you most Russians would agree with me."

So what did that really mean? I couldn't help feeling this was simply the opinion of one Vassily Okhlopkhov-Medvedjatnikov. At the same time, I wondered if I was receiving a complicated education in what we might all have to learn if we were ever to co-exist with a superpower adversary. Nor could I help wondering too, if I, as an American trying to survive in the foreignness of Russia, would have attempted to overpower my lover with *my* point of view.

Yet there were times when our joy and playfulness together left me astonished with happiness. To him our happiness was "like music that I am afraid will not last." Our laughter was color and our physical harmony like a pastel Impressionist painting. Like a child, Vassy marveled at the prosperity of America and the tolerance the Americans had for each other, whether in traffic jams or the crush of a rock concert. He adored the fresh fruits and vegetables abounding in the markets and the "health" life of his "beloved Malibu." We continued to walk strenuously in the Calabasas Mountains and Vassy swam in the Pacific. We continued to work on developing a picture together, and several of the great Hollywood screenwriters were anxious to meet and know Vassy—his talent was known already to many of them. People teased us about the explosiveness of our relationship and looked on in amusement whenever we went at each other.

Sometimes after-dinner conversation was heated and free flowing, with the Americans judging and evaluating Russian attitudes—although many of them had never even been there. And whenever Vassy launched into his now familiar Love-versus-Respect theories, he rendered the living rooms dumbstruck. They couldn't understand, they said. We in America were working to harmonize the two. Vassy said they were fundamentally separate.

Then there were the times when Vassy, compulsively yet touchingly, would get very drunk and break down in great heaving sobs when we got home. No one else could possibly understand what it meant to be a "fucking Russian in America," he sobbed. "My fucking country, my beloved Russia," he would cry. "No one here understands my country. You judge us, you condemn us, you believe we have swords in our teeth. You're so conditioned, so brainwashed, even more than we are. At least Russians know about America, not only bad things. And you here imagine Russia as a concentration camp! You don't like Commies! That's your problem. Now I hear Americans think 'Russian' is the same as evil, stupidity, idleness. That's dangerous! What about our culture, our music, our ingenuity, our patience, endurance—these are qualities, not drawbacks! Yes, we are fucking different, why not? Why should we all be the same? Instead of trying to change each other, why don't we simply tolerate our differences and enjoy similarities?"

His sobs would leave me speechless, useless and even more non-comprehending. I felt stranded on a bridge between two cultures. I knew only one thing. Here was a man I loved and was trying to understand who was genuinely pleading for comprehension—almost a plea to help him comprehend himself. I thought many times that if I had understood myself better I would have been able to understand Vassy.

Often we made trips to Paris and New York. Vassy said he would never be able to see New York through anyone's eyes but mine. Paris, of course, was different; he had had a great deal of previous experience there.

Sometimes friends of Vassy's would pass through either New York or California. One friend was an American who had lived in Russia for three years and still traveled there three times a year for his company. In the privacy of a dinner just between the two of us, I asked him what he thought about Vassy's traveling in and out of the Soviet Union. Vassy's birthday was coming up and he wanted to celebrate it with his family in their dacha outside of Moscow. His papers were duly forthcoming, and after some hassle with the Soviet authorities in Paris, he had received permission. Jack said he knew the Medvedjatnikov family quite well. He said Vassy was known to have no political interests whatever, but that he would do anything to succeed in his ambition to freely travel the world outside of Russia, and to be a free artist in the West.

"Would do anything?" I asked.

"Well," replied Jack. "You know. I can't say for him specifically. But many Russians consider marriage to a foreigner a vehicle to get out of Russia. There used to be a saying after the revolution in the '30's; 'The car is not an object of luxury but a means of transportation.' Now they say the foreign woman is not an object of luxury but a means of transportation. Many Russians do marry foreigners in order to freely travel. The system forces them to do many things to become free."

"Are you saying," I asked, "that he married his French wife to get out?"

Jack shrugged. "I don't know. Many do."

"So, is he using me, too, then?" I asked.

"Using you? I'm not sure I'd put it that way," Jack replied. "I know how grateful he is to you. He's told me you have made so much possible for him. But he also loves you. You really *are* the woman of his life, as he says, regardless of how long it will last."

"How *long*? What do you mean?"

"Well," said Jack, a wary look crossing his cherubic face, "have you ever been involved with a Russian before?"

There it was again.

"I see," I said. Somehow this question was always supposed to be the answer. "And how about promises? Do Russian men keep their promises?"

Jack laughed out loud.

"There is no such thing," he replied, amused at my naïveté. "There is no such thing as a deal. They are too emotional for that, too much of the moment. In passion they'll promise anything. Then later their feelings might change, the passion shifts. And then they accuse you of being stupid when it comes to honoring their promise."

I tried to absorb what Jack was saying with a

quiet stomach. But none of what he said was reassuring. And I knew, in my mind, that my relationship with Vassy was in big trouble.

Not too long after that Vassy and I were back in
California and on one of our walks. The sun was
hot. It was about one and a half years after we had
met. We had succeeded in adjusting reasonably well
to one another. We were deep in the throes of developing a picture which he would direct me in. He
had worked with several writers and found that
none of them had touched what he really wanted to
say in the picture.

He knew what he wanted. Such definitive certainty was commonplace and admired in really good
directors. After overhearing some of his creative sessions, though, I began to wonder whether Vassy
might not be erecting obstacle courses which weren't
necessary. Whenever I mentioned it, he again explained that only through the pain of the creative
process could wonderful art be born. It was a theory
he knew I didn't subscribe to. Whenever his anguish
in collaboration became severe, I knew he was either
getting close to what he wanted, or the relationship
with the writer would fall apart. Lately, the latter
seemed to be happening. He tossed and turned during the night and seemed to be stretching the possibility of success too thin. I almost had the feeling
that at the core there was a self-destruct mechanism
at work in him. But maybe not. Maybe it was just
his way of working.

The sun was hot on our faces as we climbed the
fire trail. I had smoked a lot the night before, but not
enough to interfere with my breathing. In fact, I
never inhaled anyway and told myself the smoke
never reached my lungs. But Vassy zeroed in on my
smoking as we walked. He walked faster and faster.
When I asked him to slow down, he said, "If you
would stop the cigarettes, perhaps you could keep
up." I felt a flash of irritation. Why was he ruining a
beautiful walk, focusing on something that was my

business to stop. We began to argue. The argument escalated until smoking became an irrelevant issue. In a swift fifteen minutes, we were discussing the defects of our relationship in detail, with Vassy entrenched in his point of view and I in mine. We both became so angry that again I felt like striking him. I controlled myself and said, "Let's call a moratorium for fifteen minutes, okay?"

He glanced at his watch. "Fifteen minutes?" he asked.

"Yes."

"Agreed."

We continued to walk in silence. After about five minutes, a particularly cogent point came to my mind, but I resisted the urge to make it, remembering our agreement. We walked on. I was proud of my control. Suddenly Vassy blurted out a stream of intelligent points of his own. I pointed to his watch. "The fifteen minutes is not up yet," I said.

"Fifteen minutes," he answered. "So what? I have something to say."

I stopped and glared at him. "But we made a deal," I reminded him strongly.

"A deal? What deal?" he asked.

I said slowly and very, very distinctly, "We made an agreement five minutes ago. An agreement *not* to continue our argument until *fifteen* minutes had passed."

Vassy actually chuckled. "You are stupid to believe that I considered that an agreement. You are naïve."

I saw red. I wound up my arm and with full preparation I hauled off and swung at him. I didn't connect. He blocked my arm and I missed. He laughed at me. I was thoroughly humiliated, outraged . . . all those familiar feelings that he was capable of provoking in me. I turned and bolted down the mountain.

"But Nif-Nif," he called after me, adding insult to outrage, "I love you."

I ran and ran down the mountain. He sauntered after me. I didn't know what I was thinking. It was dreadful. All my emotional horizons were blurred. I felt completely out of touch with my own positive instincts. For the second time, I felt danger.

When I reached the bottom of the mountain, I lurched toward our car. I could have turned the key, stepped on the accelerator, and left Vassy with no transportation home. But I didn't. I sat fuming and helpless until he arrived.

Casually Vassy climbed into the car and said, "Nif-Nif, why were you so upset?"

I wanted to slug him again.

"Why?" I pounded the steering wheel. "Dammit, we made an agreement not to argue and you violated it. But then you called me stupid for believing you. What the hell kind of shit-assed attitude do you think that is? Do you want me *not* to believe you?"

"You were stupid," he answered simply. "That's all. I needed to talk sooner. That's all."

"But so did I," I answered. "And I controlled it because of our agreement."

Vassy thought a moment. "I see," he said. "Well, there is no harm done. So let's forget about it. Look at this beautiful sunshine. Look at the bluebirds. Smell this sweet day."

I was flummoxed . . . paralyzed with helplessness at the reality of *his* truth—*his* point of view—*his* way of relating to life—and my inability to penetrate his reality in any way.

We drove home in silence. I knew I wasn't going to let it go.

I didn't know it until sometime later, but Vassy was as disturbed at my behavior on the mountain as I was at his. He wrote a long letter to his brother in Moscow relating the incident, asking what it was he had done wrong. When I asked him why he had solicited help from another Russian rather than an

American, he said it was because his brother knew him better.

I saw Jack again sometime later and told him what had happened.

"From Vassy's point of view," said Jack, "he meant what he said when he said it. But a Russian has a different concept of time than we do. That is the basic difference. The passion of the moment is just that—the passion of the moment. When the moment passes, life is a new ballgame. When he said you were naïve to believe him, he could just as easily have meant you still believed in Santa Claus. The Russian doesn't live past the moment. That's why they seem to us to be so passionately self-destructive. Who knows, maybe living in the moment is the most fulfilling way to live. Their expressive arts, after all, speak to the depths of the soul. So who knows?"

I thought about what Jack said for days after that. Were the differences between Vassy and me based predominantly on how we related to the immediacy of the moment? I had to admit that the intensity of our fun and joy together was a miracle of moments. He never held back or considered the consequences of the future. I did. His happy moments were total when they were happy. Mine were not. Was I in my American way living too much in the future? Was that, in fact, what "deals" were all about? Protecting the future? Vassy seemed to throw the future to the wind. It wasn't there until it was there. On the face of it, I wished I could do the same. And yet . . .

And yet I had the continual gnawing feeling that to Vassy the future meant probable *suffering*. It was then that I realized that the danger I felt from him was not really about the future, but more about *destiny*. His destiny.

He spoke often of destiny. It was a word that heretofore had smacked of melodrama to me. Yet somehow when *he* used it, it was emotionally viable.

He seemed to be feeling that his destiny had been preplanned. He had felt destined to be with me. He had felt destined to leave Russia and travel freely.

A few weeks later, I began to feel the communication between us break down on many levels. Work on the movie project was becoming discordant. Vassy and his co-writer couldn't come up with a satisfactory script. The more I encouraged him, the more depressed and dissatisfied he became. The more I made suggestions, the more he resented it. Our arguments became intense until one evening our relationship exploded.

We had been sullen and moody with each other for about three days. Even physical communication was breaking down as our emotional differences expressed themselves in dissatisfaction with each other sexually.

Two friends of ours (a couple we knew very well) were visiting and staying with us. They were Americans who lived in Paris. They were aware of some of our problems. I was scheduled to make a quick trip to New York, which I casually mentioned to Vassy. He seemed to accept it, but I noticed a dark hostility wipe quickly across his face. We went for a hike and he was uncommunicative. When we returned, he went into his office to write and I brooded about how I could break the mood. I fixed him his favorite tea and cakes and brought the tray in to him. I set the tray on the desk and leaned over and hugged him. He smiled involuntarily and then quickly wiped it away. A flash of dread shot through me.

"I must tell you, my dear," he began, "I have been to see a doctor about your problem."

My mouth dropped open. "What problem?" I asked.

"About your sexual problem."

"You saw a doctor about *me*?"

"Of course I didn't mention your name," said Vassy, "I just discussed your sexual problem."

I was stunned. "*What* sexual problem? So things are not as intense as they were. So what? And what do you mean, *my* problem? It takes two to tango."

Vassy got up and walked to the living room. Our friends were sitting there.

"Wait a minute," I said, running after him. "Let's talk about this. And let's talk about it in front of Judy and Jerry. We're close enough to them. They've been through their own sexual conflicts."

"Fine," said Vassy, sitting down on one of the stools by the kitchen counter.

"We have problems," Vassy announced, "but Sheerlee is stubborn with her indifference. So I have seen doctor to discuss it."

Judy and Jerry nodded, delicately acknowledging the sensitivity of the subject.

I could feel myself begin to boil. "Vassy," I said, "I don't really think this is about sex. Sex is hardly ever just about sex. Why didn't you discuss it with me? Why did you go to an outsider? I didn't even realize it was bothering you this much."

"Doctor would know better," he answered.

"A stranger, doctor or not, would know more about what I'm feeling than I would?"

"Correct."

"What do you mean, correct?" I said, hearing my voice rise.

"You don't listen to what I say. Doctor did," he answered.

"But the doctor only heard it from your point of view," I said, sitting down on the stool next to him to assert myself. "I resent it that you didn't discuss anything with me. Really I do."

"Doctor was informative," he said.

"What doctor was it?" I asked. "Someone you knew?"

"No," he answered. "I found name in telephone book. Doctor in Santa Monica."

"In the *tele*phone book??" I was incredulous. I just couldn't believe what he was saying. And yet I did, I suppose, because I felt invaded. "Wait a minute," I said, trying to control my voice, without success. "How the hell could you discuss what goes on between us with a perfect stranger? And without even mentioning it to me? I mean, if you were that bothered, why didn't you say so? Why not tell *me*?"

"I wanted to discuss with doctor."

I took a deep breath. "Well, it sounds to me like you're doing a control trip again. You've tried to control how I eat, how I hike, how I sing and dance and act, and now, by God, now you're into controlling what I do with my body in bed. The privacy of my sexuality means as much to me as yours does to you."

"No," said Vassy, "a man's relationship with his sex is more important than a woman's is to hers."

Suddenly I wasn't arguing anymore. I really saw red this time. In an outraged flash, I slapped Vassy across the face so hard and so fast that I connected completely. His glasses flew across the room. His face drained of color. He reached up to hit me, but the expression I saw on his face hit me first. It was steel-cold, controlled hatred. I gasped. His arm went down. Judy and Jerry bolted toward us. Judy grabbed my arms and Jerry grabbed Vassy's.

Vassy's implosive hostility made my blood run cold. It was what he *wasn't* expressing that chilled me. What was really going on inside of him? I wasn't sure I wanted to know.

Immediately I disengaged myself from my own emotional violence. I was shocked that I had finally succeeded in hitting him so unexpectedly but I was stunned at the expression of cruel finality on his face.

Vassy released himself from Jerry. His expression didn't soften.

Judy let my arms go.

"Jesus," I said, "I'm sorry, Vassy. I didn't mean to hit you so hard. But you had absolutely no right to invade my privacy by going to a doctor without consulting me."

Vassy crossed the room, leaned over, and picked up his glasses. He put them on.

"Is finished," he announced.

"What is finished?" I asked.

"Our relationship," he said, "is finished. I will now leave."

I laughed out loud. If I sounded slightly hysterical he certainly was being ludicrously melodramatic.

"Oh," I went on, "I see. Now you are going to just refuse to discuss the responsibility we each have for what just happened."

"Correct."

"Oh."

He straightened his back, put his hands on his hips, and walked to the refrigerator for vodka.

"You are violent," he said. "I find your violence too frightening."

"Yes," I said, "I was violent, and I'm sorry. But what about your violence to my feelings? What the hell would you *expect* a woman to do when you say *you* as a man are more important than a woman?"

"Never mind. Is finished," he answered.

I stood up. "What do you mean, finished? Are you serious?" I looked over at Judy and Jerry. Judy spoke up.

"Vassy," she said, "don't you think maybe you are afraid of your own violence? I saw the expression on your face. You could have killed Shirley. I think you were afraid you might."

Vassy shot a contemptuous look at Judy. "Is finished," he said. "I am leaving."

I no longer felt like laughing at his melodrama. I realized he might mean it.

"Wait a minute," I said. "You are really serious. What about our movie, what about working out our relationship, what about courage?"

For a long moment Vassy said nothing. Then, looking thoughtfully at his glasses, he said, "I know I will regret this for the rest of my life, but it is my destiny. I am leaving."

I felt helpless. His male infantilism I did not even *want* to cope with anymore and his addiction to suffering was beyond my empathy.

But Jerry and Judy went over to him.

"Vassy, try to express what you are feeling," said Jerry. "Before you make any rash decisions, please explore what's really going on inside of you."

Vassy walked toward the bedroom. "No," he said with conviction to himself. "Is my destiny." Vassy slowly disappeared down the hall. I followed.

Quietly Vassy packed his two pairs of corduroy trousers and his grandfather's dress shoes. Neatly he placed his six shirts and two sweaters into his suitcase. He gathered his mother's pictures, the icons of Christ beside his side of the bed, and his English-language tapes. He walked to the bathroom and boxed up his Water Pik and his Russian hair tonic. He stuffed his jogging shoes and hiking shorts into a plastic bag, and his toothbrush and electric shaver into his brown leather kit.

I looked around our room, paralyzed, watching him spirit himself away. He picked up his suitcase and threw his leather jacket over one shoulder. Then he glanced down at the ancient Russian Bible he had brought with him from Moscow.

"The Bible must stay here," he said. "My Bible will always belong to you. It belongs here in Malibu with you."

Tears of sorrow and futility filled my eyes. I knew he was really leaving. Had he planned all this, or was it happening spontaneously? He seemed unable to exercise any free will over what he considered to be his destiny.

I followed him to the front door. He leaned into the living room and said good-bye to Judy and Jerry.

I held the door open for him. There was nothing to say.

He began to descend the stairs in silence, then he turned around.

"Nif-Nif," he said, his husky plaintive voice cracking. "My sunshine, Nif-Nif. Life with you was like music. And now the music is over. I will come back for my books and records someday later."

I couldn't think of anything to say. Everything was so unreal. I thought of how life was a poor storyteller.

At the bottom of the stairs, he looked up again. "I was your Honeybear, and you were my Nif-Nif. But remember, you are also prancing horse. Horse from very good stable."

I waved him through the red lacquer gate and he pulled away in his broken-down car.

The next morning, I went to New York. Vassy called me there a few days later. He cried over the telephone and told me how lonely he was. I said I would be back in a few days and we would talk. But when I returned, he didn't want to. He had moved into the guest room of an old girlfriend. Within a week, he came down with pleurisy and lay brooding and depressed in his bed. He didn't want to see me. He didn't want to see anyone. I tried to cheer him up over the telephone, but it didn't have any effect.

Weeks later we had dinner. He was sweet, but formal. He said he wanted a woman who would be his slave, who would love everything he did regardless. He wanted "an artist's wife who would sit adoringly at my feet and tell me I am wonderful." I remembered Milanka's warning in Paris. I laughed. He laughed. He said he knew he was being simplistic, but that was the way he was. I said I understood.

But it wasn't Vassy I needed to understand. It was myself.

The breakup left me with a deep well of loneliness. It was clear to me that the love affair had had no promise of permanence. I had somehow always known that. Maybe he had too. Perhaps he had been more aware and courageous than I by acknowledging it first. Perhaps the loneliness came from the abruptness even in the face of inevitability.

For months afterward his "recklessness" and the loneliness it caused him also moved me to tears. I still felt almost tied to him and responsible for *his* pain. And what haunted me more than anything was the feeling that I hadn't really understood what I was supposed to have learned from it all. Yes, I had finally known a Russian individual intimately with all that that implied. But *personally* I felt unresolved as to why we had come together in the first place.

I understood that any love relationship between a man and a woman was a learning experience for *self*, but my feelings when we parted spoke to something deeper . . . something I couldn't put my finger on. I knew I should let my feelings of loneliness go, but I had never been able to walk away from feelings until I understood what caused them.

So, with these questions still in my mind, I began to realize that it didn't really matter whether I understood Vassy. I realized that I should just accept him for the truth that was his. He needed to lead his own life, at his own pace, in his own way. Perhaps *I* was not respecting *him*. Perhaps *I* was proof that love and respect were not coexistent. When I realized the impact of that thought, I moved out of my own confusion. I finally realized that I had only paid lip service to believing that love and respect were possible. It was now time for me to mean it. As a result, Vassy and I remained good friends and understood each other a great deal better after we parted than we did when we were together. We had more distance and the emotional involvement didn't blind us anymore. We both recognized the love which was still intact and we both continued to realize how many lifetimes had bound us together.

Though my relationship with Vassy ended nearly

four years ago, his Bible still remains on my table in Malibu where he left it. He continues to insist that my house is its real home. He has realized his dream to make American films, and I know we will work together. McPherson was right. We both feel the need to spiritualize art, and when the time comes, it will happen.

He is respected in Hollywood because he is a fine artist. No one cares about his politics. They *respect* him. Love him? Many do. For him, he still maintains that love and respect are not co-existent human emotions. Most of his scripts reflect that feeling. He still insists that real creativity is not possible without suffering; in fact, he still believes that conflict is inherent in man and is, in his truth, *necessary* to life. He still believes that without struggle one cannot recognize God. He still believes in his concept of evil, that it exists as a force outside of man. He also believes that *God* is outside of man.

Thus, more to the point, he believes that the destiny of man is to suffer. So much does he believe it that I think he feels compelled to create it.

But then, don't we all seem addicted to suffering in varying degrees? From guilt, because we feel we don't deserve to be happy, from resentment of childhood wrongs or deprivations (how *long* it takes to grow up), or from failures in adult life—whatever—we all feel the pull and tug of negativity and insist it comes from sources outside of ourselves.

Yet in fact, both negativity and positivity reside within each of us. No one of us is completely in light, or completely in the dark. And most of us create our own problems. For me, since understanding myself leads to a greater expression of my positive aspects, then the journey within is the only journey worth taking. If that journey within leads to the recognition and awareness of my higher, more positive self, then I will have no more soul-searing conflict. Recognizing the God within myself, I will recognize the larger God-source, the magnificent energy which unites us all. I believe *that* was our lesson for one another. Neither of us perceived ourselves as the other saw us. But we *did* see ourselves in the other.

Now when I reflect on the violence Vassy provoked in me, I bless him for it. He put me in touch with it so I could begin to resolve it. He provided me with the gift of understanding myself better. I hadn't needed to talk to *him*, I had needed to talk to myself. His problems and conflicts were his, mine were mine. In that brief, tempestuous period of time we spent together, I saw more clearly than I ever had how much more I needed to grow. *Because* it was difficult, I learned. *Because* he confused me, I reached more clarity. And *because* we both realized our relationship was predestined by our own free will, we tried. We were preordained to make our music together in order to hear the discord as well as the harmony.

Vassy remains just as "Russian." I remain just as "American." We know we can co-exist now, but we each have separate paths of experience to pursue. Perhaps he is right when he says that love and respect are incompatible—in *his* experience. However, I don't believe he is referring to people. I believe he is referring to the conflict with the God within himself.

I finished the account of my love affair with Vassy as Mom and Dad sat transfixed.

"So you see?" I said, "I guess all relationships happen so we can learn more about ourselves."

Daddy's pipe had gone out. And Mother's tea was cold.

"Well, Monkey," said Daddy, "you do get around, don't you?"

"Yep, I guess so."

"He certainly knew how to get your goat, didn't he?" said Mother as she shot a subtle glance at Dad.

"Yep, he certainly did," I agreed. "But now I've learned *I* was the problem. Not him. Whatever he did was just him—that's all. *I* was the only one I could improve, and he just afforded me the opportunity."

"And you really both felt you had known each other before?" she asked, searching my face.

"Yes, we really did and I'm sure one day I'll learn more about that too. But for now, *this* life is the only important one."

Mother looked over at Daddy as though expecting a remark to do with the two of them.

He complied with a smile. "Well," he said, "I reckon your mother and I have probably been around the track with each other a few times too."

"I would say so," I said. "Do you want to hear about one I already know about?"

Mother straightened up in her chair as though not certain she wanted to hear what I had to offer. Then she shrugged. Daddy nodded.

"Well," I began, "it was McPherson who told me. He doesn't usually reveal such information about other people, but he said it would be a good idea if I told you about this."

The two of them leaned toward me.

"You had a lifetime together in Greece. It might have been the same time period as Vassy and me. You were both very respected barristers. Each of you was male in that incarnation."

"Oh, Shirl," said Mother, "really?"

"Really."

"Well, go on anyway," she said.

"Well, Mother, you were a liberal barrister and, Daddy, you were a conservative barrister."

"So far so good," said Dad.

"There was a controversy about the building of a temple of Eros. Mother was for it and you were opposed."

"I expect so," said Dad.

"You two spent a great deal of time arguing over the temple. You were so disruptive and unyielding with one another that the townspeople became upset with both of you. *You* were the issue to them—not the building of the temple!"

Mother laughed. "I can believe that," she said. "It's impossible for your father to see my point of view."

"Anyway," I continued, "on one particularly argumentative day, the two of you, each believing you represented your respective constituencies, had been shrieking at each other for hours. The townspeople near the court of law became exasperated and proceeded to hoist you both onto their shoulders. You interpreted that to mean agreement. In reality, they were yelling for you both to shut up. The more the townspeople shouted, the more each of you thought they agreed with your opposing points of view. Whereupon they carried you both on the shoulders of the throng to the outskirts of town, where the temple in question was to be erected. The two of you believed the decision would be made there, but instead the upset crowd threw you both over the side of the cliff."

I waited for a reaction. They were too stunned to talk. Mother broke the moment.

"Sounds familiar to me," she said finally, throwing up her hands in agreement. "I have no problem with that."

"So McPherson said to tell you that you're still doing the same thing. And that this time around you're not going to finish with each other till you stop arguing."

Daddy saw his opening. "You mean that we have to stop arguing before we die?"

"Yes," I confirmed, "that's right."

"Well," he concluded, having found his response, "that seems like a good enough reason to keep arguing!"

I leaned over and pummeled him on the shoulder. "Daddy," I said, "be serious. You'll just have to come back and do it again if you don't get it right this time."

"It's sort of like show business, isn't it?" he joked. "You just keep doing it till you get it right."

"Okay," I said, "but where the two of you are concerned, you know there must be a lot of karmic debris for you to clean up with one another."

"Not as much debris as there is in my filthy room where the keys are," Daddy said, chuckling to himself.

"Oh, Ira," said Mother, "maybe she has a point."

"Hell, Scotch," he chided, "I'm no damn fool. I know damn good and well she has a point. I've always known that. The question is, what do we do about it—die to find out? I *like* to argue. It keeps me alive."

"Maybe you've got some Russian blood in you then," said Mother, triumphant at her stab at humor. "Maybe I shouldn't associate with you because you like to suffer." Her eyes sparkled at her rejoinder.

Daddy let her have that round.

I got up and walked about. "You know what really interests me?" I asked them

"What?" asked Mother.

"I'm interested in where *I* fit into the karma of the two of you. I mean, you've given me everything. What am I supposed to give you two now?"

Both of them became genuinely serious.

"You mean," said Mother, "that you believe you chose us as parents for some reason?"

"Yes."

"And that we chose you for a daughter?"

"Yes."

"Hmmm," she mused, "that would be interesting, wouldn't it?"

"I think it would," I said, feeling an idea form in my mind.

"How do you go about finding out something like that, Monkey?" asked Daddy.

I hesitated and teased him. "Oh," I said, my voice sounding superciliously soprano, "I have ways."

"I guess that will make another book, eh?" He

laughed, and crossed one leg over the other, delicately removing a piece of lint from his trousers.

"Do you guys like being in my books?" I asked.

"Hell," said Daddy, "how can you ignore us? If we weren't around you'd have to invent us."

"Well," I said, "I think you've invented yourselves."

"Yep," he continued, "I guess all the world's a stage and we're just players on it. But your mother here should play something besides Lady Macbeth."

Mother glared at him. I saw them both going over that cliff. "Ira," she said, "I'm not going to let you get my goat anymore. You go be as Russian as you want. You're not going to intimidate me anymore."

He laughed and coughed to himself. Nothing fazed him.

"Mother," I said, "you feel kind of powerless and helpless a lot of the time, don't you?"

"I certainly do. But I'm not going to let him make me feel that way anymore."

"Okay," I continued, "but maybe there's a reason for that."

"What do you mean?" she said with a twinge of demand in her voice.

"I mean, maybe you're feeling powerless this time around because you abused power in some other lifetime."

"Oh, Shirl," she said, "I wouldn't know what feeling power was like."

"What do you mean?" Dad chimed in. "You have the power in our house. You always have. You know that. You're the boss and you know it."

"Well, I should hope so," she immediately responded, happily contradicting herself. "Otherwise you'd make a darn fool out of yourself."

"Okay, you two," I said in an attempt to divert another skirmish, "you just keep on. I suppose it does give you energy. But if I happen to stumble across more about what all of us were doing together in past lifetimes, that should keep you arguing for another ten years."

"Well, Monkey," said Daddy finally, "the nice thing about all of this is there's a shit pot full of stuff none of us knows anything about for certain. All we really know is we don't know. But you go ahead." He hesitated a moment. Then he said, "Maybe you'll find out what you were doing with that ex-husband of yours too."

It was like a dull thud on the floor. I adjusted my back into place as I did whenever I felt challenged.

"Okay, Daddy. Maybe I will." I didn't feel he had gone too far. On the contrary. I was getting as deeply personal with them as a person could get. Why shouldn't he do the same with me?

"I'll tell you one thing," I said, "I'll bet you and Steve had some relationship together too. You disliked him the moment you met him and he felt the same way about you, and it never changed. I think you were just a father in search of an excuse to dislike the man your daughter was marrying. And anyway," I said sadly, "we had some good years between us. He's been a big support with this spiritual search of mine. He agrees with me on a lot of it. He has his problems, Daddy, but don't we all?"

"Okay," said Daddy, "we won't talk anymore about that sonofabitch. You have a beautiful daughter, so it was worth it."

"That's right, Ira," said Mother. "Let's drop it. Shirley has her own way of doing things. And Steve was one of them. It was something she had to do."

"That's right," I said flatly, not wanting to continue. I didn't want to discuss it anymore. The breakup of my marriage to Steve was something I didn't want to discuss with anyone. And hadn't. He had been an integral and important long-lasting part of my life. I needed to sort it out and it was taking some time. It was too complicated to make sense to anyone else, even my mom and dad.

"Well," said Mother diplomatically, "it certainly

has been wonderful seeing you. I hope Sachi had a good trip back to California. You tell her to let us know when she gets a good part."

Mother had a sensitive way of smoothing over other people's difficult moments. She was remarkable at easing tensions other than her own. She also had an impeccable sense of timing. Dominick was downstairs waiting to take them to the airport.

"Will you call Bird Brain and tell her we're on our way?" asked Daddy.

"Okay," I said, "but what should I call her?"

"Mrs. Randolf," said Daddy. " 'Bird Brain' is a 'term of endearment,' don'tcha know."

"We really love her," said Mother. "I don't know what we'd do without her."

"We'd get the eggs and the forks at the same time," said Daddy.

We adjourned from the living room and I helped them pack up their odds and ends.

I drove with them to the airport. As I watched them walk onto the plane with their canes and proud strides, I noticed that their very presence had drawn a crowd. It wasn't me the people were looking at. It was definitely *them*. They had that aura of silent command. It was clear. They were the stars of their own production.

As I walked back to the car, I was determined to investigate what we had all been to each other before we were born.

With my show now closed, I knew just where I could go to find out.

Part Three

The Dance Within

Chapter 14

New Mexico is called the land of enchantment. It's on all the license plates.

As I drove from Albuquerque to Santa Fe, I saw once again it wasn't a false claim. It was sundown when I arrived. The splendor of the chiseled mountains glimmered violet-orange in the last rays of the setting sun, their jagged teeth outlining the horizon, while shadowed foothills hugged the dry desert floor. Tufts of crackling sagebrush rolled over the highway. Windblown clouds splashed the evening sky like a multiprinted backdrop from Metro Goldwyn Mayer. I loved driving alone on the highways of the Southwest. The grandeur of open space made me feel anything was possible. And it was the only terrain I had ever seen where snow blanketed the scrub brush and trees grew out of stark dry desert. It had a purifying effect on me. It was triumphant in its statement, seeming to symbolize the harmony of survival.

I had been coming to Santa Fe for several years now. There was a very evolved spiritual community in residence here, drawn because of what the Indians termed "the high vibrational energy" of the place. Santa Fe means "holy faith." The Indians claimed the land was enchanted. They said the Great-Spirit blessed it and whoever lived there would be blessed too.

I drove through Santa Fe, where tourists had gathered for the annual arts festival. Chic, cozy restaurants were crammed with vacationers wearing turquoise and coral necklaces and soft Indian serapes and shawls. As I drove, the desert stars blanketed the night sky like tiny dots of crystal.

The house I had rented was on the outskirts of the north side of town. The manager of a hotel nearby had set it up for me—milk, bread, fruit, and coffee in the refrigerator. I was going to stay for ten days and what I intended to do would require all the peace and quiet I could find.

The Indians of New Mexico lived in harmony with the laws of nature. Therefore the Great Spirit was a part of their lives. The unseen, invisible God-truth was the basis of their reality. They weren't threatened by its power. They were in harmony with it.

The mountain peoples I had lived among in the Andes and the Himalayas were advanced and attuned to that same unseen reality because nothing interfered with their recognition of it. Their perceptions were keener. They seemed to be able to "see" with their hearts with more clarity. I felt that they sensed a higher dimension because they were unfettered by technology and twentieth-century pressures.

I had come to respect deeply the spiritual understanding of peoples whose greatest teacher was nature. Of course, I respected the intellectual prowess of modern man as well. But when I began to integrate *spiritual* recognition with my intellectual education, I felt like a complete person for the first time in my life. That "something" that had been missing was the awareness of my spiritual self. Yet how could I prove it? It was not to be measured by scientific means. I was barely able to describe it. It was transcendental, untranslatable into words. It was an integration one just had to experience to understand. And after experiencing it, life was never the same.

I hadn't come to Santa Fe as a tourist. I came to work with a woman who administered past-life recall treatments through the process of acupuncture. She had learned to work with Chinese techniques, using acupuncture needles which unblocked nerve channels to release past-life experience. Placing the needles at strategic meridian points, it was possible to accelerate incarnational information. Just as acupuncture needles could be used to physically block off connections which the brain might otherwise signal as pain, so they could be used to unblock connections, having the effect of opening channels of recall in the brain. According to traditional Chinese wisdom, the human body is imprinted with every incarnational event the soul has experienced. When the needles are placed around the third-eye area (the middle of the forehead) or the psychic meridian points (the right and left shoulders), or the galactic points (around the ears), the patient begins to experience scenes and memories and vignettes of lives they have lived in the past. The needles are very, very fine, producing almost no sensation when first piercing the skin. But as the patient lies relaxed and nonresistant on the table, the needles begin to have the effect of pentathal. It "feels" as though it is impossible to lie to yourself. Pictures begin to unfold in your mind's eye as the needles stimulate memory patterns locked in the cellular memory of the physical body.

Chris Griscom is a very experienced acupuncturist in psychic therapy. She has administered to hundreds of patients over the years with rather amazing results. At first, I had undergone the treatments just to see what would happen. I knew I had had many incarnations, which I had been told about by McPherson, Ramtha, and others of the channeled guides, but until I worked with Chris, I hadn't gotten in touch with anything I could say I had experienced myself. I had tried meditation, transcendental and otherwise, but nothing happened that I could be "sure" of.

Along the path of my spiritual search, I felt a longing more and more to understand *why* I had lived before and what I could learn in this present incarnation in relation to those past lives. For me, it was as Einstein said: "Knowledge is really nothing but experience." I wanted the experience. Since each of us *is what we are consciously aware of*, I wanted to become aware of more. I was intensely curious as to what raising my consciousness might reveal of my higher unlimited self.

So I had been working with Chris for some time. I had lain on her table with her needles delicately quivering from various areas of my body and allowed myself to let the imagery flow into my mind. It was difficult for me to accept at first. As the needles stimulated the cellular memories in my body, pictures of different time periods and events filtered into my consciousness. I thought that I must be "making the pictures up." I thought it was all my imagination until I stopped to reflect on what indeed imagination actually was. Each time a vignette of experience swam into view (the effect was similar to watching a film unfold in the mind's eye), I wondered where it came from. I knew the mind was capable of the most rococo creative fantasy. But then, what was fantasy? For quite a while I questioned the legitimacy of my imagery. Why was I picturing a desert, a caravan, a sixteenth-century monastery, a Peruvian Indian village, an African mother, and so on. I wasn't consciously aware of having created the images. They just happened. Yet I protested to Chris that I *was* creating the images in a free-associative way. She agreed. But she said I was creating the images because they had come out of my own experience. That *was* imagination. The acupuncture pressure points opened up the paths to the intuitive right-brain area (yin). The left brain (yang) must not be permitted to close those paths. And when I dispensed with the objections of my finite mind and got out of my own way, the pictures became more specific. They were rich in texture regarding clothing, body movement, sound, emotional attitudes; but, more than anything else, and increasingly, the images that came up were imbued with a conscious understanding on my part of why I was remembering them today.

As I said, Chris was experienced in past-life regression. She explained that the higher unlimited self always puts the earth-plane self in touch with those memories that are the most beneficial in clearing problems one is experiencing in the present incarnation. Since we have all experienced many, many incarnations (in many forms from the beginning of time) the unlimited higher self scans the blueprint of the soul's history and chooses the emotional experiences which relate to karmic trouble spots. Rarely are the recalled experiences pleasant because there would be no point in going over territory that has already been resolved. The purpose of living is to clear the soul's conflict. The purpose of getting in touch with past-life experience, then, is to isolate the areas of emotional discord so that the conflict in relation to today's incarnation can be understood. All of life is based on the *totality* of the soul experience. What we might feel as "evil" behavior only enables us, the "victim," to realize ourselves more fully. Thus the Buddhist theory of "bless your enemy, he enables you to grow" suddenly makes sense.

In the beginning, I found the sweeping benevolence of what I was learning unacceptable. I believed that there *was* evil behavior in the world. Examples were legion—in history, and around us in our lives every day. I felt that evil behavior needed to be resisted, fought against, defied, and stamped out. But as *I* proceeded to experience more and more of the "evil" visited upon me in the past, I found I wasn't reacting judgmentally to what had happened to me. I realized that instead it had been a learning process. A learning process that I had *chosen* to experience.

The learning process which is karma is not punitive. It simply follows the laws of science—for every effect there was a cause—so that in the human condition, karma translated as experience, *all* experience. Karma begets karma. *But every act of reconciliation, rather than retaliation, is a karmic step forward.* Positive karma begets positive karma. It is an ongoing process until we have ultimately been through the panoply of all human experience and recognize the total reality of our relationship to all there is.

Chapter 15

I settled into a routine in Santa Fe. My house was sunny and pleasant with many windows and an enclosed patio where I did my yoga in the open air. The house was decorated with Spanish furniture and Indian artifacts. Over the fireplace hung an *Ojo de Dios*, or Eye of God. It is a hanging decoration made from yarn and sticks. The center is the eye of God and is made in the shape of triangles which form a square around the circumference. It looks like a bird's-eye view of the Great Pyramid.

The Eye of God had been adopted by the four cultures of New Mexico—Indian, Mexican, Spanish, and Anglo—and hung in nearly every house. Some historians believe it dates back to Pharaonic Egypt, others believe it was brought from Peru. The Yacqui Indians of Mexico were thought to have introduced it to the American Southwest. In any case, all cultures used it now in a dominant spot in the home, symbolizing good fortune, good health, and long life as—the native Indians claim.

Each day I woke up to Ojo de Dios about eight o'clock, did my yoga and my mantras, had some breakfast (fruit, toast, and decaf coffee), and drove the forty-five-minute trek to Chris's home, which was located on a historic landmark in a small town called Galisteo.

The old Santa Fe Trail led into the modern freeway, which in turn led to a turnoff that I followed
into the flatlands of the sprawling New Mexican
desert. Indian pueblos dating back to A.D. 1250 dot-
ted the countryside, with cottonwood trees swaying
above them. Ristras (red peppers tied together) hung
in the sunlight from every available rafter.

The Sangre de Cristo Mountains loomed gently
in the morning light. The mountains, a part of the
Rocky Mountain Range, had been named by the
Spaniards. The blood of Christ, they were called,
because of the reddish cast on their snow-covered
peaks at sunset. The Rio Grande River flowed twenty
miles west from its source in Colorado to its ultimate
eighteen-hundred-mile-distant destination, the Gulf
of Mexico. I imagined the Pueblo, Navajo, and Hopi
Indians—whom archaeologists feel inhabited the areas
as long as six thousand years ago—roaming the surrounding plains. The Spanish explorers first came to
the area in 1558 (sixty-two years before the Pilgrims
landed at Plymouth Rock), and their influence was
predominant everywhere. Adobe structures, looking
like natural humps of clay, blended into the hills,
serving their inhabitants as cool protectors in the
summer and warm protectors in the winter.

The morning air was crisp and dry. And I was
moving eighty miles an hour on the ramrod-straight
open road before I realized it. Geological formations
in and around the mountains and mesas in the distance were not obscured by vegetation. Cloud formations splashed against the turquoise sky reminded
me of the jewelry I loved to wear whenever I was
here. "The sky-stone" the Indians called their gem-
stone, and they used its vibration against the skin to
be in harmony with nature.

Coming into the sleepy clay-baked community
of Galisteo, where about two hundred inhabitants
lived, I saw adobe (oven-dried brick) dwellings with
flat roofs right out of Biblical times. The town was
situated on a knoll in the valley with an extensive

view in all directions. The waters from the mountains converged into streams which were now dry in the heat of the summer. A horse and two stray dogs blocked the main thoroughfare—a dirt road winding past a store marked "Groceries." It had a creaking screen door.

Three small children waited for a dilapidated orange school bus. Mail to the community was delivered to rural P.O. boxes along the highway.

Carefully I maneuvered around the animals and followed the dirt road across a wooden bridge, gusting dry dust under my rear wheels. There were no street signs where dirt roads converged. One used landmarks and directional navigation.

I remembered that Chris's place was on the other side of the central community, veering to the left. Passing hollow metal shells that were once cars, and burros ambling lazily along side paths, I made my way to what I remembered was a wooden fence surrounding her house, set apart from the others in the community because of rangeland around it.

She was waiting for me, waving in the stark sunlight, surrounded by high untended shrubs and sagebrush. I recognized the chaparrals and cottonwood trees towering over her house. They had grown taller since my last visit. And Chris had grown too. In fact, she was eight and a half months pregnant.

With a happy waddle she met my car and we embraced. I patted her stomach and asked her if she had made contact with the soul inside. Indeed she had and it was a boy. Chris was of medium height, with dishwater-blond hair which framed her full, open face in soft waves. Her clear blue eyes literally shone from the depth of her being and gave you the feeling she could see through to the depth of yours. Better still, she assured you that you had nothing to hide. Her lips were plump and moist, which bothered her today because she said she had been exposed to the sun for too long while running the rapids the previous week! She spoke with a soft lilt. Her gentleness was powerful and commanding.

"Hello, my friend," she said. "It's been a long time and I've missed you. But I know how you've been doing."

Chris had no television and rarely read newspapers or magazines. She proceeded to outline, chapter and verse, my life in the past few months as though she had been living it along with me. One adjusts very quickly in spiritual circles to the truth that there are no secrets. Everyone involved with spiritual progress develops their psychic capacities. They plug into the spiritual energy and "see" whatever they wish to attune to. The more developed they become, the more they "see." They tune into the electromagnetic wavelength of another person and soon the process becomes similar to that of a radio.

Chris ushered me inside her home. Soon we were eating grapes at her long wooden dining-room table, bringing each other up to date with our lives on both the physical and spiritual planes.

She had been working with several groups of serious clients—patients from various parts of the U.S. who were making quantum leaps in their spiritual development. The more they understood their past-life complexities, the more clearly they functioned in their given endeavors today. The past-life information was not limited only to events and relationships either. It included teachings relating to the human mind, electromagnetic frequencies of accelerated thought, the transitional experience of moving into higher consciousness, and how the body made its adjustment to spiritual enlightenment. The body, being the temple for the soul, went through subtle physical changes as each stage of spiritual development was reached. It became more pliable, more flexible, and more sensitive to its environmental stimuli.

Chris and I talked of how psychic energy was experienced as electromagnetic frequencies moving

through the mind and body and how the consciousness of everything expands as a result. Moving
through our auric fields, psychic energy is perceived
by others, not so much as discernible light, but more
as a feeling of well-being which is communicated to
other human beings who may not realize what is
actually occurring.

"So many people," said Chris, "are moving so
swiftly into their understanding of these dimensions.
It has changed their lives and the lives of those
around them. Their lives are becoming more positive
in every way." She looked down at her bare feet.
"The world may seem to be in a polarized mess right
now, but there are new human beings ready to make
a breakthrough. The bell doesn't toll until the time is
ready. And the time is now. People are beginning to
understand that. Their spiritual understanding is so
much more powerful than their intellectual understanding. *That* is what will prevent us from blowing
ourselves up."

As we sat together, I was once again reminded
of my own pursuit. From the time I was small, my
curiosity motivated me to search for what I could
only define as the missing link. What was it that had
compelled me to travel so much for years and years,
uncovering whatever I didn't understand in each
foreign culture? Now I understood. I had been searching for a missing dimension in myself that I hadn't
yet touched. I hadn't realized that what I was looking for was in the backyard of my own spirit. I could
sit happily for days having a discussion such as the
one I was having now with Chris.

I explained that I was particularly interested in
pursuing previous lifetimes with my parents.

"Oh," she said, "that's very important. Our parents set the tone for how we'll ultimately relate to
the world. They know our trigger points intimately
and unless we can resolve those points with family
members, the same fate awaits us in adulthood."

"Well, Chris," I said, "don't our families cause

those conflicts in us just because of what goes on? I mean, I see so many reasons for my own insecurities in my parents. So what's the big deal in tracing down past-life stuff? Why do I want to do it so much?"

"Because," she said, "when you realize that you chose them in order to work through certain emotional problems yourself, you don't blame them anymore. When you learn not to blame your parents, you learn not to blame anyone else. Family life is the most intense of environments. Each member of the family is keenly intuitive about the behavior of the other. We feel victimized by the family because they start with us when we're infants. Sometimes we get stuck in the emotional behavior pattern of victimization. Then we choose mates that will perpetuate that addiction to victimization. If we'd just realize that the family choice is one each of us makes in an attempt to clear ourselves of the problem, we wouldn't extend it into our adult lives. But because we are not aware of our own responsibility in the matter, we abdicate the potential for growth."

"So," I said, "the household is the symbol of basic, fundamental emotional drama that we chose to work on?"

"Yes," said Chris, "and we use families to translate emotional symbols at an early age. For example, a child always relates more to the tone of voice than to the words themselves. The intuitive interplay hones his perceptions so that he can be more discerning in the world. If a child chose a domineering father, it's because he wants to work out a problem with domination. [Shades of my father.] If a child chooses a passive mother, perhaps the task is to allow the mother to experience what it is to be dominated. [Shades of my mother.] There are so many inner scenarios involved with each human soul. Only the soul knows why it has chosen its drama. And the more the soul understands, the less problems of confusion it will feel.

"You see," Chris went on, "if we taught our children that they chose us as parents, the child would learn early on to take more responsibility for his fate. That is why enlightenment is so crucial. We are not operating with enough knowledge in our society. This way the child either gives up because of the authority he experiences, or he becomes rebellious. But his soul intuitively knows that he can't legitimately blame the parent for his situation, whatever it might be. A damaged child *chose* to experience that. And if he can't resolve it, he carries it forth with him. He's stuck in victimization and is using it to perpetuate the pattern. A recognition of his own responsibility in the matter would unlock the pattern and he could let it go. But how can he do it if he isn't taught why he's there in the first place?"

"Very tough," I said. "Sometimes I look back and can't remember how I got into this myself. No one really taught me, although certain individuals set me on a path that helped me search out myself. And when what I learned 'felt' right, I knew I had it."

"Sure," said Chris, "you can't go on if you don't feel it. So how are your mother and father?"

I leaned back in her chair with the tragi-comedy of their relationship scampering through my head.

"They're so wonderful they're like a soap opera," I said, laughing. "They are so tied together at every level. I understand myself so much better by watching them interrelate. But sometimes it becomes too much. They must have some incredible karma going with each other."

Chris giggled, holding her stomach.

"Oh, yes," she said, "that's quite clear. The intensity of their commitment is spilling all over the place. I can feel it through you."

I reflected on how the process of karma worked. It wasn't chronological and linear. In other words, they might have spent a perfectly placid lifetime in association with each other while they worked out a more intense karma relating to someone else. It was clear, though, that this time around they were concentrated on each other. They were living a cocoon existence, completely wrapped up in each other, and had done so since I could remember.

"You know," I said to Chris, "sometimes I get the feeling that I've worked out most of my stuff with them except for witnessing what they do to each other. It gets me upset."

"Sure," said Chris, "your role this time is probably to point out what they've got to learn from each other, rather than how it relates to you."

Chris got up and led me outside. "Let's go do some work," she said.

We walked through a patio area in between her house and her clinic. A tricycle (her youngest daughter's) rested overturned on its side under an ancient maple tree. Two goats nuzzled each other in their stalls behind a fence and chickens clucked when they heard Chris coming.

Chris's clinic was behind a glass-enclosed greenhouse where she raised fruit trees and herbal plants. The clinic was one simple room built of stone. Inside the temperature was several degrees cooler than anywhere else. There was a bathroom with an old-style pull-chain flush toilet and a tiled Spanish sunken tub just adjacent to the clinic room.

A wide massage table covered with clean sheets and a blanket stood in the center of the room. There were two windows with rustling trees outside.

I dug out my tape recorder and batteries and tapes. Using an extension cord, I hung the recorder from a hook on the rafter above the table just over where my face would be, so that I could record every nuance of what would occur.

A small table by the door had alcohol, herbal medicines, and Chris's gold and silver acupuncture needles on top of it.

I undressed and climbed onto the table. I could hear birds chirping from the trees outside. Flies buzzed around the room from the open door. Chris stretched out her arms and directed the flies toward the open door. Whether it was the arms or the direction, they left. Gently she closed the door and instructed me to relax.

She pulled the needles from their alcohol container and brought them to the table and wiped them dry with clean gauze.

"My guides will help direct me with the needles today," she said. "They have a chronological plan of working with you during these sessions."

Chris had her spiritual guides just as I had mine. We both knew they worked together. Her guides were proficient in body meridians and energy points of the body. The primary guide was an ancient Chinese doctor who was always present when she worked.

As soon as I relaxed, I could feel the presence of the other entities in the room. Let me explain. When one works with the help of spiritual dimensional guides, it's necessary to tune in to their presence. We live and operate in what I would call the visible dimension of life, measured by height, width, breadth, mass, and time. I was learning to recognize the invisible dimension where there are no measurements possible. In fact, it is the dimension of no-height, no-width, no-breadth, and no-mass, and as a matter of further fact, no-time. It is the dimension of the spirit. It cannot be confined or defined and by many people it is not even recognized as reality. But I was learning that the invisible dimensions were, indeed, very real.

Chris went into a moment of meditation as she tuned into her guides. I felt a breath of cold air pass over my body, which always accompanies the presence of a spiritual guide in a room. I began to tune in to the presence of her guides too. I have not yet been able to "see" the energy of the invisible dimension, but she can. She sees their presence in light colors which have form. She also "sees" the auric

field of every human being. In other words, she is
what we have come to call a "sensitive." Her consciousness is specifically aware of energies which
most of the rest of us can only assume are there. For
example, I "feel" when Ramtha and McPherson are
around, but I can't *see* any evidence of it. I just
"know" it and go from there.

"Okay," she said, "I know what they want me
to do. This is going to be a kind of crash course
today. Your body is holding certain memories that
you need to release. I will place the needles at meridian points that will facilitate the release."

"You mean," I said, "that they can *see* the memory patterns my body is holding?"

"Sure," said Chris. "They see from the dimension of pure energy. Every cell in your body is holding the energy of experience, not only from this
lifetime, but every lifetime. We always have to keep
in mind that our concept of linear time is too limited.
Holographic time is the actual reality."

Chris put three very fine, thin gold needles into
the Third Eye point in the center of my forehead.
She gently twirled them to stimulate the utmost effect. There was some pain.

"I'm using the gold needles today because they
stimulate a higher frequency than the silver. You
have scar tissue in here," she said. "Your Third Eye
area is holding some traumatic pain. Never mind,
you'll get to it when you're ready."

I grunted, but was not too happy about the
prospect. I remembered what had happened when I
visited the Inca museum in Lima, Peru. I had walked
by a glass case that housed several skulls. Each skull
had a hole in the center of the forehead. As I gazed
at the skulls in horror, I had a strange memory of
what it was. The museum keeper had not even
needed to tell me that the Inca high priests had
chiseled holes in the center of the forehead to open
up the psychic energy of the Third Eye. The Third
Eye is an especially sensitized area for spiritual aware-

ness. Clairvoyant capacity, perceptive levels of discernment, the eye of God are supposed to center in the Third Eye. It is the eye that "sees" beyond the earth-plane dimension.

Again, Chris twirled the needles. The pain came again. "This is *dense* scar tissue," she said.

"Well," I said, "I had a small cancerous growth removed to the side of that area about twelve years ago. Could that have something to do with it?"

"No," she said, "it's something more. As a matter of fact, the growth probably came as a reaction to a memory the body was still holding in that area. The body remembers everything. The soul imprint is on every single cell in the body. We carry the memory into each incarnation and those memories need to be resolved and cleared if we are to go on to a higher enlightenment. Total acceptance of experience is what we're after. That's what we're all struggling for. When we totally accept experience without judgment, we are operating on a higher level of understanding and thus a higher frequency. The body, mind, and spirit are then in an aligned enlightenment."

"So what are these needles doing then?" I asked.

"They are stimulating the body to remember experiences so you can release the trauma. Each energy meridian point is stimulated when I twirl the needles. They then activate the cellular memory in the area. The Chinese were very advanced in this. They knew the body was a messenger system. The body is how we know we're here in this dimension— the dimension of mass, the dimension of experience. The body never lies. It tells us when we're sick, when we're anxious, when we're in pain. The body knows everything. We don't listen to it enough. The pain from the needles focuses on what the body remembers and needs to clear. Don't force anything though. Just let it happen."

Chris put more gold needles into my upper shoulders and behind my ears. She gently twirled them.

"Now breathe light into the needles. That helps ease the memory pain while stimulating the actual memory."

Breathe light into the needles? I visualized the location of each needle and projected light into them with my mind. I breathed deeply.

"Now relax," said Chris. "Let your mind go. Don't evaluate and don't let the left brain judge what you are thinking. Give your right brain more space. As a matter of fact, don't think. Just let the pictures come."

I breathed more light into the needles as she had instructed. Then I did some deeper breathing. The breath of life, as the Indians called it. *Prana* energy. I lay there wishing there were words in the English language which could more aptly describe the experience. We were so linear-minded, so proof-minded, so suspicious of our own soul power. How could I prove I had a soul? Why *should* I? It was a dumb expectation. The whole process of measurement and evaluation was an exercise in futility unconsciously designed to keep us in the muck and mire of our own limited thinking. Maybe we were addicted to helplessness because, intellectually, it was the only thing we could prove.

Thank God I was lying on this table with needles quivering from my forehead, my shoulders, and my ears, believing that I could get in touch with lives I had lived before so that I could clear up some confusions I had in this lifetime. Yet if, fifteen years ago, anyone had told me I would be into this, I would have thought they weren't playing with a full deck of cards.

Chris slid the sheet away from my torso and put two more needles into the center of my chest.

"Now breathe more light into these," she said.

She twirled them gently. There was no pain. I waited.

"If I don't have any pain there, does it mean I don't have anything to clear?" I asked.

"Well," she said, "perhaps you have cleared a great deal of it, or perhaps it's not relevant to what you're looking for now. The body carries memories from every incarnation you've ever experienced, but there are many of those memories that you haven't chosen to work on this time around."

"And my soul remembers everything and knows what I've chosen to work on now?"

"Right," she said. "To make it clearer, though, your higher, unlimited self is what knows and remembers everything. What we want to do is try to get in touch with that. That intuitive perception comes through the right brain. When you touch that, you are then working with your God self and will understand that you already know everything there is to know. Therefore, *you* are your own best teacher and your own guru, so to speak."

Chris replaced the sheet gently over the chest needles so I wouldn't get chilled. The cool wafts of air were coming more intensely around the table.

"All my guides are here now," she said. "So are yours. Let's turn on the recorder and begin."

"Okay," I said, "so I just lie here and relax?"

"That's right," she answered. "And *allow* the pictures in your mind to unfold."

That was not easy for me because I liked to be in control of my own creative process. I always analyzed why I was thinking something. It served as a clue to my subconscious. But what she was talking about was the superconscious.

"Where will the pictures come from?" I asked, interrupting the flow immediately.

"They will come from your own higher self, your higher consciousness, your unlimited soul— whatever you want to call it," she said. "All of your previous lifetimes of experience reside in your God self. *That* is what serves as your counselor, your guide, your teacher. You know what I'm talking about. Try to listen to it."

I lay back and closed my eyes. I could hear the

hum of the tape recorder dangling above my head. I heard a fly buzz against the screen of the open window. A dog barked in the distance. The branches of the trees creaked in the breeze outside.

I felt my mind begin to drift away from its own consciousness. I tried to relax it into blankness, for I had learned some time ago that you don't force anything when your goal is to be peaceful in your center.

Suddenly and with rapid speed, I realized I was seeing quick montages of pictures. It came so easily that I thought I was simply free associating. It didn't even occur to me to say anything aloud.

"What are you getting?" said Chris. "I know you're getting incarnational pictures because I'm getting them too."

She startled me. I thought I was just drifting around in my own brain, but she was saying it was significant.

"It's nothing," I said. "I'm just seeing lots of flashes of pictures. It's nothing. I'm just free associating. Let's wait until something happens."

"No," said Chris. "Wait a minute. Something *is* happening. Stop judging and evaluating what you're getting. Leave your mind out of this. Just get out of your intellectual way. Tell me what you're seeing."

"Well," I said, "it's sort of disjointed. Almost outrageously so. I don't know if I can talk as fast as I'm seeing the pictures. I feel like I'd rather just look at the pictures I'm making up."

"First of all," she said, "you may feel that you're making up what you see because that is the only way you have of explaining it. But you are making the pictures for yourself based on experience. Just trust that. Where do you think fantasy and imagination come from?"

"I don't know. Yes, I do. I understand what you're saying. I just can't believe I'm not making this stuff up. I mean, it's crazy."

"Tell me what you're seeing," she commanded

again. "It is *not* crazy. Your higher self is communicating to you. Listen to it."

Okay, I thought. I'll just express what's happening out loud and deal with it later. I was completely aware of my surroundings as I lay on the table. It wasn't at all like a hypnotic trance. Yet I felt I was the participant and observer at the same time. It was as though I were experiencing two levels of consciousness simultaneously.

This is what happened. I voiced all of it so I would have it recorded.

The pictures came in the front of my mind as though I were watching a film inside of my own head. They had texture, sometimes smell. There were experienced tactile sensations and definitely what I would call a recalled emotional reaction.

For example, I saw myself buried in sand up to my neck, feeling intense pressure on my body. I wasn't frightened. I was hot and unable to move my arms. Just as I asked myself what it meant, the picture shifted. I saw myself as a pirate with a peg leg, limping along a waterfront with a knapsack over my shoulder. I laughed at that image. I knew it was me, yet the image was that of a man. I remembered McPherson telling me that each of us had shared an incarnation as pirates. I wondered if that was it. And was I seeing that picture as a reminder that McPherson might be participating in this session as one of my guides? Up to that moment, I hadn't thought of him. Immediately the pirate image disappeared.

A tall, lean Egyptian-looking woman dressed in a purple and gold robe glided toward me. I couldn't see myself. I only saw the woman. It was my mother in this lifetime! She had a long aquiline nose and inky black hair. She was a queen of some kind, with subjects flanking her as she glided toward me. Then, as though I should associate the queen identity with those that followed, I saw an African native woman sobbing with an infant in her arms. The baby was hungry, but the mother, who was nude from the waist up, had no milk to feed the child. Her breasts hung limp and dry. Again, it was my mother. But I wasn't the infant. As I was attempting to zero in on who I might have been the picture changed again. A Roman or Greek athlete was running in the sun—a tall and powerful blond man—running as though in a race with his head held high and free in an exalted state of physical power. The athlete was also my mother! Suddenly I realized I was getting a rundown on some of my mother's incarnations. They were necessary for me to see for some reason.

Another image . . . high priestess of some kind with an archery set on her shoulder. Her robe was orange and fell from the other shoulder. Again—my mother. So she had had several incarnations of power, if I was properly integrating what I was seeing.

The picture shifted again. The montage of images was coming faster now. I felt the cool wafts of spiritual energy intensify around the table I lay on.

I saw a crystal pyramid off the east coast of what is now the United States, only it was on land. It gleamed in the sun, but there was much more moisture in the air than there is now. The drops of moisture glistened in the atmosphere around the pyramid like a shimmering curtain. I could see the air because of the particles of moisture. I couldn't see me, but I could feel myself breathe in the moist air which served to filter my system with each breath. Could I have been seeing the authentic atmosphere of Atlantis before it sank? Again, I felt ridiculous with my speculation. I was comfortable with believing that Atlantis had existed intellectually, but to pictorially confront what it might have been like to be there in personal terms was difficult, even for me, to accept. Again, the doubt changed the picture in my mind's eye.

Dark clouds and lightning clashed over the pyramid. The sound was deafening in my head. Somewhere in here I stopped talking and the needles behind my ears began to ache.

"What are you getting?" asked Chris. "Are you getting bad weather? That's what I'm seeing."

I opened my eyes. She was *seeing* the same pictures I was?

"Don't let it go," commanded Chris. "This is important. They're telling me it has to do with abuse of power in that lifetime. Keep the image going. Trace it down."

I shut my eyes again. The crashing storm persisted. Why was I seeing this?

"Ask your higher self why it's showing you this image," commanded Chris.

I did. Instantaneously I got back: "Because you had mastered the knowledge of weather control in this particular incarnation, but abused your power, you were insensitive to the consequences of your manipulation." The words came in English but it was the thought behind the words that I felt more deeply. I had *mastered the knowledge of weather control*?

My conscious mind raced to my appreciation of wild and stormy weather conditions today. To be in the center of crashing lightning, rolling thunder, and pelting rain gave me as much pleasure as anything I could think of. Could this feeling be related to a former existence?

The storm image disappeared and in its place were various kinds of craft floating in the air above a desert. They were shaped like huge flower petals with windows and seemed to be the mode of transportation for people who lived on earth. They weren't necessarily extraterrestrial, but I couldn't be sure. They made no sound and had no fuel. They were propelled along electromagnetic ley lines like invisible highways of energy in the sky.

I think it was at this point that I made the decision that even I wasn't "imaginative" enough to make up what I was seeing. Somehow I was seeing reality although it was no reality I had ever consciously experienced before. I let go completely and just allowed my higher self free expression.

The next set of pictures peeled off like a sliding set of stills across a huge projector screen.

I saw myself hanging from my little finger. I felt pain in the same finger. I saw myself as a nun with black scuffed shoes (my perspective focused on the shoes). I saw a particularly horrible image of myself with a hatchet embedded across my left eye. As I lay on the table, my left eye seared with pain. But as soon as the image changed, the pain left. I could hardly voice the pictures in rhythm fast enough to keep up with the images.

"Just do what you can," said Chris. "They just want you to see incarnational experiences that relate to what you can learn now."

"But," I protested, "who are *they*?"

"Your guides, as well as your own higher, unlimited God self," said Chris gently.

"Okay," I said in frustration, "but how can I be seeing these things and still consciously carry on a conversation?"

"Because," she said, "you are operating on two levels of consciousness at the same time and you are going to have to learn to do that for the rest of your life if you are serious about communicating what you learn. You soon will be able to channel your higher self at all times and use it in this earth-plane reality. Both are real. You will just have more dimension to your existence when you integrate the two. And this is something like what it will feel like."

More pictures were coming now.

I saw crystal doors standing in sand—again the desert. The doors were standing like solid portals but nothing grew around them. There was no vegetation. Only stark desert. It disturbed me for some reason. Because there was no life.

Then I saw a flashback in time which I knew was prior to the desert picture. Somehow I knew they were related. The flashback picture had lush, opulent green gardens with pink and turquoise water fountains. Gracefully lean people moved and walked along crystal walkways. They didn't talk. They communicated telepathically. Animals and birds, similar to those we have now, scampered along the crystal walkways in and among the people. They seemed to be in tune with one another. I could feel the people playfully command the animals to do something telepathically, and the animals responded immediately. I saw one of the people walk to a tree, pick a piece of fruit, and materialize another in its place. There were buildings made of something white. I couldn't tell what the material was. The clothing was a crystal fabric of some kind and the same fabric was used as hair decoration.

"I'm seeing some kind of extraordinary civilization," I said to Chris. "I see crystal and lots of orange and pink hues like rainbows in the air. What is it?"

"Ask your higher self," answered Chris. "Whenever you have a question, address it to your God self."

Okay, I would. In my mind I asked my higher self what I was seeing. The answer came in English as though spoken from within my own mind.

"You are seeing the civilization of Atlantis," it said. "Very advanced it was."

"Why does everything seem to be crystal? Why are the people wearing crystal headdresses?"

"Because," it answered, "crystal worn on the body amplifies the higher consciousness, particularly if worn about the head area."

I continued to observe in my mind's eye the longest and most detailed picture I had experienced.

I guessed it was because I didn't question it. And somehow I knew it was related to the stark picture of the dry lifeless desert previously seen. I asked my higher self what the relationship was.

"You were seeing what happened to Atlantis after its destruction. You were also seeing an aspect of the future in your present incarnation," it said.

My heart felt as though it had stopped. I silently directed my next question to my higher self in my mind. "You mean, we are going to blow ourselves up and I was seeing the result?"

My higher self didn't really answer. It said, "We will show you in more detail later."

Immediately, the picture changed again. I was on a battlefield. I couldn't make out where or when. I had a sword and some metal material around my shoulders. There was another warrior advancing toward me. The warrior stabbed me in the stomach. As I fell forward, the picture changed completely to another time period. I walked up to another warrior and stabbed him in the back. Both times the warrior was my mother!

Then I saw myself as a ten-year-old child who had been run over by a horse-drawn cart. The cart had rolled over my feet, crushing them. The feet had had to be amputated. I had learned to navigate quite easily with the stumps. I was not unhappy about my fate. I was playing in a meadow and as I looked closer, I recognized the person who was taking care of me was my father today. He had accidentally run over me and felt it his duty to devote the rest of his life to my upbringing. I felt a warm glow as I re-called this picture.

The scene changed again. I was in a monastery. I was a young Buddhist monk wearing a saffron-colored robe. An older monk came to me to say good night as I lay on the stone floor of my religious cell. As I looked up into his face, he made the sign of the cross over my face and smiled. The older monk was Vassy!

In my conscious mind, I remembered how Vassy always made the sign of the cross over my face whenever we left each other.

By now, I was feeling emotionally exhausted. I was having difficulty assimilating all that I saw. I guess I needed more time to process the experience.

"I believe we've done enough today," said Chris.

"Ask your higher self if there is anything else you should know."

I directed the question again.

"Yes," said my higher self, "you must be careful of your diet during this time period."

I didn't know what that meant. I asked for specifics, but I was beginning to feel uncomfortable on the table. I couldn't concentrate. My lower back hurt and I needed to stretch my legs. I couldn't get any more answers. It was as though I were out of touch. I felt as though I were blocking.

"All right," said Chris, "they say that's enough for today."

She put down her paper and pencil and leaned over me. Lightly, but with sharp movements, she extracted the needles from the meridian points. The Third Eye needle had already popped out.

"You certainly are rejecting the Third Eye area," said Chris. "I wonder what that's all about."

"I don't know," I said, rather confused.

"Well, we'll see."

I got up from the table and slowly stretched my muscles. I felt half in and half out of this world, but still conscious of both levels of reality.

"It's imperative," said Chris, "that you take an apple cider vinegar bath tonight. Natural apple vinegar helps the body clear the negative energy from some of the events you recalled."

"Okay," I said. "Can I have a drink when I get home?"

Chris stopped to think. "Well, if you feel you must, it's probably all right, because it will help you get out of the way of your left-brain intellectual perceptions, but alcohol slows down the vibration of the body and it will make it more difficult for you to get in touch with those higher frequency dimensions. Be sensible about it. You know what you're here for, so listen to yourself."

I dressed and we went back to her house, where her five-year-old daughter waited to be fed.

I sat at her long wooden table drinking apple juice, eating grapes, and reflecting on what had happened. I had so many questions, yet I knew my skepticism wasn't productive. There really was a difference between what I had just experienced and free association. This experience definitely felt structured. I also had come up with images which genuinely shocked me. In free association with psychotherapy, the thoughts were random and always related to experiences of familiar territory that had been part of my life in this lifetime. Yet the gnawing doubt that I might have been making it up persisted.

"Go take your vinegar bath," said Chris. "Don't ponder too much. Relax in the tub for at least twenty minutes. Go to bed early tonight and we'll continue tomorrow."

I climbed into my car and drove back to Santa Fe with the incarnational images tumbling over and over in my mind.

I stopped at the market for the apple-cider vinegar and went home straight to the bathtub. The body has an affinity for higher octave frequencies, Chris had said. Be careful how you treat it. As the body clears out the trauma of the physical memory, the residue spins off. Cleanse it. Let it go. I looked down at my legs and feet as I sat in the bathtub. Those legs and feet had a memory of their own? Each cell in the body had a memory imprinted by the soul itself? If so, it could be that each of us had carried an emotional blueprint through incarnation after incarnation and the blueprint was what manifested in body and face. So when we thought we *knew* someone upon first meeting them, we were actually recognizing the soul as it shone through the face, with each incarnational experience being part of the development of soul *and* body.

As I lay in the tub thinking, I wondered how long it would be before scientists would find ways to verify the evolution of the soul in the same way that they had verified the evolution of the body.

I thought of all the books I had read—and tried to understand—on quantum physics . . . the new physics, they called it. It sounded very much like ancient Eastern mysticism.

A few quantum physicists were saying that it looked as though subatomic particles actually possessed a consciousness. With photons, for example, they observed a "reality" whereby activity seemed to be occurring on as many as twelve different dimensions. We were used to defining reality in terms of what our senses told us, that is, our conscious experience, plus measuring in terms of height, width, depth, and abstract dimensions like linear time—but Einstein had already taught us that time in fact *has* no dimension.

Therefore all serious attempts to describe "reality" are forced to speculate on the metaphysical (*beyond* the physical). That could mean then that our perceived physical world is not the only reality, or perhaps not the *whole* reality.

Quantum physics was saying that what we perceive to be physical reality was actually our cognitive construction of it. Hence reality was only what each of us decided it was.

Ancient Hindu wisdom claimed the same thing, that each individual was recognized as being the center of its own universe—which is not arrogant when it is understood that each individual is a manifestation of God and therefore personally involved with Divine Energy.

The new physicists were saying that the key to understanding the universe was in understanding ourselves, for we alter the objects we observe simply by observing. We are then not observers but participants.

Werner Heisenberg, winner of the Nobel Prize for physics, shook the scientific world by saying that "at the sub-atomic level there is no such thing as the

exact science." Such was the power of our consciousness that we couldn't observe anything at that level
without changing it. "What we observe," he said,
"is not nature itself, but nature exposed to our method
of questioning. Therefore, quantum physics leads us
to the only place there is to go—ourselves."

Einstein said that past and present and future
time were all the same because they converged in
our consciousness *now*. Time existed in toto.

I looked over at the wooden chair beside the
bathtub. Science said that something is organic if it
has the ability to process information and to act
accordingly. The wood was made up of cells which
were made up of atoms which were made up of
protons, electrons, and neutrons, which were made
up of subatomic particles, one of which was photons. *And photons were vibrational energy which had
consciousness*. It was the "consciousness" of the pho-
ton which interacted with the consciousness of the
scientific observer. The dancers and the dancing were
one.

I remembered reading that when Werner Heisenberg asked his professor and friend Niels Bohr
how we could ever understand the makeup of the
atom if we didn't have the language for it, Bohr
replied, "First, we have to learn what the word
'understand' really means."

When the Buddhist masters implored their students to describe the sound of one hand clapping,
they were really inspiring their students to get more
in touch with their own thought processes where
linear dimensions were concerned. Eastern systems
of thought had always understood the limitations of
linear dimension.

Maybe what I was experiencing with multidimensional consciousness was part of the quantum
physics reality. My body was made up of subatomic
particles and each one of them possessed a consciousness. When the subatomic consciousness was
stimulated, I saw their translation into images.

Yogis who had learned to raise their consciousness could see their past-life incarnations as well as incarnations of other human beings. They saw their reality in light vibrational frequencies—which was exactly what the new science said photons were.

Quantum physics said that all particles exist as different combinations of other particles. That the cause and effect of that interaction created force. Could that process also be termed the karma of subatomic interaction?

According to Mahayana Buddhism, the appearance of reality was based upon the interdependence of all things. The ancient Indian vedas claimed the same truth.

The old physics taught us that we were essentially unrelated to events in the physical world of atomic and subatomic structure; that they interrelated regardless of our existence as human beings.

The new physics was teaching us that we were inextricably involved. That not only were we involved, but that such atomic structure might exist *because* of our consciousness.

As John and McPherson and Ramtha and the Eastern mystics had said, "Nature follows mind."

No wonder we human beings felt so isolated from the physical reality of our environment and science. No one much was helping us realize that not only were we part of it, but we were responsible for its existence.

I lay in the water thinking about enlightenment and what it meant. Wasn't it the process of removing veils of ignorance and judgment and preconditioned prejudice from our concepts? Wasn't it the attempt to understand personal truth so we could reach a higher level of consciousness?

Was physics about the same process? It would seem so, particularly if the physical world came down to a question of the consciousness of the atom! At the very least, spiritualism and mysticism were concepts to be taken seriously by explorers in the "physical" world. Broadly speaking, the two paths were converging toward the same truth—the truth of expanded consciousness and hence, finally, to the realization of the God-force.

Enlightenment was a state of being. Subatomic structures were also a state of being. This did not make the two states of being one and the same, but it surely created some sense of identity between the two.

I remembered Niels Bohr saying, "Those who are not shocked when they first come across quantum physics cannot possibly have understood it."

So, to be open-minded was the first step toward enlightenment.

The wind began to blow outside the bathroom window. I knew the wind was there, but I had never seen it. How would I describe the wind except to define the effect it had on something else? No one has ever seen atoms either. But we know they are there, interacting with cause and effect.

The great thinker and scientist Giordano Bruno, to whom Sir Isaac Newton paid so much respect, was burned at the stake as a heretic because he envisaged multitudinous solar systems, saw parallel planets such as ours, envisaged life on other worlds, and publicly stated what he believed.

René Descartes saw visions which left him helpless to continue to relate to linear dimensions as he had before. His conclusions were reduced to: "I think, therefore I am."

Aristotle believed that the mind, spirit, and soul were more important than the "physical" world.

As I lay in the now tepid water, I wondered if the mind could be located in parts of the body other than the head. Under the needles, I almost felt that my legs and arms and torso could think. What did that mean? As a dancer I sometimes felt that my *body* was remembering a long forgotten combination of steps.

Wilder Penfield, famous neurosurgeon and brain researcher, claimed, after exhaustive research, that, in his opinion, the mind was not lodged in the brain. The mind had no specific centered location within the body. The mind appeared to be everywhere—in muscles, tissues, cells, bones, organs. There seemed to be no separation between the one mind and other consciousness within the body. It all operated psychically.

Was this why it was possible to stimulate cellular mind memory and come up with a past-life experience?

Did we perhaps have several levels of subconscious perception going on at the same time? When the needles stimulated the subatomic structure of the cells, were they then stimulating an interior memory of cause and effect? If subconscious experience, which admittedly controlled a great deal of exterior behavior, also included karmic cellular memory, could we then consider that that "interior" karma governed a great deal of our exterior karma? It seemed a logical possibility and led to the concept that the new age of consciousness-raising was really all about becoming more aware of the interior truths in our subatomic structure.

Maybe this was the realized state of being in the achievements of Jesus Christ, and Buddha, and the Indian avatars and yogis of today. The avatars claim to have raised their electromagnetic frequencies in order to resonate to a higher level of awareness. That was why they could see "reality" beyond the accepted linear dimensions. The Indian masters claim that when they reach that state of being, they cease to feel the need to manipulate others or even to recognize negativity. There is no conflict in them, interior or exterior. They are one with themselves and the perfection of the universal God energy and hence can control individual energies.

I remembered the lama-priests I had seen in Bhutan. In icy, subzero weather they came to a frozen lake, submerged themselves in a hole cut into the ice, and meditated until the ice around them melted and steam rose from their bodies. They explained that they had simply raised their vibrational frequencies. Were they accelerating the electromagnetic energy of subatomic particles in their bodies?

They claimed the faster they accelerated their frequencies, the closer they approached the Divine God-force which they described as a white light so bright we couldn't see it. They said that an individual's electromagnetic frequency can alter the state of physical reality and that the human mind could alter the "fixed" reality of fire burning and ice freezing by changing its attitude toward that fixed reality. The important point, they said, was that there were *no* fixed laws where consciousness was concerned. That we could use our power of consciousness energy to manifest positive or negative reality for ourselves. It was all up to each individual. *We* were responsible for our reality.

Carl Jung spoke about "primordial images" and "archaic remnants which were without known origin."

He said that one day we would understand where they come from instead of being astonished and bewildered when they present themselves to our consciousness. "When we do understand," he said, "we might be able to control and use this information coming from the past, at will, since it is all part of our memory pattern."

J. Robert Oppenheimer said that the general notions about human understanding which are illustrated by discoveries in atomic physics were not wholly unfamiliar. They had a history not only in Buddhist and Hindu thought, but also in our own culture. "What we are finding," he said, "is a refinement of old wisdom." I had always wondered why Oppenheimer quoted a Hindu Sanskrit text at the moment he witnessed the first atomic blast at White Sands.

When I first encountered the concept of what

mystics called the Akashic Records, I had no idea what it meant. I read, and was told by my guides, that all experience and thought was "stored" in this etheric energy. I had understood intuitively, but not intellectually. I knew *Akasha* meant ether, but how could ether store anything?

Then I read Sir John Woodroffe's *Mahamaya: The World as Power, Power as Consciousness*. In it he defines Akasha as the ultimate substance having vibratory movement that acts as the medium for the transmission of light. Akasha was one of the gross forces into which the primordial power (Prakrti-Sakti) differentiated itself. Matter was vibrations within the Akasha. Matter was electrical charges of light trapped in the fabric of space-time.

Jack Sarfatti, the physicist director of the Physics-Consciousness Research Group at Esalen Institute in Northern California states also that matter is nothing but gravitationally trapped light.

The new physics says that electrical charges of light are what cause thought pictures. Could it be that what I was seeing under the needles were remnants of electrical charges left over from ages long ago? Was this what Jung meant by archaic remnants and primordial images out of an unknown past?

I knew I was probably being simplistic in my assumptions, particularly where physics was concerned. But I hadn't been the only one "feeling" the connection of physics and mysticism.

Of one thing I was certain, both mentally and intuitively. The path to understanding the reality of the world without was to understand the "reality" of the world within.

Chapter 16

I had a dense headache when I woke up in the morning. I knew I had "dreamt" "archaic remnants and primordial images," but I couldn't remember any of them. I took a warm shower, did my mantras, and went to the sunlit patio to do my yoga. The blood flushing through the yoga postures would clear the headache.

I was now relating even to yoga differently. I had always done it because it simply made me feel wonderful—a kind of steady vibrating well-being was the effect. It gave me energy and a sense of peace, emanating, it seemed, from the blood along my spinal column.

The yogic tantra tradition maintained that there was unlimited energy locked in the central nervous system located along the spinal column of the human body. If it is released, it flows up and down the spine. Along the way it passes through the seven centers of energy (chakkras) that govern various functions of the body. The chakkras, they say, are the knots of centered energy by which the soul is connected to the body.

With yoga and proper meditational techniques, the energy at the base of the spine (*kundalini* energy) can be aroused until it moves up through each chakkra dissolving the knots binding the soul until it reaches the brain and a feeling of the liberation of the soul is achieved.

In the average person, those seven chakkra energy centers are closed or "unawakened," allowing only the barest amount of vibrational current necessary for functioning. The person is walled into himself and sees the outside world from a closed and limited perspective. When the chakkra centers are opened, he sees with a more unlimited vision.

When the seven chakkras are open, you feel an extraordinary sense of elation. You feel that you radiate from within and are capable of manifesting anything you desire in your life.

I concentrated more than usual on the yoga today because I sensed something extraordinary was going to happen under the influence of the needle stimulation and I wanted to be as balanced as possible if that were true.

I had some fruit and toast while I sat in the yard. The sun burned warmly on my skin, the southwestern breeze cooling the perspiration. I heard the telephone ring inside. I didn't answer it. I didn't want to talk to anyone. I wanted to just be, not aware of time or schedules or obligations. Soon I got in the car and drove back to Chris's place. The scenery of mountains and mesas was a painting.

When I arrived, Chris asked if I had had any dreams. I nodded, but confessed I couldn't remember them.

"Try to write them down," she said, "as soon as you are consciously aware that you've had one. They are extremely important. You are continually learning in the sleep state. Your higher self is teaching and guiding you. That is why sleep is important. You are in touch with the spiritual plane when you sleep. And the spiritual plane contact is essential to all life. The soul needs the contact."

I remembered reading about an experiment conducted over a period of time on several people, who volunteered to be prevented from dreaming by being woken up every time dreaming started, for as long as two weeks, in order that doctors and psychiatrists could study the effects of dream deprivation. There was no damage to the physical body, but the subjects, in varying degrees, became extremely agitated, hostile, and heavily hallucinated. The doctors concluded from the experiment that the subconscious mind needed to express itself during the sleep state. If not, the mind went into a state of confused hysteria. Perhaps what was actually happening was the result of the soul's alienation from its natural habitat, the spiritual plane, the connection which could only occur while sleeping unless the individual was using meditational techniques to achieve the same result. Perhaps the spiritual plane, which we tuned into while sleeping, was as common a plane of reality to each of us as the earth plane.

Only the brain-wave activities were measurable during the sleep state. There was, as yet, no way to measure the activity of the soul, simply because it was energy that functioned on an invisible and undetectable dimension, something like the subatomic particles I was learning about.

Chris and I walked across the yard to her clinic. I wondered what was in store for me today. I wondered if in fact my consciousness would be creating another "reality" I would see. Not in the sense of making it up, but more because, as physics and mysticism claimed, consciousness was the forerunner of everything. At least I was learning to let my mind go. Learning not to obstruct the flow. I knew what I had seen was real to me. What I was beginning to sense was that I was seeing what my consciousness had created in the past. I wasn't "seeing" what I was creating *now.* I was, perhaps, seeing what I had in fact created *then.*

I lay on the table while Chris went into her meditation, tuning in to her guides. The cool wafts of air passed over and around my body again. Soon she brought the needles to the table and proceeded to insert them.

"They say we're going to use some new points today," she said, "as well as the points from yesterday."

She inserted the needles into the Third Eye (again the resistance), the shoulder points, the ear points, and the chest points. Along with that, she inserted a needle in my stomach, just below the navel.

"This meridian point is the center that helps separate the pure from the impure," said Chris. "The Chinese say that it is directly related to the colon on the physical plane because it connects with the elimination of impure body waste. But on a psychic level, it connects to the separation of pure energy from impure energy. It looks as though we're going to do some really important work today."

She twirled the needle. There was no pain. She stopped a moment and meditated.

"Yes," she said, "they're also telling me to insert one under the chin just above the throat. That is the communication center, the place where you express yourself. It is what the ancient Chinese called 'the point that controls crowds.'"

When she inserted the throat needle, there was resistance again. The needle wouldn't go in.

"That's interesting," she said. "You need to clear a lot here."

Again she tried.

"It's not going in very far," she said, "but it will do."

She twirled it lightly. There was a dull ache. "Now," she said, "breathe light into this needle. It's apparently very important that we use this point today."

I breathed in white light. I visualized it pouring in through the needle.

Suddenly there was a dense ringing in my right ear. Chris turned on the tape recorder above my head. She twirled the needle in the colon area again.

A dull ache happened there too. My ears stopped up. I couldn't hear anything in the room. Then there was a dense ringing in my left ear accompanied by a tingling in the feet like a sting of electricity.

A stricture tightened up my throat. What was going on? I told Chris what was happening.

"Yes," she said, "I see your aura changing color. Your auric field is lighting up even brighter than it was."

I lay back and breathed very deeply. I inhaled for about fifteen seconds and exhaled for fifteen seconds. I continued the deep breathing for about three minutes. Then I heard (inside my head): "Breathe in the color pink."

I visualized a deep, bright pink and drew it into my breath. I continued to breathe.

"Your auric field is vibrating the color pink," said Chris.

"Yes," I said, "I know. Something told me to breathe in pink."

"Okay," said Chris. "Keep going. This might be very exciting."

I hardly heard what she said because I felt myself make contact with what I can only describe as some other energy. It felt very familiar but new. Then I *saw* the energy. It was an exquisite coppery color.

"Your auric field is changing color again," said Chris. "It's a rusty copper color. Quite beautiful. What do you see?"

It was an effort for me to talk now because what I was experiencing took all of my concentration.

"Remember to try to relate to both levels of consciousness," she said. "Express what you're feeling so you can straddle the two levels of awareness. Just relax and allow whatever will happen to happen."

I breathed deeply into the center of myself as though I were getting my psychic balance. Then a picture swam into my mind, at first diffused, but then very clear. It was absolutely astonishing. I saw the form of a very tall, overpoweringly confident, almost androgynous human being. A graceful, folded, cream-colored garment flowed over a figure seven feet tall, with long arms resting calmly at its side. Even longer fingers extended from the arms. The energy of the form seemed more masculine than feminine to me. The skin of the being was ruddy and its hair was long to the shoulders and auburn colored. The face had high cheekbones and a straight, chiseled nose. The eyes were deep, deep blue and the expression was supremely kind, yet strong. It raised its arms in outstretched welcome. I got an Oriental feeling from it, more Oriental than Western. And I had the intuitive feeling that it was extremely protective, full of patience, yet capable of great wrath. It was simple, but so powerful that it seemed to "know" all there was to know. I was flabbergasted at what I saw, *and* what I felt about it.

"Who are you?" I asked, hardly daring to hear what it would say, nor what to make of this kind of dimensional experience. The being smiled at me and embraced me!

"I am your higher unlimited self," it said.

"Chris," I said loudly, "is this crazy? I think I'm seeing my higher self. Could this really be happening?"

"Of course," she said. "*This* is not crazy. This is what it's all about. This is what you've been looking for. Your auric field is spinning every color of the rainbow. It's a celebration."

"Oh, my goodness," I heard myself say stupidly to it. "Are you really there?"

It smiled again.

"Yes," it said, "I have always been here. I've been here with you since the beginning of time. I am *never* away from you. I *am* you. I am your unlimited soul. I am the unlimited you that guides and teaches you through each incarnation."

"Listen," I said, "why do you have a form and why does it look like this?"

It smiled again.

"Because," it said, "you need to see me in the form of an earth-plane dimension. The form of the soul is the form of the human body, in any case. The only difference is that the soul is a form without mass. But if you could see the light form of a soul, you would see a head, two arms, a body, and two legs. The soul is high-frequency light without mass. That is the only difference."

How could I be making up such language, I thought to myself. I had never consciously even had such a concept.

"Well, why do you seem so masculine to me?" I asked.

"I only seem more masculine than feminine because I am powerful. The energy of the soul is powerful, but it is androgynous. That is to say there is a perfect balance between the positive energy which is male and the negative energy which is female, or yin (feminine) and yang (masculine). The masculine positive energy is thrusting and active. The feminine negative energy is receiving and acceptive. Both are equally necessary to achieve life. One cannot operate without the other."

I heard the words inside my mind. The visualization I was seeing was above me. I seemed more interested in the information I was receiving than I was in questioning the phenomenon itself. Fascinated by the concept of two energies in the same body, I asked, "Is it a fact that the masculine, positive side of the brain is on the left?"

"That is correct," it said. "And the negative, feminine side is the right side of the brain. You already realize that the left side of the brain controls the right side of the body and the right side of the brain controls the left side of the body."

"Yes," I said, "I remember which is which by reminding myself that the male power structure rules the world and that is why most people are right-handed!"

"Very good," said the being, whom I will refer to from here on as higher self or H.S. "And masculine priorities, such as assertiveness, intellectual pursuit, science, organization, mathematics, and the like are in vogue and have been for some thousands of years. But that will be balanced by the feminine, right-brained priorities of receptivity, intuition, feelings, artistic pursuit, and the like, very soon. As you know, we are now in the Aquarian age, which is a time of feminine energy. It will be necessary to balance the energies of yin and yang, positive and negative, before the end of this millennium. The human race has been operating with predominantly only one side of the brain for too long. But the change is coming."

The image of H.S. stood calm and centered. I had the impression that it wouldn't assert itself unless *I* motivated it to do so. I looked out the window at a tree outside. It was swaying in the breeze.

"Listen," I said, "if I asked you to help me stop the movement of a tree, could we do it?"

"Try me," said H.S.

"Okay," I said. "That tree outside. Let's stop it from swaying."

"Very well," said H.S. "Feel my power become your power. Know that together we can accomplish anything."

I tuned in to this energy of my image of higher self and melded with it.

"Now," it said, "ask the tree for permission to control its movement."

"Ask the tree for permission?" I asked, suddenly understanding the more refined subtleties of karmic interreaction.

"Why, certainly," said H.S. "All life must work in harmony, balance, and respect for all other life. There can be no abuse of power without reaping consequences. You will hear the tree respond to you. You will know how it feels about it."

"Trees can feel?" I asked.

"Of course," said H.S. "All life vibrates with feeling. And the *natural* state of feeling is love. The state of love is achieved by simply *being*. Nature is a manifestation of the state of simple *beingness*. There is no judgment or morality attached to *beingness*. It just *is*. And that which *is*, in its purest sense, is perfect balance. Do you understand?"

I opened my eyes and looked up at the tape recorder realizing that it was impossible to record all of the two-way conversation. What was happening, though, left me with the certainty that I'd never forget one word of this literally ethereal conversation.

"Chris?" I said, "are you hearing any of this?" I asked.

"Not in detail," she said. "I just feel an intense communication with your higher unlimited self. You should see your aura. It's incredibly beautiful. Bright, bright copper color now. Keep going."

I returned to H.S., who seemed to be waiting benevolently for me to ask permission from the tree to stop its movement.

I felt myself tune in to the branches and leaves of the tree outside. I had never had a problem talking to nature. Flowers, bushes, even rocks were entities I felt akin to, and almost capable of conducting a relationship with. However, until now I had felt this was a fairy-tale attitude that simply gave me childish pleasure. But this was different. This was enjoining the question of my own power in relation to nature. Abuse of my power was not something I had thought much about.

"The tree," directed H.S.

"Okay," I answered. I looked out the window and from my solar plexus, where my heart feelings lay, I asked if it was all right for me to stop its swaying branches. An interesting thing happened. I felt the tree not only give me a "yes," but also communicate that it would stop *itself* in harmony with my desire. In other words, the act of requesting permission would enable the tree to manifest what I wanted because *both* energies would be utilized.

I watched through the window. I could see H.S. even though I had shifted the direction of my eyes. H.S. lifted its arms outstretched toward the tree. The tree continued to sway in the breeze. Then as if on cue the tree stopped swaying—completely ceased its movement. It was incredible. The tree literally stood stock-still. Several birds landed lightly on its branches and looked in at me through the window from the outside.

Of course it could all have been an accident. But as I had already learned, there was no such thing. All energy moves in relation to the laws of cause and effect.

I looked up at H.S. in my mind. The arms came down gently. "You see?" it said. "You did that. You can use your energy for anything. But you need to recognize me in order to do it."

I felt confused and exalted at the same time. I had so many questions, yet they all came down to one.

"Then what is the difference between you and God?" I asked.

"None," it said. "I am God, because all energy is plugged in to the same source. We are each aspects of that source. We are all part of God. We are all individualized reflections of the God source. God is us and we are God."

"And *you* are me."

"Precisely."

"Then how did we get separated? Why are we not all one great unified energy?"

"Basically, we are. But individual souls became separated from the higher vibration in the process of creating various life forms. Seduced by the beauty of their own creations they became entrapped in the physical, losing their connection with Divine Light. The panic was so severe that it created a battlefield known to you now as good and evil. Karma, that is, cause and effect, came into being as a path, a means, a method, to eventually eliminate the artificial concepts of good and evil. Eventually, too, souls lodged in evolved primates that later became Homo sapiens. Reincarnation is as necessary to karma as karma is to reincarnation. This is the process which allows each soul to experience *every* human condition as the path back to full spirituality and eventual reuniting with the God force."

"Then does everyone have a higher unlimited self of their own?"

"Exactly," said H.S. "And each higher self is in touch with every other higher self. All unlimited souls resonate in harmony with each other. The reason you do not recognize that truth on the earth plane is because you are not in touch with the individual soul energy of your higher selves. But you will get there because there is no other place to go to achieve peace. Peace on the outside comes from peace on the inside. Peace on the inside comes from understanding that we are all God."

"So then the conflict in the world is basically a spiritual conflict?"

"Exactly. Most of your wars are being fought over the interpretation of God. And the wars that are not, are being fought over values that have replaced God as the highest principle. There is nothing but the God Principle. Everything flows from that. To believe that technology, or oil, or money, or even a free, open society is more important than God is a mistake. It is not the truth. One cannot fight and kill over the freedom to worship God without violating the God Principle itself in the process."

"So what will happen to us then?" I asked.

Higher self shrugged its shoulders. I felt it was me shrugging my shoulders.

"You will each have to deal with your own inner selves," it said. "Your inner selves in relation to knowing that you are God. However, the discrepancy comes in your not understanding that every other person is God also."

"But down here we believe that people are people, and God is God, as though we are separate from God. I mean, almost everybody believes that."

"Precisely what is causing the problem," said H.S. "You will continue to be separate from each other until you understand that each of you *is* the God source. Which is another way of saying that you are One. You are having problems with this principle because your spiritual development is not advanced enough. You each need to become masters of your own souls, which is to say, the realization of yourselves as God."

"But how do we deal with murderers and fascists and criminals in the meantime?"

"You must expose them to spiritual principles. None of these souls is happy being what they are. Destructiveness is not a natural state. Rehabilitate them to spiritual values. For example, you are already aware that your prison systems only exacerbate the problem. Put spiritual understanding in the prisons, not punishment. By the way, do you understand what the Bible meant by an eye for an eye and a tooth for a tooth?"

"Well," I said, "I thought it meant that if someone smites you, you smite them back."

"No," said H.S. "It means that a person who takes the eye of another will inevitably experience the same trauma. It is a karmic statement, not a statement of punishment. You reap what you sow. It is a manifestation of the cosmic law of cause and effect which is administered by the souls themselves, not by the authority of the penal code or a government or even by God. The God energy is no judge of persons. In fact, there is no judgment involved with life. There is only experience from incarnation to incarnation until the soul realizes its perfection and that it is total love. . . ."

There was a pause as H.S. waited for me to respond. "Do you understand?" it asked.

I sighed to myself. "Oh, yes," I said, "I understand. But I think it will be difficult to communicate. I mean, everybody, including me, is all wrapped up in their own perceptions of right and wrong. I mean, the basis for morality in the world is knowing the difference between right and wrong and you're saying there is no such thing."

"That is correct," said H.S. "Go to your Bible studies. It is very clear. The downfall of man, symbolized in the story of the Garden of Eden, was caused by eating the fruit from the tree of *knowledge* of good and evil, not simply from the tree of good and evil, but from *recognition*, which is to say, the *creation* of good and evil. Until mankind realizes there is, in truth, no good and there is, in truth, no evil—there will be no peace. There is only karmic experience with which to eventually realize that you are each total love. The recognition of incarnational experience is essential to the understanding of this truth. When mankind realizes there is no death, it will have taken a giant step in understanding the God Principle existing in each individual."

"Oh my," I said, sighing, "why is it so difficult to love ourselves, to forgive ourselves, to even believe we're worth loving? I mean, how did we get off on such a wrong track? Was it meant to be like this? Do beings on other planets have the same karmic problems we have?"

"No," said H.S., "not all. You must understand that there are trillions of souls with histories pertaining to other spheres in the cosmos. The earth is not the sole sphere which supports life. Life exists throughout the cosmos. Some of it is similar to earth life. Much of it is not."

"Well, what happened to the others then?"

"Some souls have never incarnated, choosing only to oversee the creation of life, evolving it from the spiritual dimensions. Other souls waited until the physical forms had evolved to a crystal base before incarnating. These soul beings never lost touch with their divine light because crystal makes it possible to resonate to a higher level of divine consciousness."

"Are they more advanced than us then?" I asked.

"In a sense only," said H.S. "They are only more advanced because they are spiritually more sophisticated. They understand the scientific principles of the energy which is the spiritual God-force. They use their spiritual science to their advantage and they played intricate roles in the evolution of mankind. But it would be incorrect to say that what you know, or sense, as 'extraterrestrial' life is more advanced than your own in terms of soul *experience*. It would be unfortunate if human souls regarded extraterrestrial life as higher and more advanced than themselves simply because they traverse the universe. For you see, each soul is its own God. You must never worship anyone or anything other than self. For *you* are God. To love self is to love God. Actually some of the extraterrestrial beings, as advanced as they are, feel less love for self and the God-force than certain humans. So you see, it would be incorrect to compare the progress of the evolution of souls. Every soul is part of God and progressing according to its own pace, its own requirements, and its own karma, extraterrestrial or earth plane."

I hesitated. "Do you mean that our karmic earth-plane lesson has to do with being patient?"

"One of our lessons is patience, yes. Impatience caused us to become seduced by the pleasure and sensuality of the material earth plane originally. But human souls are on the path back to God. It has obviously been a long and arduous process, but there *is* progress."

My mind tumbled.

"So we, as souls, have devoted ourselves to evolving life on this earth so that ultimately we will realize once again that we are all part of God?"

"That is correct," said H.S., smiling.

Again, I had to remind myself that in this circumstance I was actually teaching myself. "So," I went on, "then both the creationists and the evolutionists are correct in their theories of how life developed?" I was beginning to understand this connection for the first time.

"That is correct," said H.S. "Although both have missed the point of the role the soul played. The creationists believe that 'God' was responsible for creating all life instantly. The evolutionists don't recognize the role of the soul at all. Neither has understood that the soul of mankind is responsible for its own destiny. *We are our own creators.* We, as souls, evolved life, working within the cosmic laws of the God-spirit. When we fell out of the flow of those natural laws, we experienced panic for the first time. The fear created negativity, which we have been contending with ever since."

There was so much for me to deal with that I began to feel a real sense of overload, yet I felt I needed to know more immediately.

"Have patience," said H.S. "Patience is one of your particular learning tasks in this incarnation. You know that. For now, what is really important to your growth is that you have finally 'seen' me. You *know,* now, that I exist. I created you as you created me. No relationship you will ever have or ever had is as ecstatic as this knowledge. Nothing can compare to knowing the unlimitedness of yourself. Whatever you need, you have only to ask. That is what was meant by 'ask and you will receive.' "

Tears came into my eyes. I couldn't answer, not even in my mind. I moved my legs to focus on their stiffness so that I wouldn't continue to cry.

"Tears are necessary," H.S. said. "For every tear you shed adds time to this life. You, as a human soul, have been through a great deal. You have seen only some of it. Do not repress the feelings. Release them. That is the purpose here. To cry is to have a liberating tonic. The energy required to repress feelings causes strain in the body and in the spirit. Let go. There will be no conflict if you release your feelings. Life is for expression, so don't be judgmental of how you feel. Use your intuitive understanding to express externally and don't agonize over what you do not understand. With the quickening of your soul, understanding will become more and more clear. Remain in flow with me, for in doing so you help your self and God. All happens for the purposeful good. Remember, where there is no resistance, there is no harm. Resistance creates conflict. It causes the energy flow to turn back on itself. What you have just recognized and connected with is the tapestry of interwoven energy which was blocked from its original source. Do you know the meaning of evil?''

I couldn't even think, much less answer.

H.S. went on. "Evil is nothing but energy flowing backward rather than forward. Spell your *live* backward and you have *evil*. The etymology of words is not accidental. All life is a question of energy.''

I stopped crying. I'd never heard evil defined in this way before.

"You are the energy flow," H.S. was saying. "If you allow any resistance to the flow of energy, you create polarity. Polarity creates conflict. Conflict creates dis-aster, which is the nearly complete disassociation from the spiritual, God source. You have just understood that. Open your resistance. Allow your energy to flow back to the God source. You will be protected because you will be aligned with me and I am part of God.''

I lay on the table trying to comprehend what had happened, realizing at the same time that I understood perfectly. But to live in this understanding would mean taking complete responsibility for the knowledge.

Chris handed me a tissue. She had remained silent during all of it.

"I think I need to get up," I said.

"Yes," she answered, "I think so. But ask your higher self if there is anything else you need to take home with you."

I closed my eyes once again and looked up, knowing that I had reached overload.

"Only one more point," it said. "We will be doing more specific work in the days to come. Specifics that relate to your life today. There is much you need to understand and confront. You need to keep your channel to me clear. Therefore I would recommend eating moderately; vegetables, fruit, and water. No dairy products. Engage in only harmonious movement, such as your yoga. Do not concern yourself with schedules, time, or telephones. Be with nature. Pay little attention to linear information. Breathe deeply to keep the channel open. Stay away from vexing people and remember that I am with you always. *I am you.*"

I nodded.

"One more point," it said. "My compliments that you have never used drugs. This is an important reason for your progress."

I found myself laughing. "With the spectacle I've just witnessed, no drug could compete."

"That is certainly true," H.S. said, and together we knew I had had enough for the day.

Chris helped me off the table. "Spectacular," she said. "We got most of it on the recorder. The rest you'll never forget."

I could hardly walk. My back ached and I had no mobility in my legs. I headed immediately to the bathroom. I needed something earth plane and familiar under me! I blew my nose and splashed water on my face. I walked back into the room, half expecting to see Chris's healing entities in body form.

Chris was lying on the floor on her back, her stomach protruding high above the rug under her.

"Does this happen often?" I asked. "I mean,

you heard what happened. Do many people have this experience?''

She smiled. "Many, many, many," she answered. "And when each person experiences the higher self the conversations are almost identical. The lessons are always the same. 'There is no such thing as evil or good. There is only enlightened awareness or ignorance.' That is the great truth. Judgment of ourselves and others is our problem. *That* is what causes fear, conflict, resistance, and despair.''

"Are people shocked by what they hear their own higher selves tell them?'' I asked.

"Many are,'' answered Chris. "Because it goes against what they've been conditioned to believe. However the shock is what causes them to understand that what they are experiencing is real rather than 'made up.' ''

"And what about some of the pictures I saw; like Atlantis, for example?''

"They are the same with everyone. They describe subdued colors of pink and violet and orange hues with fountains and crystal structures and many people wearing crystal headdresses. Atlantis is always described the same way, even by people who never were aware they believed it existed. So you see, conscious awareness is everything. The higher self is aware of everything. Our task is to become consciously aware in this dimension so we can integrate our awareness into our lives.''

"So you're not surprised by anything I experienced today?''

Chris smiled. "Not at all. It is truth. And I've heard it all before.''

I sighed deeply and slowly bent down to pick up my shoes. They weighed a ton. I sat down on the chair and dressed as though it were a new experience. The material of my blouse had a new textured meaning against my skin. I felt weightless and longed for the sun and fresh air outside. I wanted to touch earth, flowers, anything organic and alive. And hun-

gry! I was famished. I felt hot tingling in my hands
and feet like an electronic pulsation. My head was
clear and open. I was drowsy, yet alert as I'd never
been. I felt self-contained and autonomous. When I
spoke, my voice sounded richer, lower in tone, with
less anxiety. There was heat in my lower spine where
I knew the kundalini energy was rising.

I slowly walked outside as if I were on air. The
colors of the flowers in Chris's greenhouse were
shimmering vibrantly in the sunlight.

I felt I could dip into the vibrations of their
colors and enjoy them as mine.

I looked at my watch. The time didn't even
register. I felt that I was in the past and present at
the same time. I saw everything around me in mathematical perfection. Everything fit. My time on the
table was meant to happen. Everything I'd "seen"
was meant to happen. There was a reason for everything. A plan. A perfect, gigantic puzzle of perfection and each live entity on earth was a precious part
of the puzzle. Life itself seemed only symbolic of the
soul, as though it were only thought essence which
would never cease, never die. Life was God once
removed. And everything was energy. Vibrating,
pulsating, vital *energy. And* that energy was *love* energy expressing itself in millions of ways until it
finally understood the totality of itself.

I grasped at words that would express my
thoughts and feelings and for the first time, I understood that poets were the true translators of God.
William Blake's famous poem came to mind:

> To see a world in a grain of sand
> And a heaven in a wild flower.
> Hold infinity in the palm of your hand
> And eternity in an hour.

Chapter 17

*T*hat night I slept outside in a sleeping bag under the stars. Chris had suggested it because she said that the soul and brain map the celestial navigation of the stars if there is no roof obstructing the view of the heavens. And as we mapped their movements, we learned.

I found that my sleep was deeper and the rest more profound, as though I were being taught all night, and the contact with the spiritual plane inspired peace and a sense of well-being. I slept less time, but it was the quality of the sleep, not the quantity.

The following morning, I experimented with connecting to my higher self without the use of Chris's needles. It was there every time. If I had misplaced something, I asked H.S. where it was. I was always guided in the right direction. It was never wrong.

I asked H.S. what to eat, who was on the other end of a ringing telephone, what direction an address might be. It was astonishing how correct the answers were. I wondered how long it would last. The answer came: "As long as you can find me, you can find anything."

And so my concern that I had never had a really "revelatory" experience evaporated. It had always bothered me that I seemed to be progressing slowly and surely, but without any major revelation. Not so anymore.

Getting in touch with my unlimited soul was an extraordinary event, a milestone in growth and understanding and an experience that flooded me with joy. I felt that this was some kind of coming of age for me. Yet if anyone else had related that discovery to me about themselves, I guess I would have thought they were "dreaming."

I, at least, had a framework from which I could view what had happened to me. On the drive to Chris's place I thought about how I had been pursuing a search of my own identity from the time I was very small, and how the process of search would proceed from this point. The teachings of the Bible, the Mahabarata, the Koran, and all the other spiritual books that I had tried to understand flooded back to me: *The Kingdom of Heaven is within you. Know thyself and that will set you free; to thine own self be true; to know self is to know all; know that you are God; know that you are the universe. . . .* The spiritual masters had all said the same thing. They had each taught that the soul is eternal. They had each alluded to having lived many times before, even Christ: "I came before, but you didn't recognize me." They had each taught that the purpose of life was to work one's way back to the Divine Source of which we were all a part. And the karmic events that we encountered along the way were only to be experienced and understood—never to be judged. Each of the great books had warned *against* judgment, *against* the moral trap of good versus evil. The laws of cause and effect were the underlying principles of all their teachings: *Judge and you will be judged; hurt and you will be hurt; love and you will be loved; give and you will be given to.* They taught that circumstances never mattered. They were only the field on which our truth was played out.

Yet here we were in a world where everyone was engaged in some process of moral judgment. Each person or group believing that their morality was the true word of God, blind to the cosmic harmony that *every* point of view served the purposeful good in the long run. I saw how we were viewing the destiny of mankind and our individual selves from a limited perspective. From a short-run perspective. We were not seeing the entire forest; we focused on our own individual trees.

Yet in the immediacy of each individual's trauma, the seeming tragedy would be eliminated if we went into the eternal nature of our selves and understood that *nothing* then can be "tragic." Nothing is wrong. Nothing is wasted, and nothing ever dies—nothing. We were each an eternal universe unto ourselves. And to realize the transcendent wonder of that truth was all that mattered.

I thought again about *energy*. It seemed that through the examination of energy, science and spirituality would eventually have to meet. They were two different approaches to the same truth. Each spoke of energy as the glue that held the universe together. Spirituality accepted its existence and science attempted to prove it. Spirit was faith without science. Science was proof without faith.

The spiritual approach to universal truths and harmony always recognized the unseen dimensions from within consciousness. The scientific approach recognized those same dimensions from without. Yet the new science was close to saying they were the same. That consciousness was everything. Both aspects were necessary for human utilization. Unless we could put these tools of understanding to use, what power could they have for us?

As I drove and reflected on my having experienced lifetimes both as a male and as a female, I wondered why I had chosen to live life as a female this time around. There had been such focus on the feminine energy of the modern world. The women's liberation movement, the role of the female in the decision-making process of political power, and the feminine attitudes toward relaxing tension in the world in order to avoid the annihilation of civilization.

Why had I chosen to express myself through the energy of the feminine, the yin energy? Then I thought the yin energy manifests predominantly from within. The masculine yang energy manifests from without. The yin is intuitive. The yang is powerful.

The yin energy is also the holder of the unseen, the nondimensional. The yang is the unseen expressed in the seen. The yang is the active energy. Once yin energy is expressed from unseen to seen, it becomes yang energy. Thus women who express their yin energy are expressing in a yang manner. When a man goes within to contemplate the unseen, he is utilizing his yin energy. Both are necessary.

To be perfectly balanced, didn't each individual need to equally recognize both energies within their given body? To have a balanced peace in the world, it seemed necessary to have a balanced peace in the individual, which meant the recognition of equally expressed yin energy from within, and yang energy from without.

I wondered why all the prophets and masters had been men, until I remembered that the prophets were *manifestors.* They had expressed *externally.* The female held the knowledge of the unseen, the cosmic secrets, so to speak. The male always used the female as his internal support system, his intuitive counselor. Each was necessary to the other. The female held the unseen truth of *what* to do. The male activated the power of *how* to do it.

We were now in the Aquarian age, which was the feminine age of expression. More men were endeavoring to understand their intuitive capacities and more women were endeavoring to express their own power externally. We seemed to be striving to bring into harmony the seen and the unseen.

Scientists were striving for the same balanced principle, "sensing" more and more "unseen" elements that could not really be measured. Their existence could only be accepted. The same acceptance was becoming true of the unseen energies of yin and yang. They were clearly *there*, just immeasurable. They were energies with nondimensional perimeters. What was true in scientific terms could also be true in experiential human terms.

If, as science says, energy never dies, it merely changes form, then life, which is also energy, never dies. It, too, merely changes form. Since energy is never still, because nothing remains inert, then energy must continually have a changing form. There was no doubt in my mind that the life energy simply changed its form from lifetime to lifetime, just as nature did from spring to spring.

Yet the only way any of it made sense was when it related to our own personal experience. If you hadn't *felt* it, you couldn't know it. Knowledge was experience. Even Einstein, toward the end of his life, claimed "that propositions arrived at by purely logical means were completely empty of reality." He went on to say, "It is very difficult to explain this feeling to anyone who is entirely without it. I maintain that cosmic religious feeling is the strongest and noblest incitement to scientific research."

I drove in the brilliantly clear Santa Fe morning, filled with calm joy. The journey within was the most fulfilling of any traveling I had ever experienced. And the specifics were only beginning.

In contrast to the dramatic intensity and revelation of the previous day, my next experience with Chris and H.S. was sheer delight. It could have been a child's fairy tale. While on the table, I stretched out this recall for nearly five hours. I didn't understand why my higher self had guided me to experience it again until after it was over.

This is what happened.

Chris had been guided to insert the gold needles under my chin, just above my throat. The same communication points that "controlled crowds." I saw why as the pictures unfolded.

The first image that was guided to my consciousness was so unusual I had trouble with its meaning. I saw myself with a herd of elephants in the bush jungles of the subcontinent of India. Green foliage surrounded clear green-blue water. It was a time period thousands of years ago. As the images progressed, I consciously questioned my higher self to guide the meaning of what I was seeing. I was living with the elephants. Immediately I understood that I could communicate with them telepathically. I was so well acquainted with their habits and feelings that on command they obeyed me. I was about twelve years old with dark eyes painted with tree bark that I had crushed, powdered, and mixed with water. I wore a bright-colored pantalon wrap of some kind and around my arms and neck hung bracelets and necklaces of a brightly colored metallic material.

The elephants and I were playing a game as we moved slowly from dense, thick jungle surroundings to open, rolling plains spotted with watering holes of still, clear blue water. On my command they would pass me from one trunk to another while I laughed with delight. Sometimes one would swing me up into a tree where I would stay until I was retrieved by another. Sometimes they would gently roll me over in the soft mud before tossing me in the water to get cool and clean with the baby elephants. I was totally carefree and totally trusting of the elephants and they of me. They lifted me up with their trunks and trumpeted to one another, shouting the next command of the game.

Whenever I wished to take charge of the play, I would communicate what I wanted telepathically. They responded immediately. Sometimes they all galloped for me in vast circles, trumpeting their joy in being alive. I felt the exquisite power of communication on both a collective and individual basis. It was an astonishing sensation of playfully benevolent power.

I asked H.S. how I'd come to be in this Rudyard Kipling situation. It said that I had lived in a nearby village with my father. He had once been kind to the bull elephant of the herd. My father had since died and my life as a result was in danger. The bull elephant sensed my danger (the specifics of the danger weren't evident) and scooped me away from the village. He had remembered my father's kindness and responded in kind. The bull took me to the herd and protected me, handing me to a cow elephant who watched over me. I was a fragile infant but I always felt comfortable with these great, gentle creatures. The level of perception of both animals and humans was keener then than what we know now. So I had grown up with the elephants, visiting the village once in a while to eat cooked food and enjoy the company of humans.

My higher self identified my name as Asana. My relationship with the elephant herd had become legendary throughout the countryside. I became known as the princess of the elephants and could communicate with a given elephant hundreds of miles away.

On another level, and in the midst of the recall, I reflected on my fascination with elephants today. I had pictures of elephants all over my apartment in New York and many wooden elephants that I had brought back from India strode across my mantelpiece. I had never understood why I was so drawn to elephants. As far as I could remember, I had never even met one.

I had seen a painting in a museum of an old bull elephant preparing to die alone among the trees in the Indian countryside and had stood before the painting sobbing to myself. I never understood that either. When I rode the elephant on Fifty-first Street, I was not in the least apprehensive. I felt I *knew* her.

Years before I had purchased a whole series of

National Geographic pictures of elephants depicting the love and affection they showed for one another. I had plastered them all over my walls and never understood why I had been so moved.

Suddenly my love for elephants was beginning to make sense.

As I lived and played among these gentle giants, I felt myself radiate an understanding of what they were feeling. I knew each one individually and respected each one's pecking order in the herd. I presided over the births of the young, and if one of my friends injured herself, I used more sophisticated human healing techniques to nurse her back to health.

The elephants became my army of protectors, commanding the attention of everyone in the countryside. Though there was really nothing to protect. We led a free, harmonious, sometimes humorous life. The elephants loved to push my wrist bangles up and down my arms with their trunks. They enjoyed the delicate movements and the sounds the bangles made when they clanked against one another.

Whenever I commanded them to take me to the village, they encircled the community until I returned to the wilds with them. Sometimes I brought young children to play with us. The elephants were gentle and playful. They tossed the children the same way they tossed me. Sometimes a child was frightened and cried. The elephants didn't understand. They had never heard or seen me cry.

Then an event occurred in the village which was a learning experience for everyone involved, including the elephants. A friend whom I loved was killed in an argument. Shocked and miserable, I cried and cried, screaming and wailing with the all-out grief of which children are capable. My hysterics were confusing and distressing to the elephants. From my mind pictures, they understood who the culprit was. The male elephants in the herd wanted revenge. Their anger on my behalf got through to me and, alarmed, I communicated to the females that they should stop the males. It would only lead to more slaughter. Together we persuaded the males to refrain from violence. The males agreed but not until they thundered through the village, trumpeting, and deliberately encircled the dwelling of the man who had killed my friend. The man was terrified. He understood the elephants knew what he had done. Yet he also understood that they were controlling their vengeful instincts.

The other villagers watched the behavior of the elephants with reverence. They, too, knew the herd could flatten their homes with very little effort. Instead a covenant was established between the elephants of the countryside and the humans in the village.

The elephants commanded that no violence should occur among the humans themselves, or the herd would stampede through the entire village. It thus became necessary for each villager to maintain peaceful co-existence with all his neighbors. As a result, the level of peace-keeping *consciousness* rose in the village, peace-keeping became something to be *worked at*, with disputes being talked out rather than fought over, and with the elephants as the spiritual monitors. The communication among the people improved, as well as the communication between humans and animals.

The people of the countryside came to revere the example of the great, gentle pachyderms, while recognizing their own subservience to power. A delicate balance of understanding kept the peace. The villagers knew that each was responsible for the high level of awareness of every other individual in the community. Collectively they were only as strong as their weakest link. And the elephants always sensed who was the weakest link and surrounded that person with patient warnings. They could perceive negative vibrations in a human being quicker than the humans themselves. They would point out which human was liable to cause trouble and I would talk to him, explaining once again the consequences to the community should he continue down the path of negativity.

As I continued to live with the elephants, I was fascinated not so much with their talent for reasoning as with their talent for the power of being, of living in the moment. They flowed with life, living day by day completely for what it offered, but never forgetting the past. The elephants understood the energy of the moonlight and the meaning of each dawn. Together we held festive celebrations outside the village during nighttime ceremonies. I taught them to dance and they loved to perform for the appreciation of the villagers.

As the recall progressed, I asked my higher self why I had been able to empathize so completely with the great creatures.

H.S. said that this lifetime had been crucial for me and so pleasant because I had mastered the art of communicating on a collective level while respecting each individual in the process. I had learned the lesson of democracy, which required individual respect in a collective environment, and empathy with the complication of human intelligence. I had not yet manifested that understanding in this incarnation, but if I would draw on the memory of what I had accomplished in the past, I would evolve again to that understanding this time around. It would be necessary for me to accomplish that understanding in the days to come and that was why I was being shown this particular incarnation. Not insignificantly I was also to relearn the importance of understanding nature through animals. *They were completely without judgment* and an example of what humans needed to evolve toward in that respect. The elephants were also symbols of "never forgetting," which was necessary for me to understand with regard to humans. "We must always remember," H.S. said, "that locked in our memories is the knowledge that we have never forgotten anything either.

"We humans should never forget our capacity to connect with the collective spirit of animals. Their energy is essential to our future growth. The animals are on the earth for a reason and our disrespect for them has become alarming. They are totally without ego. Animals would teach us if we would listen. Pulsating in their collective consciousness are the lessons of the past. They are dumb and unable to speak for a reason. They communicate on other levels, which are there to help us hone our levels of perception with nature."

As this delightful recall receded from my mind, I was reminded again of its underlying theme. Respect the quality of life, the unquestioning acceptance of living with nature and animals while pursuing a sensitive progression of intelligence. And while understanding the will of the collective majority, be intricately aware of the needs of the individual.

I breathed a sigh of completion when it was over, because I understood.

An addendum to this tale is worth mentioning, even at the risk of sounding completely outrageous.

First, let me say that I was learning that the *theme* of each incarnation was more important to understand than the specific incarnation itself. The theme of the elephant-princess incarnation, for example, had been the co-existence of the collective in tandem with the individual. I had mastered it on an emotional and spiritual level where animals were concerned. They had been instrumental in my learning it so that I could have an effect on the humans in the village.

But as this particular recall was unfolding, another lifetime swam in and out of my consciousness, as though it were important for me to regard the two in relation to the same theme.

This is what I "saw."

I saw myself involved with the sociopolitical

questions of the Founding Fathers of the United States.

When I asked H.S. *who* I had been during that lifetime, it said, "It doesn't matter. The theme of democracy is what was important. You had an incarnation during the writing of the Constitution and the Declaration of Independence. You were involved, as were many, with the establishment of the New Spiritual Republic of the United States, and along with many others who lived then, you were deeply involved with the question of majority rule and respect for the rights of the individual. You drew on your lifetime with the elephants because your soul memory remembered your accomplishment of the same theme. You see how the holographic picture works?"

Yes, I could see it, but it seemed outrageous to connect the two.

"Nothing is outrageous when it comes to the learning of life themes," said H.S., "because the soul learns in many ways. You must learn to decipher what the lessons are in each given experience. You will find yourself repeating the same themes in different circumstances each time until you complete the understanding. That is what you did here. And you will be confronted with the same theme again as the United States continues to deal with its theme of collective and individual rights in the future. This country exemplifies the highest understanding of this theme to date, but there is still much to work out."

I was beginning to see the point.

And so I have no idea who I was or what I was doing during the Founding Fathers' days. I only know that the spiritual and sociological meaning of what they attempted to establish in 1776 had moved me deeply during my school years and does even today. My political activism in this lifetime has been motivated by a desire to see a return to their original intent.

Our founders were spiritually inspired men and

women seeking escape from the political and religious oppression of Europe. In the personal background of each one was a recognition of the mystical truths relating as far back as Pharaonic Egypt. They desired to spiritualize their New Republic and used ancient symbols to express the roots of their beliefs. They designed the dollar bill with the Great Pyramid of Giza on the back, and the Third Eye above it.

They were spiritually aware, and in terms of leadership today, it seemed to me essential that leaders also have a spiritual support system which would keep them in touch with the recognition of their own higher knowledge in order to propel society toward a peaceful world.

Chapter 18

In the days that followed, each incarnation that was shown to me carried with it a theme and meaning I needed in order to understand myself more fully today. I was shown more than I could possibly relate here. Suffice it to say that I realized I was coming to a point where, if I were to be happy and effective in fulfilling the reasons for my coming into this incarnation, there was now an urgent need for me to clear up my own unresolved conflicts. In order to continue to grow in this incarnation and to expand my awareness of unseen dimensions, I would need to clear out the emotional residue of trigger points that still bothered me.

It was obvious to me that people who operated only from an intellectual reality were becoming less and less at ease in their worlds. *Nothing* made "intellectual" sense anymore and, as reason failed them, they were becoming bitter and cynical.

Our battles and conflicts were not with governments or with our culture or society. They were with ourselves. But I began to see that nothing would really threaten us if we were aware of who we were and what we came from. The more we quickened our soul's awareness, the less we would be polarized by authority and fear.

Higher self explained that many souls on the spiritual plane were waiting to come into the earth-plane dimension so that they could proceed toward working out their karma. That was why life in the body was so highly valued. Karma was not resolved on the spiritual plane. It could only occur on the plane of experience, the physical plane of mass—the earth.

H.S. said that each soul knows it will eventually come into the light of understanding even if it takes several hundred lifetimes to complete one theme.

Life was not about survival. It was about spiritual evolvement. To operate with survival instincts alone, one had to polarize against something. To operate with instincts of evolvement meant there was no conflict because there was no resistance.

If we proceeded with the knowing awareness that we *elect* to have each experience, we then approached trauma from an expanded consciousness. When our conscious awareness was expanded, we came into a more perfect alignment with the Divine Source and the trauma disappeared. Tragedy is tragedy because we *perceive* it as such. Thus we remain on the treadmill of negative blindness, not understanding what the purpose is, not learning. We are judging our predicament and polarizing our energy flow at the same time.

Survival implies struggling against. Evolvement implies embracing the flow. Since all energy flows to the God source, the alignment induces peace and perfection.

The nourishment and sustenance of the soul comes from the God source, not the earth source. There is no loneliness of conflict when one is aligned with that energy because one is aligned with true self.

Each event happens according to what is necessary for the soul to learn.

The days unfolded like budding flowers as I experienced and understood more and more. And as each session impacted on my conscious mind, I understood that most of the lifetimes shown to me represented my *lack* of use of spiritual power. Of course, there had been many completion incarnations, but to see them wouldn't have been useful. The conflict had already been resolved. And even in the completion incarnations I had only completed one aspect of whatever it was I had come in to complete, only an aspect of a wider spectrum of karmic resolution.

Of one thing I was certain. What I was doing *felt* right. I wasn't unhappy or disturbed by what I was learning. Not in the least. As a matter of fact, it was a kind of liberation of understanding to realize that my life today was a result of the lives that had preceded it, that I was the product of many lives and would be again. It made sense. There was a harmony to that—a purpose—a kind of cosmic justice which served to explain everything in life—both positive and negative.

Perhaps I was searching out more details in my past lives than most people. Perhaps even those who understood what I was doing would prefer to know less about past lives than I. Perhaps it was safer to pay lip service to the theory while refraining from becoming too specific. Maybe to others I was too vigorous in my own personal investigation. But that was *my* truth. It was my way of doing things. Once I was curious about anything, I overturned every rock on the path.

To those who would insist that my cosmic-justice theory was too convenient, I could only say that it made just as much sense as flailing at the world. To those who would insist there is no such thing as harmony or purposeful good, I could only suggest that they weren't looking at the grander picture.

All of life, both its sad spectacles and glorious triumphs, had meaning if one observed it without judgment. Everything happened for a reason. Life was like nature. The beauty was in the *being* and every event in nature was tied to a chain of interdependent events. I was pursuing a curiosity of the chain of interdependence.

I would allow myself the freedom of considering any truth that might be hidden, yet nevertheless real.

So whenever I felt skepticism about my search, I learned to let it go. The truth I was seeking was more important to me, regardless of where it took me. I decided to trust what I felt was my higher self. As I learned what that meant I found myself reflecting on how I had been living my life in *this* incarnation prior to my spiritual understanding.

I had so often been anxious about time schedules, promises I had made, responsibility, and pleasing others. My life had often been so busy that I felt I'd never accomplish all that I wanted to or that was necessary. That had changed now. Somehow I had relaxed, trusting that there would indeed be time. With the release of that anxiety I had suddenly discovered I was living totally in the present—no longer calculating how much time I would have to devote to the next problem, nor regretting what I had not given to what was past. *Now* was what mattered. As I trusted my spiritual power I found that I had more clarity of thought because it was void of anxiety. Therefore I accomplished more in a shorter period of time. It was astonishing to me how the spiritual freedom from anxiety worked. Since I felt that everything that occurred in my life was occurring for a good reason I just let things flow. And as a result my lack of resistance enabled me to manifest just about anything I desired.

As I worked day after day with Chris and her acupuncture needles, I'd go into an altered state of consciousness even though I was simultaneously aware of my conscious state.

My higher self conducted incarnational scans and isolated which lifetimes it was necessary for me to relate to. Often I saw overlapping pictures, one image tumbling over another. Then H.S. would stop-

frame an incarnation in time and show me a picture
of an aspect of it. I couldn't always understand what
the pictures meant, but somehow I understood the
emotional reasons for seeing them. The lifetimes often came up as movable paintings.

I was dancing in a harem, attempting to spiritu
alize the movement.

I was a Spanish infant wearing diamond ear-
rings, and in a church.

I was a monk meditating in a cave.

I was an infant lifted by an eagle and deposited
with a primitive family in Africa, where I became
frustrated because they were not as advanced as I.

I saw myself as a child in a swing looking up at
the sun.

I was a ballet dancer in Russia. I lived in a home
which had a veranda. I wore velvet skirts and played
the balalaika. I sat in a swing with books and a pen
and paper. I loved the sunshine of the Russian spring
and searched for strawberries that had been buried
under the snow. There were no other people in the
Russian incarnation. I was looking for Vassy, but
there was no one.

The picture flashed to Brazil, where I was involved with voodoo of some kind, misusing the power
of the occult.

The picture flashed again. I was on the Arabian
desert with a caravan, looking up at the stars.

Again a flash—I was doing Chinese tai-chi.

Then another: I was a Japanese woman in a
brightly colored kimono shuffling along cobblestone
streets in the morning light on my way to a Buddhist
temple.

Another: I was swimming in a cave. An alligator
slept on a riverbank nearby. I knew it, and was
afraid.

Then an incarnation came up that upset me so
intensely that I didn't want to go on.

I was a young boy of about eleven. As I "looked"
closer I realized I was an Inca youth in Peru. I was

being trained by tribal priests to use my Third Eye power. In an attempt to accelerate my perceptions, they had chiseled a shallow hole in the center of my forehead.

It was horrible. I remembered my reaction to the skull I had seen in the museum in Lima. A searing ache began to throb in the center of my forehead as I lay on the table. One of the gold needles popped out.

I didn't want to go any further. I asked Chris if it was necessary.

"Ask your higher self," she answered.

I did.

H.S. said, "If you want to progress, you must clear the psychic pain buried in this memory pattern. We would suggest you progress even further in learning how to function in two dimensions of consciousness simultaneously. You have carried the scar tissue in your Third Eye for other lifetimes as well as into this incarnation. You should release it. Don't deny the experience."

I breathed deeply. All right. I'd go ahead.

The picture came in again. I was in a spartan stone cell. A priest lovingly attended me, administering herbs and tonics to my Third Eye indentation. I was in confusion with the acute pain and felt that I was being forced beyond my understanding. He tried to explain. I had some sort of herbal gauze wound around a spongy plug that had been inserted into the indentation. It was humiliating to me as well as excruciatingly painful. I hated both the psychic and the physical violence, but couldn't control either. The priest held me in his arms, rocking me as he continued to explain that this method would lead me to a higher level of clairvoyance. He said I had been chosen to divert the path of the community from evil. I became hysterical with anger and humiliation, wrenched myself out of his arms and ran from him.

He made no attempt to follow me. I turned back

toward him. The last thing I saw was the priest raising his arms in some sort of melancholy benediction.

It was at that moment that I realized the priest had been Vassy! And the theme was overcoming evil.

As each incarnation came up, I experienced some kind of emotional body pain. I say emotional because of the memory it aroused. The pain didn't always correspond to what I was seeing. I asked H.S. the reason for that.

It said that each of the incarnations I had viewed had ended in a painful death. It wasn't necessary to show me the death. What was important was my lack of understanding while I had lived. However, each area of pain I felt related to each death. I needed to move through the bondage of the pain of those deaths and release it. But I also needed to understand that the deaths would not have been painful had I been in alignment with my spiritual power. Pain was nothing but resistance; resistance to the God energy caused by fear.

Without fear and resistance, death would simply be a transition to another dimension.

Reviewing the incarnations, I realized there had been an unresolved mystical understanding in each one of them. The theme had been my lack of utilization of my own spiritual power even when placed in mystical situations.

At least I had recognized Vassy in one of my past lives.

It was at the end of the week that I recognized others.

At the end of each day's session, Chris and I reviewed the meaning. She was always fascinated by the exquisite interweaving of themes. She had been through marathon treatments such as mine with many and warned me to go easy on myself as I was taking in an overwhelming amount of information.

Each day I left her ranch to drive home slowly in the sunset. I never saw anyone else and reviewed my tapes while soaking in the hot vinegar bath each night.

My dreams were intense, complicated, and symbolic. I often woke with a headache. I wondered again if I was going too far. But then I just couldn't do anything halfway.

I ate fresh vegetables and fruit and drank at least eight glasses of water each day. Sometimes I didn't know what I was looking for in the sessions. Along with learning, it was an adventure within myself which entertained and stimulated me more than anything I had ever done.

I found new levels of meaning in the simplest act. If a bird sang outside my window, I longed to know the hidden message of its song. When the sun drenched hot on my skin, I wondered if intelligence lived behind the sun's gaseous rays. I drove alone for hours into the desert night until the moon sank below the granite mountains.

And when I lay out under the stars, I felt connected to everything above me.

It was a wondrous time for me.

Sometimes I found myself crying. Other times I was overcome with joy. I was expressing myself *to* myself.

I meditated on the smallest speck I could see until I felt it become infinitely huge. Then I meditated on a mountain until it became a speck. The more I found the center of myself, the further out I could go in understanding.

I went into the hills and found a big tree. I encircled it with my arms and asked H.S. to tell me the tree's secret to peace.

H.S. said, "It is standing still."

I began to lose my sense of time. An instant was an hour. Sometimes I would forget where I was.

Other times I didn't recognize landmarks and drove past a familiar turnoff. New York and Hollywood were another planet. The fast pace of survival there seemed denigrating and way off the mark when life's important priorities were considered. The wind-chased movement of a white cloud seemed infinitely more important. In fact, everything seemed infinite. Nothing had limits or perimeters. Everything had meaning. Nothing was wasted or gratuitous. And somehow all of life seemed to fit into a puzzle of perfection. The world and its chaos fit into the puzzle of peace too For the chaos, seen in the full flow of time, was just the necessary drama chosen to be played out on this stage called earth.

It wasn't until after my last session with Chris that I realized what I'd been looking for. Of course, H.S. knew all along, but "I" wasn't aware of it.

I had had a good preparation when it finally came. I mean, I understood that I was seeing predominantly violent and traumatic incarnations because within those memory patterns lay the unresolved conflicts I needed to clear.

There were two notable incarnations, never to be forgotten, that helped me see more clearly today.

I will relate them in the order that they were revealed to me because the sequence probably has some significance, although I'm still not sure what it is.

The scene opened in the wild, desolate Gobi Desert near Karakorum. (One of my favorite books in childhood had been *The Sands of Karakorum*, about a Western couple who braved the deep wind-blown shifting sands of the desert on a journey searching for a lost city where their best friend had disappeared.)

I saw a caravan of tents and camels starkly alone against the dry, barren ocean of sand.

Inside one of the tents, I (as a young woman) lived with my father, mother, and two other sisters. We were Mongolian nomads and subjected from time to time to the raids of roaming bandits. The bandits were merciless, inflicting indescribable cruelties upon their victims if their demands were not met.

Other than the pressing fear of these bandits, the lazy desert life was lean but harmonious. We tended our camels and horses within the caravan and I was particularly interested in weaving brightly colored cloth interspersed with small mirrors which we had picked up at a trading-route junction.

At this point, it's important that I begin to identify each character of the incarnation. The father was my father of today. The mother was the present lifetime sister of my father. My middle sister (I was the eldest) was Chris, and my youngest sister was Sachi.

So there was an immediate connection to the significance this incarnation had for me today.

The "story" unfolded.

I was about sixteen and in the full flush of puberty. I was attracted to a young man of about twenty who lived with his family in a neighboring tent. It was understood that he and I would someday marry, but not until my father consented. I was a beautiful young woman who could be desirable on many levels and my father had the cunning of a Mongolian trader. As a woman in that culture I was simply an attractive possession to be bought or sold when the proper time came. And the young man, as well as my father, regarded me in those terms. The young man was my ex-husband, Steve, in this present lifetime.

My father was dominant within the family circle as all desert Mongolian fathers were, but his lordly role could easily be compromised by bribery, or intimidation.

One evening, following the meal (chunks of camel meat roasting over a spit as we dunked hunks of dry bread into fermented milk), the family settled in for the night. A thick rug covered the sand floor of the huge tent with multicolored pillows scattered in strategic resting places. Silks hung from the interior of the tent and a pile of untanned skins lay heaped in a corner. There were fur skins being cured outside, waiting to dry in the sun.

The stars outside looked so close, I could have picked them from the sky like zircon plums.

I heard a rider in the distance thundering across the sand with more speed than usual. When he came into view, I saw it was one of the feared bandits. Alongside his black Arabian stallion, he guided two galloping camels.

I quickly ducked into the tent and told my father of the approaching bandit.

He said nothing, but I could see he was afraid.

Soon the bandit reached our caravan and made for our tent immediately. He whipped open the front entrance flap and stood before us looking for all the world like Genghis Khan to me. His flashing eyes were like bruised olives and his face was covered with a ragged beard and moustache. His hair hung long and black, tied in the back with a thin piece of leather. He wore black muslinlike robes with a red crimson cummerbund around his waist. He straddled the rugs in our tent and brandished a long, jewel-encrusted sword. He was menacing in the extreme, but we knew he wanted to make some sort of deal.

The bandit surveyed the interior of the tent. My father smiled ingratiatingly and attempted a friendly gesture of welcome. The bandit ignored him. He surveyed our furs and skins, but moved on to scrutinizing the three sisters. I realized he was there to steal a woman.

My father realized it too. This was one time when it wasn't a question of what I was *worth*, but whether I would live.

The bandit pointed to me and said he would take me and go in peace. Otherwise, if I wouldn't go willingly, he would ransack our tent, kill the other occupants, and take me anyway. He said he needed a woman and *I* was to be his possession.

That didn't leave my father much choice. He looked at me.

I somehow found the bandit rather attractive. I was not at all afraid of him. In fact, I found him adventurous and thrilling. I pictured him on long desert rides under the stars as my protector.

My father saw that I wasn't afraid, which made his position and decision much simpler. He shrugged.

The bandit shrewdly observed the interplay between us and before any other bargaining could take place and without any leave-taking, he swept me out of the tent and flung me onto his black stallion. He replaced his sword in its sheath, seized the reins of the two camels, and vaulted to the back of the horse, encircling me with his arms. He dug his feet into the sides of the animal and urged it into a gallop with the two camels following behind.

I wasn't afraid. To me it was an adventure. I knew I would be safe with the bandit because he regarded me now as his possession.

I realized that the bandit was my mother today.

The pictures of my new life with the bandit tumbled over each other as a jumbled montage. There were starry excursions alone with him across the wild endless sands and howling winds of the desert. There were groups of other bandits with whom he did business and before whom he proudly flaunted me. I cooked for him over desert fires and shared his bed, a luxurious stack of mountain-animal furs. He talked to me but didn't really communicate. He regarded me as a comfortable shadow who caused no difficulty or inconvenience, yet was always there. I was reasonably happy but sometimes missed my father and the young man to whom I was supposed to have belonged. I seemed to be extremely passive, not exactly accepting life, but instead adjusting to what I believed was my incapacity to alter it. I had very simple attitudes and responses which carried little emotional involvement.

That detached sense of being carried over into what happened next.

Chris stood up and prepared to put another needle into my throat. Up until now, she had not been able to penetrate that past-life scar tissue. My throat was even more resistant to the needles than the center of my forehead had been.

"They're telling me I should use a needle here today," she said as she gently jabbed it into the soft tissue of my throat. This time she succeeded, but it quivered a little.

"Please go on," she said.

I was sleeping on the furs in the tent. By now I was pregnant. I was pleased about the pregnancy because it would give me another human being to relate to. I was sleeping alone because the bandit was away.

Out of the silence, someone entered the tent. I called out. He answered. It was the young man from the village who had tracked me down and had come to claim me for his own.

As soon as he saw that I was pregnant, he became furious. His eyes blazed and he yelled at me. He wasn't angry with the bandit. He was angry with *me*. I was *his* possession and now I had been contaminated with the mark of another man.

He fell down upon me and proceeded to violate me in the harshest kind of lovemaking. As he raped me, he seemed to be eroticizing his own violence along with indulging himself by using me with proprietary and possessive commands. Yet I found I was enjoying the erotic struggle myself, my only concern being the welfare of the baby.

In the full throes of our sexual embroilment, someone flung open the front entrance flap. It was the bandit. He looked down at me with the young man, pulled him off me, and yanked me roughly to my feet. He was not angry with the young man. He was angry with *me*.

He dragged me out into the desert. The dawn was coming. The young man followed. The bandit took his sword from its sheath. The young man also unsheathed his sword. I knew the bandit was going to kill the young man and then me. The young man, though, suddenly cowered in front of the bandit and, as though to try and save his own life, he lunged at me. Holding me around the neck from behind, he very deftly slit my throat. The bandit looked on with an implacable expression tinged with sadness.

Blood spurted down my shoulders and arms. Making placating noises to the bandit, the young man bound my hands behind me and tied me to a stake he embedded in the sand. He was using my death to save his own life. The code of the desert required that the woman pay for adultery with her life.

I, knowing I was going to die, looked over at the bandit. He was sorrowful but stern. I looked up at the young man. He was paralyzed, more with terror for himself than for me. He stood watching, making not a move now.

Again, I seemed not to react to what was happening to me. I felt no pain on the table, and although the images were horrible, I was watching the other players more than myself.

The young man turned away from me, leaving me tied to the stake. The bandit shouted to him. The young man put his arms in the air as if to say, "You do what you want."

The bandit allowed him to leave. The young man climbed onto his horse, and without looking back, rode away into the sun, leaving me to bleed in the desert heat.

The bandit sorrowfully broke camp, piled all his belongings onto the horse and camels and rode away too.

I was left alone on the desert to experience the vicious attacks of predatory birds as I slowly bled to death.

Now on the table the pains in my throat began. The needle fell out and, once again, I didn't want to go on.

How does one deal with a recalled memory such as this? I realized that each of us humans had been through a panoply of horrors, but what was I supposed to learn from this? I had always been afraid of birds. They were possessed of a power that left me feeling helpless. Was this memory what caused such an unrealistic fear?

"Release the fear," said Chris. "It will be cleared for good. We can review the rest of it later." She twirled the needle in my throat.

I breathed light into the needle. The ache was terrible, a gnawing, pounding ache.

The picture of myself dying stayed in my mind. The sun was high now. I had nearly expired completely. The scene was too grisly for me to focus on for much longer. At the same time that I felt reluctant to focus, I saw myself decide to leave my body and let go and die.

The feeling of terror and pain left me as soon as I left my body. I looked down at myself. I tracked the young man after he left me. I saw him return to my father. He told my father that the bandit had wounded me and left me to die.

My father believed him and upbraided him harshly for not defending me. But there were, after all, two other daughters left who might bring him a more promising arrangement in the future.

The young man then began to bargain for my youngest sister (Sachi). Sachi refused to be sold to him because she had fallen in love with *his* younger brother. The younger brother was my brother of today! The two young people went off together, leaving both of the men who had been responsible for my fate to fight between themselves. I heard my young man swear revenge against my father's soul, and he vowed he would continue until he succeeded in destroying him in a future lifetime.

The picture rolled away until it disappeared.

I stopped for a moment. I began to put some pieces together. Then I said to Chris, "You know, what is significant to me here is that my father and my ex-husband disliked each other from the moment they met. It was an almost chemical dislike based on absolutely nothing conscious. They each went after the other in a proprietory way, as though I were to be protected *by* each *from* each. I never understood it. And each of them believed that the other was not good for me. I loved them both, but they couldn't bear each other."

Chris chuckled quietly. "A little karma going down," she said. "It happens in every family. But look at the karma your mother, as the bandit, and your father have to work out. I mean, she really abused her power unmercifully in that lifetime even though it was the code of the desert to steal women. How do you feel about that?"

I thought about it, trying to be as objectively honest as possible. "Well," I said, "somehow I feel more interested in what happens between the two of them. I always have. It's as though I haven't particularly held any subconscious grudge against either of them, but instead have agreed to come into this lifetime as their daughter to help them work out their problems with each other. Is that possible?"

"Yes," said Chris, "and gracious! You chose such a magnificent entity in your mother in order to work through many issues which were necessary for you. She has taught you to love without judgment. She has reminded you that each of us has been a tyrant at one time or another. She has been through it all and is blossoming in that understanding, just as you will. Your father is still straddling the fence between understanding the latent power he possesses and putting it to use, but he will. They are both going to progress rapidly because you are. The two of them have an urgent and intense karmic tie, but the enlightenment of one individual soul elevates every other soul on the planet. Your mother was your chosen one to learn through. She exuded the ideal which best served what you needed to learn. That is why she attracted you as a potential parent.''

That was putting it mildly, I thought. What rang so true, in terms of myself, was my observation of Mother's apparent powerlessness in this present lifetime. Whatever her reasons were for drawing that victimization to herself, I didn't want that to happen to me. So even though she drew a great deal of frustrated helplessness to her this time around, she served as a lesson for me to avoid the same fate. For that lesson, I would be eternally grateful. I had certainly chosen a superb teacher. As far as my parents together were concerned, they expressed their repressed emotions to each other much more fully when I was around than they did when alone with each other. My lesson in all of this, then, might be to simply sit back, be patient with their karmic intensity, and let them argue and flail away at each other until they finally got it all out. Their love for each other was obvious. But that kind of love was not what the experience of life was all about. It was about forgiving *self* so each of them could fall in love with their own beings.

A few other points about the desert incarnation.

Since I was a child, I have felt a mystical attraction to the desert—not the Mojave Desert or the Sahara Desert, but the Gobi Desert. It was always a desert with Mongolian inhabitants that fired my imagination. They were wild and rough, answerable only to the God whom they worshipped with fear and awe. The howling wind was their constant companion and the expanse of the heavens above their only reminder that they weren't alone. Why I would romanticize the Gobi Desert after having experienced such a lifetime, I don't know, unless perhaps I had worked through my problem with the people who had victimized me and had as yet not worked through the trauma with the birds, the sun, and slow death.

There were so many threads that bound that lifetime to my present one that it is virtually impossible to look at and understand all the connections. *And* what had happened to me on the desert was the result of events that had preceded it.

For example, after the Mongolian experience with the young man who slit my throat, I wondered what I had done to him previously that required me to go through such a violent and slow death.

I asked my higher self. What came up was an incarnation in Rome. I was a Roman soldier who had incarcerated a woman and her daughter. They slowly starved to death in a cell after having contracted leprosy because of the filth. The woman was the soul of the young man. And the young man was my ex-husband today!

The karmic law of cause and effect was staggering in its implications. The drama never seemed to end. I marveled at the rich canvas of human history. What movies could be made out of karmic drama! If only Hollywood would become interested in how karma works for each member of the human race. It would no longer be simplistic good guys versus the bad guys stuff. It would be all of us in the soup of emotional conflict together. I longed to see a film where poetic justice was spread over several lifetimes. Then we could learn something about how the harmony of life's purpose works. Violence would not be mindless; it would have meaning. And when the meaning was understood, it would become far less provocative and dangerous. Perhaps people would find themselves monitoring their own behavior, knowing that *they* were the final judge of their actions and master of their own destiny.

Human understanding would accelerate immeasurably if each of us had the certain knowledge that whatever we visit on another, good and bad, would be experienced by us. Again, I thought about leadership. Each person in a position of power must feel the loneliness of not seeing the "meaning" when facing a decision that involves the possible death of others. It isn't the death that is the issue. It is the robbing of the vehicle of experience—the body—which is the highest cosmic crime. The only route to God is through the earth plane, the karmic experience which occurs in the body. To kill another is to terminate the soul's opportunity to find God.

If the sole yardstick to my time with Chris and her needles was entertainment, I would have to say it was the most dramatically involving experience I had ever had the privilege of viewing. And, as always in the best entertainment, it all had real meaning.

The last incarnation I saw was the most dramatic in relation to my life today.

It began in Russia (there it was again) during the time of the czars. I served in some meaningful capacity at the royal court. It was a life of luxury: sleigh rides in the deep snowy countryside with sleigh bells celebrating our smooth speed. (I could feel the icy weather and hear the bells as I recalled this incarnation. It was as though I were there again.)

There were huge velvet skirts, muted tones of color, long tables of caviar and vodka. French was spoken with Russian accents as the people of the court talked of Impressionist paintings and the sophistication of Europe.

Abject poverty riddled the countryside as well as the mainstream of society, while the elite attended symphonies, the ballet, and opera. The poor lived in shacks partially underground in a desperate attempt to gain warmth.

I saw all the images in a generalized, abstract way. They served to establish the basic conditions in which my involvement occurred.

The Russian Orthodox religion was powerful

within the royal court. Satan, personifying evil, was a real and terrifying symbol. The prevailing philosophy was that the poor were trampled by Satan because that was their destiny. The rich were rewarded by God. That was their destiny. However, the members of the royal court felt inferior to Europeans because they were ashamed of the primitiveness of their peasant country. As they hobnobbed with French intellectuals, they spoke of how the peasant class was not ready for democracy. They were "savages" who needed to be ruled in order to protect them from themselves. They were capable of killing without thought, more animal than human. I saw those same judgmental, elitist people devouring legs of lamb with both hands while seated at luxuriously set banquet tables.

Moreover the settling of arguments was not done with analytic diplomacy. There was usually an eruption of physical violence, then much laughing and crying. Passions ran rampant.

I lived my life protected within the seclusion of the court. I had a son I adored. He was my life. He was about six years old as the picture stop-framed. He had high cheekbones (a physical attribute I recognized immediately) and tawny-brown skin. I recognized him as Vassy. (So he *had* been my son in a previous incarnation.)

Then the picture changed to the backwoods of the United States during the Civil War period. I was a woman living alone in a log cabin with my young son. Again, the son was Vassy! He was very upset with me and seemed to be preparing to run away from the log cabin where we lived. He bolted from the door half in jest and half in earnest. I ran after him. He ran to a cliff where he was used to playing, but lost his footing and fell over.

The picture switched back to Russia.

Vassy, who lived at court with me, was a shy Russian boy who felt deeply about the plight of the poor. Often he would leave the court to play with friends on the outside, taking with him precious objects which he would present to his friends so they could sell them for food. I was aware of his Robin Hood tactics and said nothing.

A new picture came up. A man from a village outside asked to see me. I agreed. He was representing a group of the poor and stood before me outlining the desperate conditions under which he and his family lived. He said his people needed help and recognition from the royal court to ease the burden of their impoverished existence.

I listened and was moved, but felt helpless to do anything. The man asked if I could work out a way to sell some of the royal treasures so that other unfortunate human beings could survive. He said he would take responsibility for the disbursement of the funds so that it wouldn't have to become royal policy. He was genuinely distraught, and had displayed a great deal of courage in asking to see me in the first place. This man was Steve, my ex-husband.

I listened and sent him away with the promise that I would give his problem serious consideration.

I then contacted him and took to donning a peasant robe to disguise myself. I left the court on numerous occasions and met the man so that he could familiarize me firsthand with the conditions of life that he spoke about.

The peasants welcomed me into their pitiful shacks, offering me their homemade wine and what food there was. I accepted what they offered and enjoyed myself at the same time. I listened to their stories and sang their songs with them. My son came with me and introduced me to his poverty-stricken friends, giving them money every time he left. I found his childish gestures of charity embarrassing. The problem was so overwhelming that small gestures seemed paltry.

Yet the poor became a contact point of loving reality for me. I enjoyed their company and wanted to help them. I was then forced to consider whether or not I had the courage to see it through.

I went to someone in a position of great power in the court. His rank was not clear. I only knew it was the soul of my present-day father. He was sympathetic, but unmotivated to rock the boat. He said the fate of the poor was their destiny and he had been told by his spiritual counselor that to interfere with the karmic destiny of anyone would be a spiritual crime. His spiritual counselor was the soul of my present-day mother. I was seeing how complicated our karmic intertwining had been. When I went to her to plead the case for the poor, she said it would be evil and the work of Satan if the royal family interfered with their karma. She said Satan worked in devious ways. One should continually be on the lookout. My son looked on. I could see how she influenced him.

I felt caught in the middle. I was a product of the Russian Orthodox Church, too, with a deep belief in the polarities of good and evil. And Satan came as a wolf in sheep's clothing. If we didn't believe in Satan, we were being seduced so as not to recognize him.

I was confused and felt immobilized. I wanted to help the people I had come to love and empathize with. I saw myself pacing back and forth in confusion. I wanted to listen to my own inner voice, but I was afraid to incur the displeasure of those who might be correct about their evaluation of Satan. And I was also afraid of being ostracized by other members of the royal circle.

I stopped going to the village, unable to accept the hospitality of the poor in good conscience. The man who approached me in the first place began to lose hope as he watched my dwindling courage and inability to do what I knew was right.

When he mustered the bravery to confront me one more time, I refused to see him and had him sent away.

Sometime later, I learned from my son that the man had become discouraged and was ill. His family, as well as many others in the village, had depended upon him. Now he was too depressed and ill to function.

One by one his family died around him, leaving him helpless to prevent it.

Still I did nothing to help.

He became more and more angry with me. Then disease swept his village.

I was so horrified, I became even more paralytic.

Whole families were wiped out until finally there was no one left.

The man could not understand my lack of moral courage. On behalf of all those I refused to help, he vowed to seek monetary revenge against me. He was aware of the principles of karmic destiny when he made that vow. It mattered not whether he would seek revenge in that lifetime or a future one.

There was another character in this incarnation who was silent but powerfully affected by the conditions of the poor. He was a chronicler of some kind and kept a diary so there would be a written record of events. That writer was my brother, Warren. My mind flashed to his passionate obsession to tell the story of the Russian Revolution through John Reed.

The pictures stopped. I didn't need to see any more. I knew exactly what they had meant.

The karma of my father and mother was clear. Because of spiritually withholding money from the poverty-stricken peasants, they were perceiving in this lifetime that they had money problems of their own—even though they did not. And both Mom and Dad had deep compassion for the plight of the poor today, identifying with them on a profound level.

Part of the Vassy connection was clear too. He had been my son in at least four lifetimes (I isolated two others which are not worth mentioning). And in each of them, the theme was good and evil, and love and violent passion versus freedom and respect.

But the most revelatory experience was with the man from the village. My parents may have reaped money problems from that lifetime. But theirs were nothing compared to mine. As I have said, the man who had vowed monetary revenge was my ex-husband Steve. During our marriage, he had felt the need to take large amounts of money from me. And during the property settlement he demanded even more. I had never understood the basis for his desperation about money until now. He had vowed revenge against my father in the Mongolian lifetime and against me in the Russian incarnation.

In the Russian incarnation, paralyzed by fear, I had run counter to my own convictions, denied him help, and, as a consequence, there had been terrible results for him and his family. In my present lifetime I believed I was experiencing the karmic reaction, reaping the fruit of my own weakness in the past. It all fitted.

I wondered if such a belief could be helpful to the millions of people who found themselves bitter and angry at having been ripped off, cheated, and, to all appearances hurt for no reason.

There is always a reason. We are all participants in our own karmic drama from lifetime to lifetime. It is simply a learning process and if we can only persuade ourselves to think of it that way, a lot of the knocks become easier to take.

When I understood what I had just seen, I felt the tears come. To understand the *reasons* for Steve's apparently negative attitudes was moving beyond words. I didn't open my eyes. I focused in on my higher self again. It was more clear than ever.

I saw H.S. peacefully standing in the center of the me that functioned on the spiritual plane. It stood quietly and balanced. Then an astonishing thing happened. My higher self held out its arms as if to welcome another being. This new persona approached

H.S. and I realized it was the higher self belonging
to Steve. But it had the appearance of a very old
man. H.S. embraced the old man, who looked steadily down at me.

"I hope I have helped you learn," the old man
said with deep compassion and sadness. "My purpose has been only that. I love you beyond all understanding and we both agreed to lead the life we
have led in this incarnation. We have been together
through experiences that are too numerous to remember. You know that. And through each one, we
have taught each other and learned from each other.
All that you have put me through and all that I have
put you through was done in the name of love. And
the love for each other was only a lesson in the love
and realization of self."

My heart flooded with emotion as I began to
resolve all the confused tearing feelings I had had
about him. He smiled sadly again. Then something
happened that will stay with me forever.

H.S. lifted its arms in a welcoming gesture. Moving slowly into my higher dimensional picture floated
the essences of several other people. I say essences
because the forms were not literal, yet I could see
that they were the soul energies of the higher selves
of my mother, father, brother, Vassy, and Sachi.
They seemed to vibrate with individualized light,
manifesting aspects of themselves that I recognized
today. They held themselves in their own light, quivering in a subtle dance of individualized radiance.

I was nearly unable to deal with what this made
me feel. I began to cry again. I felt such an outpouring of love from them. It was so perfect. They
meant so much to me. They were surrounded in
their own light. Two other light beings joined them—
Ramtha and Tom McPherson. They stood on either
side of my small group. And the tears continued to
flow.

Then H.S. spoke again. "This is *your* perfection," it said. "This is the harmony you seek. Your

tears recognize a truth you have been seeking. Know that it is there for you, and do not lose it by struggling so hard to find it! But remember always that seeking, not struggle and fighting, is part of the path. Seeking is a necessary part of the whole, and in the imperfect world that we ourselves created there must always be a search for harmony. That is the purpose of the imperfection—and therefore the paradox, the imperfection that makes the perfect balance. Do you understand? Do you understand how we are all connected in love and light and purpose?"

I was crying so hard I was glad I only needed to answer in my mind.

"Yes," I answered, "I understand."

Apart from insights into my relationships with family, friends, and lovers, it would be difficult for me to define accurately the effect my time with Chris, and achieving connection with my higher self, have had on my life. But there are perhaps three significant areas in living where my growing spiritual maturation has assumed major importance for me: first, in energy control and resource; second, in reality perception; and third, in experiential reality.

As for the first, my energy is "phenomenal." People tell me this—and I surely know it in every phase of daily living and work. Secondly, more and more I am convinced of the truth of Flaubert's statement: "There is no such thing as reality. There is only perception." And that perception of one's own reality relates directly to the third—experiential reality.

Now, when I encounter something that seems too negative or confusing to deal with, the knowledge that I have chosen it for my own learning experience makes it less difficult to cope with. The task then becomes an attempt to investigate *why* events occur so that the pieces can be fitted into the larger picture.

Shortly after I left Santa Fe, two events occurred which exemplify, for me, the process of how one relates to life in the light of spirituality.

Part Four

The Dance of the Red Thread

Chapter 19

I had started right away to draft *Many Happy Returns*. Somehow the title itself inspired me to touch what I wanted to say easily. I found that if I entrusted the writing to my higher self, I could work nine to twelve hours a day without tiring. In fact, it didn't feel like work. It felt more like free-flowing expression. I was beginning to understand how the creative principle of trusting one's own higher knowledge worked. I was simply getting out of my own way. I wrote the first draft in five weeks.

Then an apparent roadblock occurred.

I had returned to Los Angeles, and during a session with Kevin Ryerson (the medium for the spiritual entities Tom McPherson and John), they informed me that there was a problem with the title of my book. They said a book exploring the past lives of Edgar Cayce (the celebrated American medium) was about to be published and was entitled *Many Happy Returns*. They added, however, that I would find a better title that related more personally to my own life and lives. I was unhappy, but waited for a new title to emerge. I went back on the stage.

I was playing the Orpheum Theater in San Francisco when Kevin Ryerson came to see my show. I walked out on stage for the opening number in my usual red sequined pantsuit. As soon as I began to move, I noticed a long red thread dangling from my sleeve. Having had experience with sequined material, I knew it was dangerous to pull on the thread because each sequin was attached to the same thread. The wardrobe woman was very conscientious, so I couldn't understand why this was happening.

After the opening number, I stopped, asked for some scissors and remarked that if I pulled the dangling red thread the whole costume would unravel. As it turned out, my remark was a metaphor for what transpired.

Kevin came backstage. Under his arm, he toted a pamphlet. "I think we have an interesting piece of synchronicity here," he said. I, of course, didn't know what he was talking about until I read the material he had brought with him. "Read this," he said. "Then we must talk."

I quickly scanned an article investigating the life of a Zen master in the fifteenth century called Ikkyu. He had been a phenomenal poet, inconoclast, and a religious reformer who, although an emperor's son, had spent most of his long life (eighty-eight years) as a wandering medicant (healer) monk. He became the greatest calligrapher of his time and was remembered as a legendary lover who had his most passionate love affair in his late seventies. Ikkyu was as full of contradictions as the time period in which he lived, a period of political upheaval, not unlike ours today, with riots, civil wars, plagues, epidemics, famine. Yet, at the same time there was a radical renewal of the arts, a cultural renaissance rivaling the Italian Renaissance. Ikkyu's influence on the period was immeasurable. He became a folk hero, making his greatest contribution to the Japanese culture as the father of *Wabi*, which, loosely translated, means the beauty of simplicity and the absence of materialistic ostentation through "things." He was a Chinese as well as Japanese poet.

As a Zen master, however, he challenged Zen philosophy, which not only ignored but almost denied the existence of women and therefore the importance of love and sex between men and women in human life. He called his acceptance of human sexuality and respect for the female energy Red Thread Zen, acknowledging that life itself would not exist if not for the umbilical cord that connects us to the feminine. He excoriated celibacy, and declared that his intimate relations with women deepened his own enlightenment. Although he had openly experienced relationships with many women, it wasn't until his midseventies that he claimed he had found the great love of his life. She was a blind singer of Japanese ballads and was forty years his junior. On his deathbed, he dedicated his last poem to her.

> I do regret to cease pillowing my head in her lap
> I vow eternity to her . . .

As I read the material, I felt a strong sense of familiarity. Kevin said he had felt "compelled" to give it to me, that it must have something to do with my own past-life experience. Somehow in my intuitive higher mind, I felt that perhaps I might have been the blind ballad singer.

A few days later, we had another session. McPherson and John came through. I questioned them about the synchronicity of the red thread on my sleeve and the Red Thread Zen of Ikkyu.

"Yes," said McPherson, "we programmed a harmless yet dramatic small event so as to attract your attention."

"But why?" I asked. "Was I the blind ballad singer? And if so, what difference does it make?"

"What do you feel?" asked McPherson, in that way that all spiritual guides have of forcing you to think more intuitively for yourself.

"Well, yes," I said, "I feel I was."

"You are correct," he went on.

Then suddenly I connected the trouble I had been having with my eyes to what I was realizing. I had been experiencing dark spots swimming across my eyes which at moments made it difficult for me to read. I asked if this was connected.

"Indeed it is," said McPherson. "Your higher self understood that you would draw this knowledge to your conscious mind and the memory of the blindness was manifesting through the cellular memory of your eyes."

I blinked and tried to recall what I had looked like. I realized that I was "seeing" with a deeper insight. I didn't see "form," I "saw" meaning and feeling.

"You had an inner sight then," he said, "a highly developed sense of being because you had not the gift of outer sight. It would be well for you to develop more of that inner sight today."

Just as McPherson said that, I had a blinding flash of insight in relation to Ikkyu. I could hardly bring myself to express it aloud, but I had long since learned not to limit or block those feelings.

"Tom," I said, "I'm having the strangest idea or whatever you call it."

"I know," he answered.

"Is it true?"

"Express your feeling," he pushed.

"Well"—I swallowed—"I have the feeling that this Ikkyu character was my ex-husband, Steve!"

Tom smiled through Kevin's face.

"Quite right," he said. "You needed to unravel the threads of your own mystery in order to come to a new understanding and thus a more personal title for your book."

"What title?"

"Well," said Tom, "to you all life is a dance, isn't that correct?"

"Yes."

"A dance of energy and lessons?"

"Yes."

"Ikkyu's Red Thread Zen was the personification of the recognition of the dance of male and female energy as we embody both male and female in each incarnational experience. His was a dramatic breakthrough in the puritanical asexual Zen philosophy of his period. He understood that all experience is connected to the female through the red thread of the umbilical cord. That was your Steve. That is why you have been so spiritually connected to him through your present incarnation and also why you and he have had this identification with Japan. This spiritual lineage has transferred to this lifetime, only in this incarnation the roles are reversed. *You* have been the public expounder and he has been the learner. Sometimes your insights are too much for him. At those moments he buckles in on himself. Just as in your previous incarnation together his insights were more than others could see. *Your* inner sight in this incarnation will enable you to be more tolerant of the pace of others who are sometimes blinded by the light. Do you understand?"

I straightened up in my chair and breathed deeply. The spots in front of my eyes disappeared as did a deep pain in my right shoulder which had been troubling me for two days.

"The pain in your right shoulder," said Tom, "has lifted because you have gotten in touch with the incarnation we have been discussing."

"Why did I have the pain?" I asked.

"It was inflicted by another Zen master and was beyond your understanding at the time."

"Did Ikkyu hit me?"

"No," he answered, "another monk struck you because you and Ikkyu were responsible for upsetting traditional Zen beliefs."

I rubbed my shoulder, unable to locate where the pain had been a few minutes before.

"All body pain," Tom continued, "or even disease, for that matter, is nothing but unresolved, unreleased karmic impurity. When the karma is understood, the energies in the body flow freely. The more karmically free one becomes, the less pain or dis-ease one feels in the body."

"But Tom," I said, not understanding why I was suddenly feeling frantic, "how can people free themselves from pain and disease if they don't know how to get in touch with their past-life karma? I mean, not everyone has you or other guides like you to talk to."

"It is very simple, really," said Tom quietly. "Very simple. If everyone was taught one basic spiritual law, your world would be a happier, healthier place. And that law is this: *Everyone is God. Everyone.* The greatest threat to Earth is spiritual ignorance. There is a hunger for this understanding. The human race is experiencing a thrust in this direction with the revival of religious fervor. But each religious faction is judgmental and intolerant of the other. Release the zealous judgment. When everyone is aligned with the knowledge that *each* is part of God, the consciousness of civilization will reflect peace—peace within. Recognize that within each individual is the divine cosmic truth that you term God."

I gazed at Tom McPherson's energy coming through Kevin's body.

"So you're saying that if we just *know* that we are totally and individually part of that God-force, *we* will experience no more pain, trauma, or dis-ease?"

"That is quite correct," said Tom quietly. "Enlightenment can come to anyone, regardless of how despicable they might seem to be. Each individual is working through his or her own soul conflict. Each person deals with his own trauma at his own pace. No one can possibly know or judge another. For each soul in the universe is part of God."

I sat still.

Then Tom said, "Do you know what a koan is?"

"No," I answered.

"A koan," said Tom, "is a question which a Zen master will pose to his student to inspire him or her to think more deeply about his own reality. 'What is the sound of one hand clapping?' That is a koan. 'If a tree falls in the forest, does it make a sound if no one is there to hear it?' That is a koan.

"Koans are intended to stimulate insight. The title *Many Happy Returns* was a koan for you. It stimulated investigative thought because it inspired and amused you. When it was jerked away from you, even deeper insight occurred. Now, with the dance of consciousness you have experienced you know more about yourself. To know self is the only thing worth knowing. Everything flows from that."

We both sat silently. I wondered what Tom as a spiritual entity would really look like if he had form. What was form? What were bodies? What were we? Were we simply coagulated thought? Were we physical manifestations of our own consciousness?

"Well, Tom," I finally said, "I guess you are my new koan. If you had form, what would you look like?"

"Quite right," said Tom. "And I can assure you I would seem different to each soul who posed that question. Reality is what one perceives it to be. If you have no more questions, I will be leaving now."

I nodded. "And if you leave, you will only appear to be gone?"

"Oh, yes," said Tom. "Nothing is ever gone. Everything and everyone is present always. Remember that in the days to come. The more you are conscious of that, the more awareness you possess. The more awareness you possess, the closer you come to knowing your higher unlimited self. The more you know your higher self, the closer you are to all other higher selves and to the Light which is the God-force."

A shudder went through Kevin's body. Tom McPherson left. But I was indeed to remember, and be grateful for, Tom's words "in the days to come."

* * *

I received a call from Christopher Adler, my friend of so many years who had written the lyrics for my show and who had thrown that magnificent "light and life" birthday party for me. In the years of working together we had become very close. Now he was distraught. "Something is terribly wrong," he said in a kind of controlled panic. "I am having ghastly stomach pains and I have a high fever, edema (water retention), and no energy, none. And the doctors don't know what's wrong." He said he was going into the hospital for tests.

I called Chris Griscom in Santa Fe immediately to see if she could tune in to anything specific. She was shocked.

"Oh my, my friend," she said after a long silence of communicating with her higher self. "The young man has disease all through his body which I see as having begun about three years ago. Shirley, it doesn't seem possible for him to make it."

I was stunned. Christopher was so healthy and vibrant.

"Well, what can he do?" I asked.

"He has to accept that he had elected to have this experience, which is not going to be pleasant. If he understands the role of his own karmic free will in this, it is just possible that he can begin a healing process."

I didn't know what to do; whether to call Christopher or not.

I called Kevin and J.Z. and asked them to check with McPherson and Ramtha.

They came back to me with the same projections. The ramifications of disease in Christopher's body were truly monumental.

I spoke with Richard Adler, Christopher's father, with whom I had also worked all these years. Neither of us could take in the dreadful swiftness and apparent finality of what was happening to Christopher.

A few days later Christopher called again. "It's

lymphoma, Shirley," he said, trying not to cry. "I have lymphoma all through me. I have cancer. I can't believe it. They took out all they could but now I have to go through chemotherapy for five weeks. I don't understand why this is happening."

I couldn't speak. What in God's name could I tell him?

Then, in a strong voice, Christopher said, "Listen, I need a spiritual game plan. I'm *frightened*. I know we've talked about your spiritual stuff and how it relates to our earth-plane life, but I *really* need to understand it now."

I talked to Chris Griscom and Kevin and J.Z. again. All of them said chemotherapy would thwart the body's natural healing processes because it would destroy so much besides the lymphoma. But they added that given his karmic prognosis it probably wouldn't make that much difference anyway.

I talked to Christopher's doctors. They said they knew there was truth in my spiritual approach to my friend's terrible problem, but they didn't understand it empirically and preferred to go through with their medical procedures. I understood that. So did Christopher. So did Richard.

What followed was weeks of visits and phone conversations; for Christopher the nauseating sickness of the chemotherapy and his confusion about whether to adopt an attitude of "fighting" the disease, or giving in to it.

I tried to encourage him to believe that he could beat the lymphoma but not from a "fighting" point of view. I talked with him more along the lines of understanding and believing that his body was perfect if he could only focus on the reality of that perfection. He was thirty years old, his heart was perfect, so could the body be perfect if he "knew" it.

The Adler family began to prepare themselves for the worst yet continually supported Christopher in his battle. I went to New York for a week to be with him. During this time I had a "vision dream"—

the kind we all have from time to time that seems so real it feels like an experience.

I walked into his hospital room where I had seen him lying in desperation, confused and determined.

This time, as I entered, he was fully dressed, his arms stretched out to me. He looked healthy and happy. He put his arms around me and we began to dance together. I looked around. We were dancing in a bubble of pure white light. He leaned over and whispered in my ear, "Now I am ready to talk about my mother."

I woke up abruptly. I knew his mother had died when he was very young and that he had been devastated by her leaving.

I called Chris Griscom and asked her about the literalness of my realistic dream.

"Yes," she said, "my guides have told me that he needs to work out a long and complicated relationship with his mother that has gone on for centuries. This is his way of doing it."

"Well," I asked confusedly, "does the dream mean he'll survive? Or will he go?"

"He'll go, Shirley," she said. "The white bubble of light around you is his acceptance of coming into the light of understanding *after* he goes on to the higher dimension."

I hung up. I wasn't prepared to accept that explanation. I wanted Christopher to live in the body as much as he and his family wanted him to.

I went into my room to do some yoga. In the middle of my yoga session my higher self began to speak to me in a clear and succinct voice.

"Why do *you* feel," it said, "that you have the right to insist that Christopher stay alive in the body when he has other issues to work out on a higher dimensional level?"

I stopped my postures stock-still. "What do you mean?" I asked out loud.

"Just what I said," H.S. answered me rather

strongly. "You know he will never really die anyway. Let him proceed with his course at his own
pace. One person can never really understand what
another is actually doing or why they are doing it."

"But," I protested, "*he* says he wants to stay
alive in the body."

"Part of him does," said H.S. "But it is clear
that his higher self needs to go on or this would not
be happening. He is leaving because he has chosen
to leave. That may be difficult for you to understand
because you value life in the body so highly. But *you*
are the contradiction. Allow him to pass over gracefully. That is his lesson to all of you."

I stood staring at myself in the mirror. Suddenly
the personalization of the so-called death experience
made sense. I had never really had anyone close to
me "die" before. Now I was understanding in the
most visceral way that Christopher was not really
going to be "gone." He was just going to make a
transition into another dimension. And the more I or
anyone else insisted that he stay alive in the body,
the more difficult we were making his transition for
him. What he would do was up to him. The doctors
would play their roles. Aspects of Christopher himself would continue to struggle, but the real Christopher would make his own decision when and whether
he would go.

After that experience with higher self I ceased to
struggle about Christopher. Grief I felt for the loss of
a dear friend and for the family who would miss
him, but I no longer had a sense of outraged despair.

He apparently made his decision about six weeks
later. I was playing my show in Los Angeles, thinking about him whenever I began the lyrics to his
opening number. One night I went home to bed
early. As I was sleeping a blazing white light filled
my head. It woke me up. I thought the sun was
shining into my room. I sat up in bed. The room was
dark but I was enveloped in a shower of light that I
felt surrounded me as well as emanated from inside

my own mind. I knew it was Christopher. The light stayed with me for the rest of the night and for days thereafter.

When I received the call from Richard I told him I already knew.

Whenever I stepped out onto the stage and began to dance in the light of my own spot, Christopher's light seemed to mingle with it. I could feel him enjoy what I was doing and what he had been so much a part of creating.

I felt that he had somehow gone home to a place where all of his questions had finally been answered and he was reassuring me that his "spiritual game plan" was well into play. He was released from his confusion and pain and terror and knew exactly what he was doing.

We all adjusted to his leaving in our own ways.

As for me, whenever I think of him I see him dancing in a shower of light, looking down on me while I dance in mine.

Epilogue

*T*o be skeptical of all I have described is understandable. I was suspicious, too, at first, except for one thing. I knew it *happened* to me. Perhaps I wanted it to happen, yet what I experienced led me to understand even more fully what the new physicists and ancient mystics were attempting to reconcile in their own minds: the reality of consciousness. Aside from suddenly seeming to speak the same language, they seemed to be on the brink of agreeing that even the *cosmos* was nothing but consciousness. That the universe and God itself might just be one giant, collective "thought." And that every bit of information stored in our own consciousness was cross-referenced with every other bit of information, not only in our consciousness but in everyone else's. That the "reality" of the physical universe was really only holographic memory patterns in our own minds. That time period upon time period lives on in the memory patterns of our mental and bodily consciousness.

The hologram of that consciousness enables us to feel one with the universe and one with everything we've experienced. We are in "reality" multidimensional beings who each reflect the totality of the whole.

I believe my intense search for self was motivated by the intuitive certainty that in myself lay the reflections of all there was. That all my curiosities regarding the outside world were in truth curiosities I had about myself. If I could know me, I could know the universe.

As the new physics and the ancient mystics now seemed to agree—when one observes the world and the beings within it, one sees that we are in fact only dancing with our own consciousness. Everything we feel, think, and act upon is interrelated with everything everyone else feels, thinks, and acts upon. We are *all* participating in the dance.

When I began to see the world with karmic consciousness, the knowledge that we all create our own paths of our own free will made me recognize the cosmic justice in everything. I understood that there was a purposeful good in all occurrences if I allowed them to provide a path of experience and understanding.

The total understanding and realization of my self might require eons for me to accomplish. But when that awareness is achieved, I will be aligned completely with that unseen Divine Force that we call God.

For me to deny that Divine Force now would be tantamount to denying that I exist.

I *know* that I exist, therefore I AM.

I *know* that the God-source exists. Therefore *IT IS*.

Since I am part of that force, then *I AM* that *I AM*.

To me, understanding spiritual principles is identical to understanding scientific principles. The two approaches to truth are searching for the same answer: What is God?

I believe that one day scientists and theologians will be sitting together on top of the same mountain of knowledge.

As far as my own life is concerned, my higher self is with me every moment. When I get in trouble, I consult with it. When I have a question, I direct my inquiry to it. It is my teacher. It is the master of my soul. It is *me*.

When I feel out of touch with it, I take the time to be peaceful and meditate until I am aligned with it again.

The flowing, nourishing, knowing awareness of my own being is as essential to me as air. I cannot prove its existence to anyone else. One has to experience it to know it.

When that happens, it is possible to understand the reason for life, why we do what we do. But more important than anything, in my experience the purpose for continuing is simply to understand SELF. The dance within and the dance without are intertwined. The Dance and the Dancer are One.

ABOUT THE AUTHOR

Shirley MacLaine was born and raised in Virginia. She began her career as a Broadway dancer and singer, then progressed to feature performer and award-winning actress of television and films. She traveled extensively on her own all over the world. Her experiences in Africa, India, the Far East, and Hollywood formed the basis for her first book, *"Don't Fall Off the Mountain,"* which became a national bestseller, as did her subsequent books, *You Can Get There From Here* and *Out on a Limb.*

QUANTITY PURCHASES

Shirley MacLaine Times Four!!!

BANTAM
SHOP-AT-HOME
C·A·T·A·L·O·G

Special Offer
Buy a Bantam Book
for only 50¢.

Now you can have Bantam's catalog filled with hundreds of titles plus take advantage of our unique and exciting bonus book offer. A special offer which gives you the opportunity to purchase a Bantam book for only 50¢. Here's how!

By ordering any five books at the regular price per order, you can also choose any other single book listed (up to a $5.95 value) for just 50¢. Some restrictions do apply, but for further details why not send for Bantam's catalog of titles today!

Just send us your name and address and we will send you a catalog!
